CREATING INTERDISCIPLINARY CAMPUS CULTURES

CREATING INTERDISCIPLINARY CAMPUS CULTURES

A Model for Strength and Sustainability

Julie Thompson Klein

Foreword by Carol Geary Schneider

Association
of American
Colleges and
Universities

JOSSEY-BASS
A Wiley Imprint
www.josseybass.com

Published by Jossey-Bass
A Wiley Imprint
989 Market Street, San Francisco, CA 94103-1741—www.josseybass.com

Jossey-Bass books and products are available through most bookstores. To contact Jossey-Bass directly call our Customer Care Department within the U.S. at 800-956-7739, outside the U.S. at 317-572-3986, or fax 317-572-4002.

Jossey-Bass also publishes its books in a variety of electronic formats. Some content that appears in print may not be available in electronic books.

Library of Congress Cataloging-in-Publication Data

Klein, Julie Thompson.
  Creating interdisciplinary campus cultures : a model for strength and sustainability / Julie
  Thompson Klein.
    p. cm.
  Includes bibliographical references and index.
  ISBN 978-0-470-55089-2 (cloth)
  1. Interdisciplinary approach in education—United States. 2. Universities and colleges—United
  States. I. Title.
  LB2361.5.K54 2010
  378.1'99—dc22
                              2009036748

FIRST EDITION

HB Printing 10 9 8 7 6 5 4 3 2

The Jossey-Bass
Higher and Adult Education Series

CONTENTS

To my colleagues and students who fought with strength and integrity against closure of the Department of Interdisciplinary Studies at Wayne State University

THE AUTHOR

Julie Thompson Klein is professor of humanities in interdisciplinary studies/English and Faculty Fellow in the Office for Teaching and Learning at Wayne State University. She has held visiting positions in Japan and New Zealand and was a Fulbright Professor in Nepal. Klein received the Kenneth Boulding Award for outstanding scholarship on interdisciplinarity, including the books and monographs *Interdisciplinarity: History, Theory, and Practice* (1990), *Crossing Boundaries* (1996), *Mapping Interdisciplinary Studies* (1999), and *Humanities, Culture, and Interdisciplinarity* (2005). Her edited and coedited books include *Interdisciplinary Studies Today* (1994), *Transdisciplinarity* (2001), *Interdisciplinary Education in K–12 and College* (2002), and *Promoting Interdisciplinary Research* (2005). Klein has lectured on interdisciplinarity throughout North America, Europe, South Asia, Latin America, and Australia. She was also Senior Fellow at the Association of American Colleges and Universities (AAC&U) and served on national task forces of the Society for Values in Higher Education (Interdisciplinary Studies), AAC&U (Integrative Learning), and the Association for Integrative Studies (Accreditation). In addition, she has advised the National Institutes of Health, National Academy of Sciences, and National Science Foundation on interdisciplinary research. Klein is currently coeditor of the University of Michigan Press series Digital Humanities@digitalculturebooks and is working on a book mapping the field of digital humanities. She is also coeditor of the forthcoming *Oxford Handbook of Interdisciplinarity*.

FOREWORD

I majored in history when I was in college and later went on to earn a doctorate in the same field. But both as an undergraduate and as a graduate student, I really thought of myself as an "early modern studies" student. Intentionally and extensively, I added numerous courses from multiple disciplines studying early modern developments in religion, philosophy, art history, literature, political science, and anthropology, always with the goal of building a fuller understanding for myself of the contours and contests of my chosen area of work.

This was, however, an entirely independent project. My mentors did not disapprove it, but neither did they at any point see it as their role to help me integrate my far-flung and multidisciplinary studies.

Early on, I began to realize that the material that really interested me—the interplay across religion, politics, and contested cultures—scarcely "belonged" at all to the "discipline" of history. Indeed, there were entire other disciplines that existed specifically to probe each of these areas of human experience: religion, political science, and anthropology, not to mention the then emerging fields of cultural studies. Where, then, should I locate myself? Should I think of myself as "interdisciplinary"? What might this mean when, across some twenty-plus years of formal education, I had never taken a single course or ventured into a single department that presented itself as interdisciplinary, cross-disciplinary, or even multidisciplinary?

My work might be cross-disciplinary, but I was a solo actor. What would it mean in practice to make some form of cross-disciplinarity a primary organizing principle for my own educational identity and institutional location—whether in scholarship or teaching?

As I struggled to make sense of all this conceptually, method-ologically, and professionally, I remained, like the majority of academics in my generation, largely on my own. Some brave spirits—many, in fact—went out and founded dynamic new inter-disciplinary fields, giving birth to the extraordinary intellectual fertility of the current academy, a fertility that Julie Klein maps brilliantly in this book. But this did not occur to me, and in any event, such areas as ethnic, environmental, and women's stud-ies seemed to have a considerably greater urgency about them than my own particular interest in post-Reformation religious and political landscapes.

I mention my personal intellectual history because I have come to believe that the disjunction I experienced—the tension between my actual work and the academy's dominant organiza-tional and educational structures—is not only widespread but absolutely commonplace. Julie Klein's fine study tells us, however, that we do not need to simply live with these disjunctions. We have reached a point where we are starting to see both how to change them, and that we must.

The twentieth-century academy organized itself firmly around the concept of disciplinary conceptual structures, problems, and methods. The institutional and psychosocial legacies of that decision live on into the twenty-first-century academy. Indeed, in Europe, this legacy not only lives on but is taking on a second life in what is known as "the Bologna process." Through the Bologna process, dozens of countries have agreed not only to set clear intellectual standards for what undergraduates need to achieve in their studies, but to do so by "tuning" specific academic disciplines. *Tuning* is a term meant to ensure that there will be a shared understanding, across institutions and countries, of what it means in terms of knowledge, methodological skills, and applied work to earn a degree in a particular subject area—whether history, biology, or business.

One could almost say that since the academy failed to clarify the meaning and standards for disciplines in the twentieth century, European scholars are working now to tidy up that unfinished business—mapping the intended contours of "the disciplines" for the twenty-first century.

But in truth, as Julie Klein makes clear in this rich and enor-mously useful analysis of the academy's actual scholarly terrain, we have already entered a different world. The boundaries have blurred, and the creative energy of our age is decidedly cross-disciplinary. Undone by tens of thousands of scholars whose interests were as unfounded as my own, the entire concept of "the discipline" has increasingly taken on the stance of fiction, and an inconvenient fiction at that.

For dozens of different but intersecting reasons—developments and tensions within established fields, creative work that cuts across fields, the deepening connections between the academy and the communities it serves, and the actual interests of contemporary scholars—both intellectual work and undergraduate teaching and learning move restlessly across the so-called disciplinary boundaries. Across all the major domains of academic work, with established fields as well as in new fields, we have broken free of anything we might think of as a disciplinary framework for pathbreaking intellectual work.

These developments notwithstanding, however, our institutional structures for both faculty and undergraduate learning remain firmly rooted in an earlier set of understandings. Disciplines, as Klein notes in Chapter Four, are "systems of power with control over resources, identities, and patterns of research and education. Disciplines constitute economies of value ... encoded in canons of work and the professional apparatus of publication."

Faced with this deeply rooted contradiction and the resultant tensions between generative academic work and the structures of actual power, American higher education has enormous work before it. One priority is that of understanding the scope and reach of the many emerging forms of cross-disciplinary work. We need to understand the world we actually inherit.

A second priority is that of providing new forms of institutional support, recognition, and reward for those who do this work, whether as scholars or in their curricular leadership and teaching. The third priority—an arena in which the Association of American Colleges and Universities (AAC&U) has joined hands with interdisciplinary scholars and teachers across the United States—is that of rethinking teaching and learning, and the larger project of providing a liberal or horizon-expanding education in light of this new interdisciplinary dynamism.

This book provides guidance on all of these issues. Klein's analysis shows convincingly that from research in the sciences to new graduate-level programs and departments, to new designs for general education, interdisciplinarity is now prevalent throughout American colleges and universities. She maps the drivers of interdisciplinary changes in scholarship and curricula and demonstrates forcefully that developing and sustaining interdisciplinary studies is essential to providing students with complex capacities so important to navigating the world of work, learning, and citizenship today.

Klein documents trends, traces historical patterns and precedents, and provides practical advice. Going directly to the heart of our institutional realities, she focuses attention on some of the more challenging aspects of bringing together ambitious goals for interdisciplinary vitality with institutional, budgetary, and governance systems. A singular strength of this book, then, is the practical advice it provides about such nitty-gritty issues as program review, faculty development, tenure and promotion, hiring, and the political economy of interdisciplinarity.

Klein's overview of campus educational practices meshes with what we at AAC&U see in our own work with campuses on the revitalization of curriculum, teaching, and learning. Spanning every kind of college and university (two-year and four-year, public and private, large and small), AAC&U members overwhelmingly are incorporating more integrative and engaged forms of learning in both general education and major programs (AAC&U, 2009). Whether the actual course of study is described as disciplinary or interdisciplinary, American higher education is now engaging students with big questions and real problems. Almost invariably, those problems span conventional disciplinary boundaries.

As Klein describes in her comprehensive overview, the American college curriculum now prioritizes integration, cross-cultural interaction, and the development of cross-functional and inter-disciplinary capacities—capacities that are precisely what today's world demands of college graduates. Whether they proceed to graduate school and engage in complex research in nanotechnology or biomedical engineering or directly to a workplace increasingly defined by innovation and globalization, today's college graduates will be challenged every day to integrate their knowledge and skills and apply learning to new settings and forms of complexity.

Klein also forcefully shows that trends in interdisciplinarity are driven not only by the changing nature of research or the demands of a globalized economy. To be a responsible citizen in today's world requires a scope and depth of learning that enables individuals to understand and navigate dramatic forces—physical, cultural, economic, technological—that directly affect the quality, character, and perils of the world in which they live. With fields changing so rapidly and unscripted problems abundant on every front, we cannot hope to teach students *a* discipline that will work for all purposes. But we can teach them that in both their professional lives and lives as citizens and community and family members, they need to look far and wide, analyze rigorously, synthesize judiciously, and take anomalies and contradictions directly into account.

Klein's work has been an important resource for AAC&U as this association has made integrative and interdisciplinary learning an ever more central part of our vision for twenty-first-century liberal learning and educational quality. In *College Learning for the New Global Century,* the signature report from AAC&U's decade-long initiative on Liberal Education and America's Promise (LEAP), the authors affirm that teaching students how to integrate their learning across multiple disciplines and contexts is essential, not optional, in the campus framework for educational excellence. The LEAP report also calls for new campus leadership and action to make intentional integrative learning a defining feature for liberal education and, indeed, for American higher education. We noted in the LEAP report that "with campus experimentation already well advanced ... it is time to move from 'pilot efforts' to full-scale commitments."

Klein's book demonstrates convincingly that the academy is indeed poised to move in precisely that direction. We are proud to partner with Jossey-Bass in publishing this important study, and we know that readers everywhere will find it simultaneously richly illuminating and intensively useful.

CAROL GEARY SCHNEIDER
President
Association of American
Colleges and Universities

ACKNOWLEDGMENTS

This book would not have been possible without the generous help of colleagues and friends who enriched my understanding as we worked together on a variety of projects:

- Diana Rhoten and Stanley Katz of the Social Science Research Council's Teagle Foundation–funded study of interdisciplinary quality assessment in liberal education
- Veronica Boix-Mansilla and Howard Gardner of the Interdisciplinary Studies Project at Project Zero in the Graduate School of Education at Harvard University
- Dan Stokols of the School of Social Ecology at the University of California, Irvine, and Transdisciplinary Research Initiatives in the U.S. National Cancer Institute
- Katri Huutoniemi, Janne Hukkinen, and Henrik Bruun of the Helsinki Institute of Technology, University of Helsinki, and the Academy of Finland Interdisciplinary Research evaluation team
- Gertrude Hirsch Hadorn and Christian Pohl of the Swiss Institute of Technology in Zurich and the Network for Transdisciplinary Research, known as td-net (www.transdisciplinarity.ch/e/index.php)
- Jack Spaapen, coordinator of quality assurance and research evaluation at the Royal Netherlands Academy of Arts and Sciences
- Gabrielle Bammer of the National University of Australia and Network for Integration and Implementation Sciences
- Robert Frodeman, Carl Mitcham, and Britt Holbrook of the editorial team for the *Oxford Handbook of Interdisciplinarity*

Others supplied vital materials and insights:

- Gail Dubrow of the University of Minnesota, about the Consortium for Fostering Interdisciplinary Inquiry
- Cathy Davidson, Susan Roth, Celeste Lee, and Peter Lange of Duke University, about the Duke model for facilitating interdisciplinarity
- Kathy Woodward of the University of Washington and Bruce Burgett of the University of Washington Bothell campus, about their campus cultures
- Peyton Smith of the University of Wisconsin, about the cluster hiring model
- Lisa Lewis and Peter Mitchell of Albion College, about their campus culture
- Creso Sá of the University of Toronto, for an early copy of his dissertation, "Interdisciplinary Strategies at Research-Intensive Universities"
- Tanya Augsburg and Stuart Henry, for a prepublication copy of *The Politics of Interdisciplinary Studies: Essays on Transformations in American Undergraduate Programs*
- Joan Fiscella, principal bibliographer and associate professor at the University of Illinois at Chicago's University Library, for advice on Web-based searching
- Marceline Weshalek of the Wayne State University Library and Information Science program, for conducting database searches referenced in the Introduction and Resources
- Sherry Tuffin of the Wayne State University Library and Information Science program, for assistance with copyediting tasks

The following institutions and forums were valuable testing grounds for ideas:

- Centre de recherche en intervention éducative, University of Sherbrooke, Quebec, with special thanks to the founder and director, Yves Lenoir
- The Australian Academy of Science Fenner Conference on Disciplinarity
- The U.S. National Academy of Sciences Task Force on Facilitating Interdisciplinary Research

- The U.S. National Academy of Sciences panel on Modernizing the Infrastructure of the National Science Foundation's Federal Funds for R&D Survey
- SRI International Task Force on Indicators of Interdisciplinary Science and Engineering Research
- Michigan State University, Central Michigan University, the University of Michigan at Ann Arbor and at Dearborn, Oregon State University, the University of Washington at Seattle and at Bothell, Edgewood College, and New York City College of Technology

For permission to adapt and update previously published material, I am indebted to the following:

- The Association of American Colleges and Universities, for portions of a monograph: Klein, J. T. *Mapping Interdisciplinary Studies*. Academy in Transition series. Washington, D.C.: AAC&U, 1999.
- Heldref Publications, for portions of a "Resource Review" article: Klein, J. T. "Resources for Interdisciplinary Studies." *Change* (2006), *58*, 52–56.
- The State University of New York Press, for portions of Klein, J. T. *Humanities, Culture, and Interdisciplinarity: The Changing American Academy*. Albany: SUNY Press, 2005.
- Sage Publications, for portions of "Interdisciplinary Approach." *Handbook of Social Science Methodology*, eds. S. Turner and W. Outhwaite. Thousand Oaks, CA: Sage, 2007.

I am also indebted to Jossey-Bass and the Association of American Colleges and Universities (AAC&U) for a wonderful publishing partnership. David Brightman, senior editor of the Jossey-Bass Higher and Adult Education series, was an enthusiastic champion of this book. Carolyn Dumore was a pleasure to work with during copyediting as was Shana Harrington in the proofreading stage. Aneesa Davenport guided the overall production process, and Carrie Wright oversaw marketing with the aid of Tracy Gallagher. Carol Geary Schneider, president of AAC&U, and Debra Humphreys, vice president for communications and public affairs, were generous in welcoming copublication and have been valued colleagues on other projects for many years.

Finally, I would be remiss in not thanking my husband, George Klein, who was pressed into service many times as a sounding board for ideas, even when he least expected it.

JULIE THOMPSON KLEIN
Detroit 2009

CREATING INTERDISCIPLINARY CAMPUS CULTURES

Introduction: A Model for Interdisciplinary Change

Interdisciplinarity has become a mantra for change in the twenty-first century. The word appears in countless reports from professional associations, educational organizations, funding agencies, and science policy bodies. It is a keyword in strategic plans, accompanied by a companion rhetoric of *innovation, collaboration, competitiveness,* and the *cutting edge.* It also echoes in the way that we describe knowledge and education today. Images of knowledge as a *foundation* or a *linear structure* have been replaced by a *network* and a *web.* Images of the curriculum follow suit, supplanting *fragmentation* and *segmentation* with *integrating, connecting, linking,* and *clustering.* The concept is not new or, as some suggest, merely a passing fad. The earliest documented use of the word dates to the 1920s, in social science research and the general education movement. Others trace the concept's origin to the 1940s, in the Manhattan Project to build an atomic bomb, and many cite the 1960s and 1970s, in a surge of educational innovation and experimentation. Current interest is more widespread, fostering the belief that interdisciplinarity is now basic to both research and education. In 1997 the editors of the *Handbook of the Undergraduate Education* (Gaff and Ratcliff, 1997) declared that a historical reversal of the trend toward specialization was underway. In 2004 Johan Heilbron called the diffusion of interdisciplinarity throughout the academy since the 1960s "probably the clearest sign of the erosion of disciplines as the predominant mode of academic organization" (pp. 37–38). And in 2009 Brint, Turk-Bicakci, Proctor, and Murphy reported that interdisciplinary research and teaching is now widely considered a notable feature of academic change, documented by a sharp increase in collaborative research, administrative advocacy, funding, and a literature of best practices.

The belief that interdisciplinarity is more important today is affirmed by a shift in requests for help. Twenty years ago, it was not unusual for the director of an individual program to seek advice about a single initiative. Today it is not unusual for a high-level administrator to request help creating a more favorable institution-wide support system. The multiple connotations of the word signal the reasons for heightened interest. Interdisciplinarity is associated with bold advances in knowledge, solutions to urgent societal problems, an edge in technological innovation, and a more integrative educational experience. Administrators, in particular, value the organizational flexibility to respond to new needs, offer new fields and forms of education, attract faculty in new areas, stimulate greater coherence in the curriculum, establish a distinct identity among peer institutions, enhance collaborative use of facilities, be more competitive in securing external funding, and forge new partnerships with government, industry, and the community. Faculty cite the ability to pursue new intellectual questions, work in new areas of teaching and research, counterbalance the isolation of specialization, infuse innovative and active-learning pedagogies into the curriculum, develop integrative and collaborative skills in students, and respond to societal problems. Students appreciate opportunities to learn about a broad range of disciplines, study real-world problems and issues, make connections between their majors and other disciplines and fields, pursue interdisciplinary majors and concentrations, find and integrate knowledge from different disciplines, and gain skills of higher-order critical thinking, synthesis, and collaboration for working in teams.

A search of the LexisNexis online news service over the past several years puts a more concrete face on the reasons for heightened interest. This century began with updates on the widely touted interdisciplinary (ID) general education program at Portland State University and recommendations to strengthen ID learning requirements at Texas Christian University. In 2001 the *Chronicle of Higher Education* heralded the birth of a new field of Internet studies. In 2004 Northwestern University announced a plan to create more interdisciplinary options, and Vanderbilt University's English department added new courses emphasizing cultural influences on literature. The year 2005 brought news of a global studies major at UCLA and a campaign at the

College of New Caledonia in British Columbia to strengthen inter-disciplinary awareness in training programs for health care professions. A search of the Educational Resources Information Center database over the same period yielded additional reports of integrative curricula in a wide range of areas, including adult learning, technical and scientific communication, information architecture, Web-based education, international business, natural resource management, and math and science courses.

The most recent study of interdisciplinary programs adds further evidence. When Brint, Turk-Bicakci, Proctor, and Murphy (2009) examined patterns of growth in nine fields between 1975 and 2000, they found that growth has been particularly strong in the areas of technological innovation and social incorporation of traditionally underrepresented populations. However, growth was not distributed evenly, suggesting that interdisciplinary organization is not likely to continue in all fields. These authors foresee new brain and biomedical fields, such as cognitive science and neuroscience, eventually becoming institutionalized in departmental structures. Environmental studies might also become more fully institutionalized as departments, though activist agendas do not fit easily within the professionalized structures of academic departments.

Others have also observed a gap between the rhetoric of endorsement and the realities of campus life. When Irwin Feller (2002, 2006) examined a number of leading U.S. research universities, he found checkered patterns of growth, stasis, and decline in interdisciplinary initiatives, with discernible variations in the willingness of administrators or faculty to accept them. Even where initiatives take hold, they survive mainly as enclaves or showpieces within the historically determined disciplinary structure of higher education. As a result, they have limited staying power, engendering only marginal changes in performance norms, resource allocations, and outcomes promulgated in strategic plans. Lacking deep roots within the core functions of hard money budgets, tenure lines, and space, they remain vulnerable. In a recent study of interdisciplinarity in research-intensive universities, Creso Sá (2005) noted further gaps, including a lack of comprehensive studies and data on research structures, programs, and funding outcomes. Moreover, evidence is mixed and fragmentary, and discussions of organizational structures and strategies are often normative or speculative.

The gaps are evident in both education and research. Changes that foster interdisciplinarity, Faith Gabelnick (2002) reported, are occurring on many campuses. Yet so is resistance. Fear of losing past routines and traditions is high on the list of objections. Furthermore, Stuart Henry (2005) warns, a new round of disciplinary hegemony is trumping interdisciplinary ascendancy with efforts to co-opt, absorb, regularize, and normalize successful experiments in the curriculum. Mindful of the same challenges in interdisciplinary research (IDR), James Collins cautions that deeply embedded cultural issues confront individuals and institutions. When respondents to preliminary surveys for the National Academy of Sciences (NAS) report, *Facilitating Interdisciplinary Research* (2004), were asked to rank supportiveness for interdisciplinary research, they indicated a trend toward more favorable environments. Yet they were also aware of the barriers: 71 percent of 423 respondents to the individual survey and 90 percent of the 57 provosts and vice chancellors who answered a provost survey believe that major impediments exist locally. Administrative, funding, and cultural barriers between departments collectively impede movement across boundaries, perpetuating institutional customs that create "a small but persistent 'drag' on researchers who would like to do interdisciplinary research and teaching" (Collins, cited in *Facilitating Interdisciplinary Research,* 2004, p. 171).

The arguments in support of interdisciplinarity are persuasive. However, promotional rhetoric and the promises of strategic plans ring hollow when interdisciplinary work is routinely impeded and discounted. Diana Rhoten (2004) came to a similar conclusion in a study of IDR centers and programs funded by the National Science Foundation. Despite all the talk about interdisciplinarity, universities are failing to walk the walk. Many are simply adopting interdisciplinary labels—without adapting their disciplinary structures and artifacts. The authors of *Facilitating Interdisciplinary Research* (2004) affirm that few universities have implemented systemic reforms for lowering institutional barriers. Even institutions with well-known profiles and a significant portion of faculty identifying themselves as having ID affiliations and commitments recognize the need to address persistent impediments. Uneven development benefits some but leaves others at the margins (Dubrow and Harris, 2006).

Simply speaking the word can "warm a room," Caruso and Rhoten (2001) quipped, generating "knowing nods" of agreement about interdisciplinarity's explanatory power, relevance, and practical applicability. Yet organizational roadblocks, skepticism, and lack of agreed-on metrics to gauge quality counter claims. The contradictory discourse is not new. For more than thirty years, Peter Weingart observed, interdisciplinarity has been "proclaimed, demanded, hailed, and written into funding programs" (2000, p. 26). Yet specialization continues unhampered. Researchers publicly pronounce openness to interdisciplinarity. Their endorsements, though, do not necessarily translate into practice. In short, affirmations of the need for interdisciplinarity cannot be taken at face value.

Facilitating Interdisciplinary Research (2004) admonishes institutions to examine their structures for supporting interdisciplinarity within the context of the larger, overarching framework that both defines and constrains it. Karri Holley (2009) echoes the call in her book on the current challenges and opportunities for interdisciplinarity. She outlines changes that foster, support, and reward faculty engagement through an active and deliberative process. Developing a new institutional culture, Holley exhorts, requires a flexible vision, structural modifications, and shifts in organizational behavior and norms. This book deepens the conceptual framework and broadens the pragmatic strategies for doing so in a model of a systemic approach to creating campus cultures conducive to interdisciplinary research and education. In the absence of a systemic approach, arguments for change are weak, plans are underdeveloped, current activities and interests are underidentified, existing resources are not leveraged to greater effect, best practices are not incorporated, barriers and impediments are not eased, and outcomes are limited to marginal efforts that cannot be sustained. The buzzword factor also prevails. In a guide to program review discussed more fully in Chapter Four, the American Studies Association cautions that terms such as *disciplinary, mul-*

tidisciplinary, and *interdisciplinary* are often just buzzwords. They replace informed arguments with superficial aphorisms such as, "Everyone is interdisciplinary today," a proclamation belied by evidence.

Interdisciplinary change entails many of the same challenges and opportunities as other initiatives. Generally it is easier to foster change within a small institution than a large one. It is also easier to work with individual enclaves than to achieve institution-wide transformation. Interdisciplinary change, however, is more complex because it runs counter to conventional ways of thinking, behaving, planning, and budgeting in academic institutions (Gaff, 1997). An old administrative saw comes to mind—that interdisciplinary programs exist in the white space of organizational charts. Today, though, the white space is more crowded. Modern systems of higher education, Burton Clark (1995) found in an international study of research universities, are confronted by a gap between older, simple expectations and the complex realities that outrun those expectations. Definitions that depict one part or function of the university as its "essence" or "essential mission" only underscore the gap between simplified views and new operational realities that are transforming the way we think about knowledge and education (pp. 154–155).

Trowler and Knight's studies of institutional change in higher education (2002) shed further light on the gap Clark identified. The standard model of "contextual simplification" assumes that organizations are culturally simple, fitting into a small number of pigeonholes. Trowler and Knight found, though, that "any university possesses a unique and dynamic multiple cultural configuration which renders depiction difficult and simple depictions erroneous" (p. 143). Viewed from an analytical telescope, differences in values, attitudes, assumptions, and taken-for-granted practices look small. Viewed from an analytical microscope, they loom large. Interdisciplinarity compounds the problem of contextual simplification because academic work is presumed conventionally to lie within the confines of departments. Faculty interests, though, cut across boundaries and are not confined to the overt reality of recognized units.

In reviewing the track record of educational experiments of the 1960s and 1970s, Keith Clayton (1985, p. 196) suggested that the "concealed reality of interdisciplinarity" may be greater than the overt reality. Some activities flourish most readily, in fact, when they are not labeled as interdisciplinary. Clayton was talking about geography, medicine, veterinary science, agriculture, and oceanography. Yet his observation is true of other domains and parallels three other related concepts. Charles Lemert (1990) called the composite set of structures and strategies that challenge the prevailing metaphor of disciplinary depth a "shadow structure," and J. Hillis Miller (1991) described new developments that cross departmental, disciplinary, and institutional boundaries as a "hidden university." Brown and Duguid's (1996) concept of canonical practices is also applicable. Canonical practices in organizations are prescribed and set down in official documents, mission statements, and other defining texts that function as road maps for members of an organization to follow. The relatively static nature of canonical practice, however, can never keep up with the complexity and variability of events on the ground, in the rough terrain missed by large-scale maps. The dynamic character of knowledge and expertise drives divergence with the emergence of new ideas, understandings, modes of work, and reinterpretations and reconstructions of tasks, projects, and roles.

Dynamism and divergence also drive another concept in this book: distributed interdisciplinary intelligence. The methods and theories of textuality, narrative, and interpretation appear not only in traditional disciplines of humanities but also in social sciences and the professions of law and psychiatry. Gender is not a conceptual category in women's studies alone. Culture is not the sole intellectual property of anthropology or the traditional textual disciplines of humanities. Sustainability is not the sovereign province of environmental studies. The concepts of information and communication have been developed in not only engineering but also in media studies and library and information sciences. Conflict, justice, and democratic participation in decision making have a presence well beyond political science and policy studies. Research and teaching on the body occur in both medicine and art history. Diversity is a core concept in several interdisciplinary fields as well as general education requirements and discipline-based majors and research programs.

THE BOOK

Every campus will not follow every strategy presented in this book because local institutional cultures, priorities, and resources differ. Campuses will also be at different stages of development. Some are just beginning to think about how to foster interdisciplinarity. Others want to coordinate current activities more effectively while keeping options open for the future. Regardless, informed decision making depends on awareness of the variety of approaches being used around the country in concert with a careful reading of the local culture. As the president of one university remarked in a consulting meeting with his cabinet, "Let's hear what is happening and the strategies being used elsewhere, then decide what makes sense here."

The book is not an encyclopedic catalogue of every program, center, and project across the country. It presents a conceptual framework for change that is concretized in a portfolio of representative strategies and practices from a variety of institutions, large and small, public and private, oriented to teaching and research intensive. The conceptual framework brings together a number of ideas from organizational theory, higher education studies, and the discourse on interdisciplinarity that are defined throughout the course of the book. The underlying premise is that interdisciplinarity is a pluralistic idea. It is embodied in a heterogeneity of forms and practices that are changing the way we think about knowledge and education. They range from informal networks and communities of practice, where like-minded individuals create alternative social and cognitive space, to new and emerging fields. Individual activities have discrete locations, but they also intersect and cross-fertilize, adding to more frequent boundary crossing and the greater pluralism and complexity of the academy today. Local context, in turn, results in added variations.

The portfolio of strategies presents current lessons of practice, based on literature review and field experience. The literature review spanned studies of higher education, institutional change, and organizational theory, as well as the voluminous discourse on interdisciplinarity that spans print publications and the "gray literature" of conference papers, reports, documents, guidelines, and, increasingly, online materials. Some readers will be familiar with these literatures. Most, however, are not, with the exception of administrators and faculty who read studies of higher education organization and management. Moreover, few members of any campus read the literature on interdisciplinarity in depth. As a result, even the most committed faculty and administrators are not fully aware of resources and strategies for interdisciplinary change, leaving them uncertain about the most appropriate and effective approaches to planning, implementing, managing, and sustaining initiatives.

My field experience consists of over three decades of teaching in an interdisciplinary program and visits to other campuses that are the best means of feeling the pulse of change and testing the feasibility of strategies. Field experience also revealed that three questions are uppermost in the minds of faculty, administrators, and planning groups:

- What changes are occurring?
- What is happening on other campuses?
- How should we respond locally?

These questions are all the more pressing in a new period of financial exigency driven by an international economic crisis. Now more than ever before, it is crucial to have answers to the questions that typically arise in order to strengthen arguments for change, anticipate and counter resistance with evidence, and inform decision making with precedents, literature, and the accumulated wisdom of theory and practice. In answering the most common questions that arise, this book benchmarks the topic of interdisciplinary change. Benchmarking is not a passive exercise in reading. Benchmarkers review literature, documents, and other quantitative and qualitative data. Yet they do not simply apply lessons from written material and the narrow connotation of numbers, measures, and standards. C. Jackson Grayson (1998) defines *benchmarking* as a form of action learning that is extended through direct observations, site visits, participation, and interactions aimed at learning tacit knowledge, culture, and structure. It is a process of identifying, learning about, adapting, and implementing outstanding practices from other organizations in order to help a given organization improve its own performance. This book guides the process for improving interdisciplinary performance.

THE AUDIENCE

The intended audience of the book is wide and large. The primary audience comprises the thousands of administrators, faculty, planning committees, and task forces across the country striving to create favorable environments for interdisciplinary education and research. Because interest is so widespread, their disciplines and fields span the entire academy, from department-based majors engaged in reforms to the expanse of interdisciplinary programs and projects identified in Chapters One and Two. Likewise, interdisciplinary research appears widely, in department-based projects, ID centers, and cross-campus initiatives. In order to serve this broad audience, the book bridges three perspectives:

- Upper-level administration, strategic planning, and policy
- Mid- and lower-level planning, management, performance, and evaluation
- Individual, small group, and project- and program-level work

The three perspectives are often treated separately, diminishing common understanding and cooperation. For that reason, the book is designed to be read in common at all levels of an institution, then returned to later for more focused discussion of specific topics by particular groups. The secondary audience for the book is threefold. First, even in a time of constrained resources, academic libraries seek comprehensive overviews and guides to the latest resources. They will find the Resources section at the end of the book especially helpful, since it provides a guide for collection building for the entire campus. Individual programs and central oversight bodies that maintain their own libraries will benefit as well. Second, professional associations, national policy bodies, and funding agencies with an interest in interdisciplinarity also need authoritative overviews. Third, individual scholars and students of higher education can use the book as a resource on the changing history of interdisciplinarity, and it can be adopted as a textbook in undergraduate and graduate courses on higher education, organizational management, and interdisciplinarity.

THE STRUCTURE

Preparing for interdisciplinary change requires two mappings. The first map is national. Chapter One provides an overview of developments associated with interdisciplinarity today in science and technology, social sciences, and humanities. As a result of the heterogeneity of activities, faculty and administrators have different connotations in mind when they hear the word *interdisciplinary*. They need a common picture of the drivers of change. Shared awareness will enable individuals to locate themselves within the larger landscape of higher education, reduce their sense of isolation, lessen ignorance and skepticism about other domains, and foster a common commitment to easing mutual barriers. The chapter also introduces a core vocabulary for campuses and ends with a summary statement of the conceptual framework of the book.

Chapter Two addresses interdisciplinary modes and types of work, empirical data, taxonomy, local mapping, and variables of change. It moves from the national map of developments sketched in Chapter One to a picture of the modes of work and organizational forms those developments take on local campuses, based on five snapshots of patterns identified in recent bodies of data and taxonomies. The chapter ends with a plan for mapping interdisciplinarity locally and, in the transition to Chapter Three, the organizational variables for interdisciplinary change that need to be weighed.

Chapter Three discusses strategies for change, central oversight, leadership, and an interdisciplinary endowment. It presents a framework for platforming interdisciplinarity through actions aimed at capacity building and creating an institutional deep structure. Based on decisions about variables and models of change, a robust portfolio of strategies can be created. Transformative and incremental approaches should be combined, as should strategic targeting and general loosening of barriers. Top-down and middle-level strategies should also be combined, along with interests that arise bottom-up from faculty work. The chapter closes with discussions of central oversight, leadership, and an interdisciplinary endowment that encompasses funding, space, and equipment.

Chapter Four examines criteria and strategies for strength and sustainability in the areas of institutionalization, program review, and the political economy of interdisciplinary studies. It begins by defining arguments in the debate on institutionalizing interdisciplinarity and critical mass factors for strong programs. It then defines five principles for interdisciplinary program review: interdisciplinarity, antecedent conditions, benchmarking, balance, and partnership. The chapter closes with lessons on the political economy of IDS programs from a new collection of case studies that illustrates the principles and other lessons about strength and sustainability.

Chapter Five covers hiring, tenure and promotion, and faculty development. Few institutions have taken a comprehensive approach to the interdisciplinary career life cycle. However, the composite body of strategies being used across campuses yields guidelines for greater intentionality and protection. Hiring and tenure and promotion policies need to be anchored in clear and supportive policies, as well as a memorandum of understanding with faculty and constituent units that will ensure consistency and appropriate criteria of evaluation. The chapter does not treat phases of the career cycle as isolated steps. Defining and implementing an interdisciplinary career model requires attention to needs that begin well before hiring, continue with career rewards, and take deeper root through ongoing faculty development.

Even with a clear conceptual framework and a strong portfolio of strategies, all parties will still find themselves confronted at some point with a number of myths. Being able to respond to them is a crucial final step for thinking about interdisciplinary campus cultures. Five myths are prominent: that interdisciplinarity is new, a "genuine" interdisciplinarity trumps all other forms, interdisciplinary work is superficial, it threatens the disciplines, and it is impossible to do. The Conclusion offers answers and a final set of questions linking the answers back to Chapters One through Five.

The Resources section provides further support and next steps for local campuses. It identifies materials for collection building by libraries, central oversight bodies, programs, and individuals. It is not an exhaustive bibliography but a representative selection of key works and strategies. It looks at overviews and bibliographies;

domains of practice; interdisciplinary studies; integration, collaboration, and evaluation and assessment; and Web-based searching and networking. The emphasis is on the past decade, though scrutiny of bibliographies will lead to earlier key publications in particular areas, and Web-based searching and networking will ensure continued updating.

The Glossary provides a summary of key definitions and an abstract of the conceptual framework for the book.

CHAPTER ONE

MAPPING NATIONAL DRIVERS OF INTERDISCIPLINARY CHANGE

Preparing for interdisciplinary change requires two mappings—the first national and the second local. Skipping to the second map shortchanges the answers to two of the three questions that are uppermost in the minds of faculty and administrators: What changes are occurring? and What is happening on other campuses? Shared awareness of the national picture will enable individuals to locate themselves within the larger landscape of higher education, reduce their sense of isolation, lessen ignorance and skepticism about activities in other areas, heighten awareness of the plurality of local activities, and foster a common commitment to easing barriers. This chapter presents an overview of major developments associated with interdisciplinarity today in science and technology, social sciences, and humanities.

The book adopts a root meaning of interdisciplinarity based on two authoritative definitions from the National Academy of Sciences (NAS) report, *Facilitating Interdisciplinary Research* (2004), and Klein and Newell (1997) in *Handbook of the Undergraduate Curriculum.* Interdisciplinary research (IDR) and interdisciplinary studies (IDS) integrate content, data, methods, tools, concepts, and theories from two or more disciplines or bodies of specialized knowledge in order to advance fundamental understanding, answer questions, address complex issues and broad themes, and solve problems that are too broad for a single approach (*Facilitating Interdisciplinary Research,* 2004; Klein and Newell, 1997).

The consensus meaning, though, is only a literal definition. The root term has many connotations, distinguishing a variety of goals and contexts that will become clear in this chapter. The differences are dramatically evident in disputes over what constitutes real or genuine interdisciplinarity. Awareness of the multiple connotations is not an idle exercise in etymology or history. Differences surface in local arguments for and against certain forms of interdisciplinarity. To help readers navigate the debate on meaning, this chapter also introduces a core vocabulary that can be used on campuses and ends with a summary statement of the conceptual vocabulary of the book.

Science and Technology

When scientists hear the word *interdisciplinary* some mention historical precedents ranging from the Greek philosopher Anaximander to Charles Darwin. By and large, though, scientists are inclined to cite modern developments in defense-related research during the 1930s and 1940s, especially the Manhattan Project to build an atomic bomb. It was the first large government-funded example of IDR. In subsequent decades, IDR became part of the profiles of the Department of Defense, the National Science Foundation, the National Institutes of Health, and the National Aeronautics and Space Administration. Scientists also tend to cite major discoveries and initiatives, such as x-ray crystallography and the human genome project. The current momentum is documented in a 2004 report from NAS. *Facilitating Interdisciplinary Research* identifies four primary drivers of IDR today (pp. 2, 40):

1. the inherent complexity of nature and society
2. the desire to explore problems and questions that are not confined to a single discipline
3. the need to solve societal problems
4. the power of new technologies

Drivers 2 and 3 are not new. However, they gained momentum in the closing decades of the twentieth century. The heightened profile of driver 3 was signaled in 1982, when the Organization for Economic Cooperation and Development declared in *The*

University and the Community (1982) that interdisciplinarity exogenous to the university now takes priority over endogenous university interdisciplinarity based on the production of new knowledge. The exogenous originates in real problems of the community and the demand that universities perform their pragmatic social mission. International economic competition in science-based fields of high technology propelled increased activity and investment from the late 1970s forward in areas such as engineering and manufacturing, computers, biotechnology, and biomedicine. Complex problems of practice in professional and vocational education have also fostered interdisciplinary approaches in law, medicine, social work, education, and business.

The National Research Council (NRC) tracked changes in a series of reports. In 1986, the authors of *Scientific Interfaces and Technological Applications* announced that almost all significant growth in knowledge production in recent decades was occurring at the interdisciplinary borderlands between established fields. The five prominent areas in fundamental research were biological physics, materials science, the physics-chemistry interface, geophysics, and mathematical physics and computational physics. The six outstanding areas of technical applications were microelectronics, optical technology, new instrumentation, the fields of energy and environment, national security, and medical applications. Four years later a new NRC report, *Interdisciplinary Research* (1990), tracked developments that were promoting increased collaborations between life sciences and medicine and between physical sciences and engineering. New intellectual understandings of biological systems, problem complexity, the costs of instrumentation and facilities, and the desire to transfer knowledge rapidly from laboratory to hospital practice have been strong catalysts for change.

These developments signaled a double form of boundary crossing between disciplines and commercial sectors, leading Rustum Roy to suggest that the more accurate term is not *interdisciplinary* but *interactive research* (2000). The escalation of boundary crossing between academic science and commercial sectors, in combination with recent discoveries in molecular and cell biology, prompted the National Institutes of Health to issue a new road map for research and funding in 2002. Collaborative teams, new combinations of skills and disciplines, a better toolbox, and new technologies are all needed to understand the combination of molecular events that lead to disease. The NIH has accelerated this trend with the aim of creating a new discipline of clinical and translational research capable of catalyzing new knowledge and techniques for patient care (http://nihroadmap.nih.gov/overview.asp; http://nihroadmap.nih.gov/clinicalresearch/overview-translational.asp).

Driver 4 is apparent in new technologies of molecular imaging, nanomedicine, and bioinformatics. In addition, new tools of quantitative and computer-assisted mathematical analysis also facilitate the sharing of large quantities of data across disciplinary boundaries in areas as diverse as medicine and the geosciences, the latter of which already experienced an interdisciplinary transformation in the mid-twentieth century fueled by the theory of plate tectonics. Driven by Web 2.0 technologies, information sharing across the infrastructure of distributed information is also enabling individuals and networks in dispersed locations to collaborate. The implications are not merely technical. In the journal *Science,* Alan Leshner (2004) observed that "new technologies are driving scientific advances as much as the other way around," allowing new approaches to older questions and posing new ones (p. 729).

In the midst of these major developments, the quiet daily flow of borrowing methods, concepts, and tools continues. The impact varies greatly, from auxiliary or supplementary borrowing to a degree of assimilation that is no longer considered foreign. Many physical techniques that originated in one discipline, such as spectroscopies, have become so fully integrated into biological research that their origin may be forgotten. Researchers also apply knowledge from one discipline in order to contextualize another, akin to the engineering profession's inclusion of social contexts of practice. When new laws comprise the basic structure of an original discipline, such as electromagnetics or cybernetics, a new domain takes shape. Methodologies of statistics, oral history, and econometrics were the foundation for other specialties as well, and other interactions led to the formation of new fields and hybrid interdisciplines such as biochemistry, cognitive science, and computational biology (Heckhausen, 1972; Boisot, 1972).

Another development, the emergence of new communities of practice, is part of a wider process of boundary work. Individuals and groups work directly and through institutions to create, maintain, break down, and reformulate boundaries between domains. The term *trading zones* arose in science studies to describe the heterogeneous interactions that give rise to new social and cognitive formations centered on common interests. These formations range from a *pidgin* zone, in the linguistic sense of an interim form of communication, to a *creole* zone, a new main subculture or native language (Galison, 1996; Star and Griesemer, 1989; Fisher, 1993; Klein, 1996). Interactions have been sources of continual advances in concepts and applications across the science of molecules and atoms, surfaces and interfaces, and fluids and solids. The current interface between physics and chemistry, for example, has been crossed so often in both directions that the authors of *Scientific Interfaces and Technological Applications* (1986) remarked "its exact location is obscure" and "its passage is signaled more by gradual changes in language and approach than by any sharp demarcation in content" (p. 53). As a result, Norman Burkhard reflected, the difference between a physicist and a chemist is no longer obvious: "Now we have chemists who are doing quantum-level, fundamental studies of material properties, just like solid-state physicists. There's almost no difference" (cited in *Facilitating Interdisciplinary Research*, 2004, p. 54).

Three implications follow for thinking about the definition of interdisciplinarity, the nature of disciplines, and the curriculum. Taking definition first, much of scientific IDR today is instrumental in nature, in the sense that it is motivated by strategic or opportunistic goals (Weingart, 2000). Economic, technological, and scientific problems tend to take priority over epistemological motivations, aligning interdisciplinarity with mangerialism, commercialism, and entrepreneurism (Sá, 2005). The heightened profile of instrumental interdisciplinarity (ID) is linked with a historical shift in the performance of scientific research from individual investigators to multidisciplinary groups driven by external demands. Some research programs have grown so large that they are stimulating new understandings in multiple fields, evident in the wide impact of the theory of plate tectonics, global climate modeling, and the human genome project. IDR may also add value to traditional fields. Researchers in nanoscience, for instance, bridge several disciplines while using their nanoscience experience to open new disciplinary research directions and applications, such as incorporating nanostructures into bulk materials (*Facilitating Interdisciplinary Research*, 2004).

As for the second implication, the argument for interdisciplinarity is often countered by a demand to protect the disciplines. Yet since the 1950s, many disciplines have become more porous and multi- or interdisciplinary in character (Bender and Schorske, 1997). Some domains, such as physics and biology, have also become so large and heterogeneous that they have been called federated disciplines. Specialization has a double effect. It reinforces fragmentation, but it also gives rise to connection and, in some cases, mutual interdependence (Winter, 1996). The inner development of the sciences has posed ever broader tasks leading to interconnections among natural, social, and technical sciences. The same object—an organism, for instance—is simultaneously a physical (atomic), chemical (molecular), biological (macromolecular), and physiological, mental, social, and cultural object. As mutual relations are reconsidered, new aggregate levels of organization are revealed, and *multidisciplinary* is becoming a common descriptor of research objects (Habib, 1990).

The third implication calls to mind the oft-remarked gap between new research and the curriculum. The gap persists, but Jerry Gaff (1997) likens scholarship to the molten mass of radioactive material that forms the core of the earth. Periodically it erupts in a volcano, or a shift in tectonic plates occurs. In accounting for interdisciplinarity in the science curriculum, Wubbels and Girgus (1997) report that faculty are incorporating new knowledge of genetics, cognition, and the solar system. They are organizing courses around complex technical and social problems and topics. They are also designing curricula that reflect the blurring of boundaries in contemporary research, including an introductory course integrating mathematics, physics, and chemistry; a joint biochemistry and biophysics program that integrates physics, chemistry, and biology classes; courses that teach general chemistry based on the context of physical materials; and project-based laboratories for general chemistry using lasers. Other reports add to the roster of examples. *BIO 2010* (2003) offers a blueprint for bringing undergraduate education in biology up to the speed of contemporary research in an interdisciplinary curriculum that integrates physical sciences with information technology and mathematics with life sciences. Pellmar and Eisenberg's 2000 report, *Bridging Disciplines in the Brain, Behavioral, and Clinical Sciences*, presents models of interdisciplinary teaching and training at all levels, from undergraduate through postdocs.

More broadly, the NAS report, *Facilitating Interdisciplinarity Research* (2004), presents a series of recommendations for science education drawn from survey data, interviews, and literature review. The top advice for educators is to develop curricula that incorporate ID concepts, participate in teacher development courses on ID topics, and provide students opportunities to participate in IDR. The report also urges a multifaceted and broadly analytical approach to problem solving and revising foundation courses such as general chemistry to include materials that show how subjects are related to other fields and to complex societal problems. Favorable policies for team teaching are recommended as well, along with modifying core course requirements to allow more room for breadth and for team-building and leadership skills. Undergraduate students, for their part, are encouraged to seek courses at the interfaces of traditional disciplines that address basic research problems, courses that address societal problems, and research experiences spanning more than one traditional discipline. The top recommendation for graduate students is to broaden their experience by gaining requisite knowledge and skills in one or more fields beyond their primary subjects. Like faculty, they also need experience in using new instrumentation and techniques from other disciplines. Graduate students might also be admitted into broad fields, such as biological sciences and engineering, with no requirement for specialization until the end of the first or second year. Institutions, in turn, are urged to offer opportunities for students to work with and learn from students in other disciplines and with multiple advisers or dual mentors who contribute diverse perspectives on research problems.

SOCIAL SCIENCES

When social scientists hear the word *interdisciplinary*, they tend to cite historical precedents such as Auguste Comte's vision of a unified social science and the founding of the Social Science

Research Council (SSRC) in the early 1920s. At SSRC the term *interdisciplinary* was shorthand for research that crossed more than one of the 'council's seven disciplinary societies, breaking down boundaries by cross-fertilizing ideas and joining methods and techniques. Representatives of five major social science disciplines, statistics, and history were brought together with the aim of producing purposive and empirical social problem-oriented applied research, including targeted programs in fields such as social security and public administration (Frank, 1988; Fisher, 1993). The first twentieth- century appearance of *interdisciplinarity* under stewardship of the SSRC, Calhoun and Rhoten (forthcoming) recall in an overview of its history in social sciences, was characterized by a desire to revive the quest for a Comtian style "science of the social" that would both analyze and address social ills. Problem focus was also a strong catalyst for the rise of applied social science concerned with societal issues such as war, labor relations, population shifts, housing shortages, crime, and welfare (Landau, Proshansky, and Ittelson, 1962). (This account draws on Klein, 2007.)

Landau, Proshansky, and Ittelson made a distinction in the early history of social sciences that illustrates the difference between two basic metaphors of interdisciplinarity identified by the Nuffield Foundation: bridge building and restructuring. *Bridge building* occurs between complete and firm disciplines, but they do not change as a result. *Restructuring* detaches parts of several disciplines to form a new coherent whole (*Interdisciplinarity*, 1975). The difference is evident in Landau, Proshansky, and Ittelson's comparison of the first and second phases of interdisciplinarity (1962). The first phase, dating from the close of World War I to the 1930s, was embodied in the founding of SSRC and the University of Chicago school of social science. The interactionist framework at Chicago fostered integration, and members of the Chicago school were active in efforts to construct a unified philosophy of natural and social sciences. The impact of these efforts was widely felt and the scope and data of disciplines altered. On occasion disciplinary spillage even led to the early formation of hybrid disciplines, such as social psychology, political sociology, physiological psychology, and social anthropology. Yet traditional categories of knowledge, structures of fields, and the organization of academic work remained intact. Social scientists also tended to emulate natural sciences, heightening concern for objectivity, precision, and quantification. In the interests of scientific analysis, techniques and instruments were borrowed to support testing and measurement.

In sum, the first phase was largely empirical and instrumental bridge building. The second phase, dating from the close of World War II, was stimulated by new developments in logic and in philosophy and sociology of science that illustrate restructuring. The difference was embodied in integrated social science courses, a growing tendency for interdisciplinary programs to become integrated departments, and the concept of behavioral science. The traditional categories that anchored the disciplines were questioned, and lines between fields began to blur, paving the way toward a new theoretical coherence and alternative divisions of labor. The emergence of area studies in the late 1930s is a well-known example. In contrast to earlier and limited forms of interdisciplinary borrowing, it was a new integrative conceptual category with greater analytical power, stimulating a degree of theoretical convergence and potential in the concepts of role, status, action, exchange, information, communication, and decision making. The behavioral science movement also sought an alternative method of organizing social inquiry based on theories of behavior that went beyond borrowing and tacking methods and concepts onto traditional categories. The culture-personality movement and decision making are additional examples. When a political scientist, for instance, adopts decision making explicitly as a frame of reference, the nature of the field of focus changes, and the work is not just politics. It is also sociological or psychological, or both.

The early history of interdisciplinarity in social science illustrates another important distinction, between methodological and theoretical interdisciplinarity. Methodological ID typically aims to improve the quality of results. In a typology of cross-disciplinary approaches in social sciences, Raymond Miller (1982) identified two types. *Shared components* include techniques of statistical inference and conceptual vehicles. *Cross-cutting organizing principles* focus on a particular concept or a fundamental social process, such as role or exchange. New engineering and technological methods that evolved from operational research during World War

II, feedback systems, and computer manipulation also stimulated borrowing of the mathematics of probability, cybernetics, systems theory, information theory, and game theory, as well as new conceptual tools of communication theory and decision theory. Techniques of surveying, interviewing, sampling, polling, case study techniques, cross-cultural analysis, and ethnography belong on the list of examples too. And in the latter half of the twentieth century, a third methodological movement emerged, stimulating new borrowings that combine quantitative and qualitative traditions (Mahan, 1970; Smelser, 2004; Teddlie and Tashakkori, 2003).

In contrast, theoretical interdisciplinarity typically fosters a comprehensive conceptual framework, synthesis, or integration across disciplines. This aim was evident in the boundary work of advancing new integrative concepts such as "behavior" and "area" and in the macrosocial theories of Emile Durkheim, Georg Simmel, Max Weber, Robert Park, and Talcott Parsons. More recent efforts include Anthony Giddens's search for a new synthesis of social sciences, Randall Collins's call for a comprehensive theory of every area of society, Jeffrey Alexander's attempt to create a convergence of major classical and contemporary sociological theories, Jürgen Habermas's work toward an encompassing theory of communicative action, and Niklas Luhmann's aim of building a synthetic framework for a comprehensive theory of everything social (Camic and Joas, 2004).

Theoretical forms of interdisciplinarity are also associated with the concept of transdisciplinarity, a term that originally connoted an overarching synthesis or a common axiom that transcends the narrow scope of disciplinary worldviews. General systems theory, structuralism, Marxism, feminist theory, sociobiology, and phenomenology have been leading examples. More recently in Europe, two new connotations have emerged: a new structure of unity informed by the worldview of complexity in science and trans-sector problem solving involving the collaboration of academics and stakeholders in society. Conceptualized as a form of transcendent interdisciplinary research, the transdisciplinary team science movement in the United States is also fostering new theoretical frameworks for understanding social, economic, political, environmental, and institutional factors in health and well-being (Rosenfield, 1992).

In the latter half of the twentieth century, the scope of IDR in social sciences expanded with two further sets of developments. One looked to the sciences. Propelled by the growing sophistication of scientific tools and approaches, new biological explanations of human behavior became possible, and the hybrid fields of cognitive science and neurosciences expanded. Technologies of brain imaging and magnetic resonance imaging also facilitate mapping brain functions with increasing precision (Yates, 2004). The other set of developments looked toward humanities, informed by new postpositivist, poststructural, constructivist, interpretive, and critical paradigms (Teddlie and Tashakkori, 2003). By 1980, Clifford Geertz proclaimed that a broader shift was occurring across intellectual life in general and within social sciences in particular. The model of physical sciences and a laws-and-instances ideal of explanation was being supplanted by a case-and-interpretation model and symbolic form analogies. Social scientists were increasingly representing society as a game, a drama, or a text rather than a machine or a quasi-organism. Crossing the traditional boundary of explanation and interpretation, they were also borrowing methods of speech-act analysis, discourse models, and cognitive aesthetics. Conventional rubrics remain, but they are often jerry-built to accommodate a situation Geertz deemed increasingly "fluid, plural, uncentered, and ineradicably untidy" (p. 166).

The mainstream disciplines remain anthropology, economics, political science, psychology, and sociology. Yet Neil Smelser (2004) cautions that describing social sciences solely with reference to the "big five" distorts reality in two ways. First, under those headings, subareas of investigation rely on variables and explanations outside the commonly understood scope of social sciences. Geopolitics, sociobiology, behavioral genetics, and behavioral neuroscience all appeal to nonsocial and nonpsychological explanatory variables and explanations. Second, another range of disciplines could be labeled behavioral and social-scientific, although not entirely so. Demography, for example, might be considered a separate social science or as part of sociology, economics, and anthropology. Archaeology might be classed as part of anthropology or an independent social science. Geography, history, psychiatry, law, and linguistics present similar complications for taxonomy. So do relations with intersecting fields such as genetics, behavior, and society; behavioral and cognitive neurosciences; area and international studies; and urban studies and planning public policy. Assignment to one category of inquiry or another would vary according to the criteria used.

Furthermore, multiple types of interdisciplinarity occur within a single discipline. Geography's broad scope is evident in a multitude of conceptual and analytical approaches, ranging from technologies of earth sciences to interpretive theories of humanities. Synthetic work of a different kind occurs in efforts to combine basic research findings from a large number of subfields in order to integrate results from cognate disciplines and merge existing and new knowledge about a particular place or region. Another type of activity occurs in applied research on societal problems (Association of American Geographers, 1995). Sociology, for its part, aspires in principle to be the most synthetically encompassing of all social sciences. Yet Craig Calhoun (1992) reports that beyond holistic and generalist claims, it is also an interstitial discipline that fills in gaps among other social sciences and working along their borders. In anthropology, connections pluralized as the discipline expanded beyond the "sacred bundle" of four fields that Franz Boas defined as biological history, linguistics, ethnology, and prehistoric archaeology. Since 1983, George Stocking Jr. (1995) notes, many "adjectival anthropologies" have emerged, and the number of subsidiary professional groups has increased. Anthropologists were also more open to poststructuralist and postmodernist thought than other social scientists, destabilizing intellectual categories at the same time a general blurring of genres and disciplinary boundaries was underway. Even economics, which patrols its boundaries more closely than other disciplines, has multiple affiliations with mathematics, political science, history, sociology, psychology, philosophy, and law (Becher, 1990).

The formation of new fields is an important part of this history. Miller (1982) identified four catalysts for interdisciplinary fields and hybrid specializations. *Topics* are associated with problem areas. Crime, for instance, is a social concern that appears in multiple social science disciplines and in criminal justice and criminology programs. The concepts of area studies, labor, cities, the environment, and the aged also led to the founding of new programs. The category of *life experience* became prominent in the late 1960s and 1970s with the development of ethnic studies and women's studies. *Hybrids* formed interstitial cross-disciplines, such as social psychology, economic anthropology, political sociology, biogeography, culture and personality, and economic history. *Professional preparation* also led to new fields with a vocational focus, such as social work and nursing and, Smelser (2004) adds, fields of application to problem areas such as organization and management studies, media studies and commercial applications, and planning public policy.

All fields are not the same, however. Some, Jill Vickers (1997) noted in an overview of Canadian studies, have congealed to the point that they have a recognized canon or foundational theory. Effecting a partial closure, they act like disciplines because they have a shared epistemological base, journals, learned societies, and, in some cases, separate departments. In contrast, "open or cross-roads interdisciplinary fields" do not necessarily settle on a paradigm, canon, foundation, or epistemology. They remain open to new ideas, especially identity fields centered on self-studies that emanated from broad societal movements for change, such as women's, Quebec, and First Nations' movements for self-determination. Moreover, in open cross-roads fields, two forces may be at work: an integrative tendency, and a self-asserting dis-integrating tendency that tries to draw the focus away from the center of existing knowledge systems, strongly evident in critical, oppositional, and self-studies. Older fields have changed as well. American studies, for instance, was one of the earliest exemplars of an interdisciplinary field. After emerging in the 1930s and 1940s, it took a more critical turn in the 1960s and 1970s and embraced a new plurality of practices that expanded in the late twentieth century to include new methods and concepts linked with cultural studies. In education, Hendershott and Wright (1997) report, change is also occurring as a result of interdisciplinary developments. Increased attention is being paid to multicultural and gender interests, evident in the titles of undergraduate social science textbooks using the keywords *diversity, multiculturalism,* and *global.* Growing numbers of ethnic studies and gender studies majors in departments of English and literary studies, though, raised concern about the lack of attention to demography, quantitative research methods, statistics, or immigration public policy. In general education programs, new understandings from social sciences are informing general and liberal education themes of citizenship, leadership, health, and family life. More broadly, a heightened problem focus is apparent across the curriculum in units and courses focusing on social problems and bridging theory and practice in service learning. And new alliances are being forged in interdisciplinary courses focused on complex societal problems such as crime, juvenile violence, infant mortality, AIDS, ethnic tensions, and pollution.

Reflecting on the latter half of the twentieth century, Calhoun and Rhoten (forthcoming) called the 1960s and 1970s a period of "reflection and intervention." The 1960s ushered in a wave of epistemological segmentation and polarization. Positivists aimed to intensify trends toward scientific universalization and hyperspecialization, manifested in the dominance of neoclassic economics. Yet increasing numbers of researchers sought approaches that would privilege a mix of theoretical prospects, disciplinary perspectives, and societal purposes. Civil tensions, political conflicts, and social movements also spawned field creation in Miller's categories of life experience (for example, ethnic studies, women's studies) and topics (for example, environmental studies, labor studies, and development studies). During the 1970s, researchers with an ID problem orientation began tackling issues in poverty studies and social medicine, using methods that brought together academic experts and local stakeholders in action research programs akin to transsector transdisciplinarity. The turn of the century has been a time of extension and computation. This development is not driven by philosophical faith in or epistemic hope for interdisciplinarity; rather, intellectual demands and design strategies responsive to disciplinary limitations have come with the advancement of science. The diversity of paradigms and heterogeneity of perspectives that motivate and propel interdisciplinary practice today, Calhoun and Rhoten concluded, also tend to complicate its processes and prospects. The very conditions of possibility are often the very causes of difficulty that stall its varied forms.

Humanities

Humanists have the longest genealogical reach, tracing interdisciplinarity to foundational ideas of synthesis, holistic thought, and unified knowledge in ancient Greece. These ideas were transmitted in the traditions of humanism and liberal education and subsequently formed the basis for the unified model of culture and knowledge at the heart of the first American colonial college. At the dawn of the twentieth century, the historical warrants for interdisciplinarity were the generalist model of culture, a synoptic view of subjects, and interart comparison. Period style was the most powerful basis of synchronic relation, grounded in common motifs, themes, and genres within historical eras. When the modern disciplines were taking shape in the late nineteenth and early twentieth centuries, the traditional humanist model also found a new home in interdisciplinary theme-based general education programs grounded in a canon of "great books" and ideas.

Over the course of the century, traditional canons of wholeness were challenged by new approaches to culture, history, and language. New forms of interdisciplinarity also arose in a history extending from the importation of European philosophy and literary theories in the 1950s to social and political movements in the 1960s, structuralism and the language-based psychoanalysis of Jacques Lacan, newer kinds of Marxist criticism and deconstruction, and, during the 1970s and 1980s, widening interest in feminism and semiotics. Further into the 1980s, an array of practices lumped under the umbrella term *poststructuralism* took root, including new historicism, Foucauldian studies of knowledge, and cultural and postcolonial critique. By the 1990s, multiculturalism was a major theme, and the belief that humanities was evolving into cultural studies was gaining favor. More recently, digital humanities has become a growing field of research, teaching, and technological innovation at the intersections of computing and the disciplines and fields of arts and humanities, media and communication studies, and library and information science.

Interdisciplinarity has been implicated at every turn. Each movement differed in some way, but together they fostered a new generalism that challenged both the modern system of disciplinarity and the older model of unified knowledge and culture. The new generalism is not a unified paradigm. It is a cross-fertilizing synergism in the form of shared methods, concepts, and theories about language, culture, and history. A new rhetoric of interdisciplinarity developed in kind. *Plurality* and *heterogeneity* replaced *unity* and *universality*. *Interrogation* and *intervention* supplanted *synthesis* and *holism*, and older forms of *interdisciplinarity* were challenged by new *anti-, post-, non-*, and *de-disciplinary* formulations. The keywords of the new rhetoric signified the defining values of critical interdisciplinarity. This form interrogates the dominant structure of knowledge and education with the aim of transforming them, while raising epistemological and political questions of value and purpose silent in instrumental ID.

The values of critical ID are apparent in Salter and Hearn's definition of interdisciplinarity (1996) as the necessary churn in the system, aligning the concept with a dynamic striving for change. In humanities, the concepts of new interdisciplinarity and transdisciplinarity are also associated with new critical and theoretical approaches. Critical ID gained a certain orthodoxy in humanities. Yet it is not the only interdisciplinary practice. Older forms of interart comparison and borrowing continue, embodied in studies of authorship, connoisseurship, and the influence of one art form on another. Even so, in conducting interviews with faculty in humanities and social sciences, Lisa Lattuca (2001) found that an increasing number of them do interdisciplinary work with the explicit intent of deconstructing disciplinary knowledge and boundaries. This trend is especially apparent in cultural studies, women's and ethnic studies, and literary studies, where "the epistemological and the political are inseparable" (p. 100).

The traditional disciplines of humanities are implicated as well. Their broadening scope led to a pluralization of subdomains that intersect with interdisciplinary fields, including "new histories" and "music." As humanities disciplines moved away from older paradigms of historical empiricism and positivist philology, increasing attention was paid to the contexts of aesthetic works and the responses of readers, viewers, and listeners. The concept of culture also expanded from a narrow focus on elite forms to a broader anthropological notion, and once discrete objects were reimagined as forces that circulate in a network of forms and actions. As a result, interdisciplinary practices today are often hybrid. Close reading of a text or technical analysis of a painting or a musical composition may be combined with psychoanalytical, sociological, semiotic, deconstructionist, or feminist approaches. Disciplinary categories have not been abandoned. Yet their meaning has broadened to encompass more subject matter, conditions of artistic production, social science methods and concepts, and previously marginalized groups and other cultures. This development was reinforced by heightened interests in history, sociology, politics, and an anthropological definition of culture that have reshaped thinking about both disciplinarity and interdisciplinarity.

Changes of this kind once again expose the limits of the conventional dichotomy of disciplinarity and interdisciplinarity. Part of the problem of interdisciplinarity, Stanley Bailis (1974) reflected, is how disciplines have been taught. They were presumed to be topically coalescent, solidified, and monolithic. Furthermore, they were rarely taught with reference to each other, and the bridges built between them tended to become separate domains or subdisciplines practiced differently within parent fields. Disciplines, in actuality, are highly differentiated, and authorized practices are contested. Reflecting on changes in the discipline of history, Carl Schorske (1997) noted a generational shift that is not unique to it alone. As a graduate student, Schorske had to learn the methods of other disciplines from colleagues. By 1995, students were taking seminars in art, literature, and psychoanalysis to acquire their analytical techniques. Students of other disciplines were also appearing in history department seminars in search of a more professional way of entering the discipline's discourse.

Changes of this kind are not easy to map either. Giles Gunn (1992) identified four approaches to mapping in literary studies that are applicable across all disciplines. The simplest strategy is on disciplinary ground. The conventional conjunctive strategy traces the relationship of one discipline to another, such as literature and philosophy. The map changes, though, if another question is asked. What new subjects and topics have emerged? Many examples appear, including history of the book, psychoanalysis of the reader, and the ideology of gender, race, and class. Each topic in turn projected further lines of investigation. This degree of complexity seems to defy mapping. "The threading of disciplinary principles and procedures," Gunn observed, "is frequently doubled, tripled, and quadrupled in ways that are not only mixed but, from a conventional disciplinary perspective, somewhat off center" (pp. 248–249). They do not develop in a linear fashion and are not traceable in all their effects. They are characterized by overlapping, underlayered, interlaced, cross-hatched affiliations, collations, and alliances that have ill-understood and unpredictable feedbacks. The final and most difficult approach is rarely acknowledged. Correlate fields such as philosophy and other disciplines have changed. These changes challenge assumptions about the strength of boundaries while working to erode them.

The charge of superficiality, though, still haunts interdisciplinary work. In considering concepts in the interdisciplinary study of culture, Mieke Bal (2002) addressed the concern. Concepts have the theoretical and analytical force to go beyond multidisciplinary diffusion, illustrated by the examples of image, mise-en-scène, framing, performance, tradition, intention, and critical intimacy. They exhibit both specificity and intersubjectivity. Concepts do not mean the same thing to everyone, but they foster common discussion as they travel between disciplines, between individuals, between academic communities, and between historical periods. In the process of travel, their meaning and use change. Their productive propagation prompts a new articulation with a new ordering of phenomena within the cultural field. The basis of interdisciplinary work, Bal maintains, is selecting one path while bracketing others. Cultural analysis is not medium bound, and it does not exist without connections to other disciplines and recognizes that fields such as postcolonial studies have been catalysts for disciplinary change. At the same time, interdisciplinary analysis has a specificity that is not lost in superficial generalisms. Informed borrowing, Bal admonishes, is crucial. "Surfing" and "zapping" produce only "muddled multidisciplinarity," not the productive interdisciplinarity that results from paying a "good quality of attention" to the subjects and objects that make up a culture.

Ultimately, W.J.T. Mitchell (1995) concluded, everything depends on what sort of interdisciplinarity is being practiced. Mitchell distinguished three major types:

- *Top down*: Comparative, structural formations that aim to know an overarching system or conceptual totality within which all disciplines are related

- *Bottom up*: A compulsive and compulsory interdisciplinarity dictated by a specific problem or event
- *Inside out*: The indisciplined or anarchist moment, a site of convergence and turbulence

The top-down model hearkens back to a Kantian architectonic of learning in a pyramidal organization of knowledge production capable of regulating flows of information from one part of the structure to another. It appears in philosophy and critical theory, in claims for a utopian convergence of theory and practice, and in the promotion of semiotics as a universal metalanguage for studying culture. The bottom up emerges in response to emergencies and opportunities. Cultural studies is a general form of the bottom-up model. The inside out is the indiscipline of breakage or rupture. It disturbs continuity and practice. Ruptures, though, can become routinized, evidenced in the rapid transformation of deconstruction into an institutionalized method of literary and cultural interpretation. The "anarchist" moment, Mitchell maintains, may well be the most important event. Like Salter and Hearn's "churn in the system" (1996), it is the time before routine or ritual is reasserted.

Interdisciplinarity, Gunn (1992) concluded, is ultimately a double-sided question: "The inevitable result of much interdisciplinary study, if not its ostensible purpose, is to dispute and disorder conventional understandings of relations between such things as origin and terminus, center and periphery, focus and margin, inside and outside" (p. 249). Relational studies of the conjunctive kind proceed from the question of what literature has to do with other disciplines. Genuine interdisciplinarity, in his view, alters the constitutive question that generates interdisciplinary inquiry in the first place, asking how insights and methods of another field or structure can remodel understanding of literature and the ways literary conceptions and approaches remodel allied fields and subject materials.

Gunn's view is widely shared in humanities, though Stanley Fish (1989) challenged the underlying premise of new interdisciplinarity on institutional grounds. Its agenda seemed to flow naturally from new theories and practices that are critical of the structures by which lines of political authority are maintained and disciplines establish and extend their territorial claims. Yet, Fish contended, any strategy that calls into question the foundations of disciplines theoretically negates itself if it becomes institutionalized. The majority of activities center on straightforward tasks that require information and techniques from other disciplines, expand imperialistically into other territories, or establish a new discipline couched in the language of antidisciplinarity but producing a new breed of counter professionals. This objection resurfaces in Chapter Four in the discussion of institutionalization.

As for the humanities curriculum, Lyn Maxwell White (1997) identified several trends in innovations, including greater collaboration across departments and merging traditional viewpoints with new scholarship. Content has also broadened to include more comparative study, informed by new scholarship on culture. Poststructuralist theories of language and meaning, coupled with new understandings of the nature of texts and reading, have changed the way traditional and new texts and subjects are taught. Faculty in English departments, for example, are adding a new plurality of cultural texts while drawing on social history and new theories of language and meaning. History teachers are applying quantitative methods from the social sciences and borrowing qualitative strategies of understanding texts from literary theory. As a result, White concluded, boundary lines have become harder to draw. In arts education, Ellen Harris (1997) reported, multiculturalism and cultural contextual studies bring history and sociology into greater focus while expanding the canon beyond its traditional Eurocentric foundation. New technology has also opened new modes of learning and understanding the creative process, stimulating new philosophical inquiries about the nature of object of study. (For a fuller discussion of ID humanities, see Klein, 2005.)

TRANSITION TOWARD LOCAL CHANGE

Summing up the most recent period in higher education, Carol Geary Schneider and Robert Shoenberg (1998) characterized it as a time of transformative change. A complete transformation has not occurred. However, every element of a new academy is visible across the country. The new academy is a broad-based movement that has grown up around the edges and increasingly within the departments of the old academy. It comprises new forms of scholarship and modes of teaching and learning, reconfigurations of disciplines, and a new relational pluralism (Minnich, 1995). Interdisciplinarity is a major variable in the new academy. However, organizational charts and taxonomies rarely capture its full extent and the fluidity of faculty identities (Brew, 2008) that Marcia Bundy Seabury and Gail Dubrow have observed over the course of their careers.

Seabury (1999), who has administered and taught in the University of Hartford's interdisciplinary general education program, reports that faculty teaching in the program usually have conventional departmental homes. Yet "if you look beneath the surface you often find people who have been covert boundary crossers all along." The complexity of their lives and interests belies the "relative linearity of their departmental careers" (p. 5). Gail Dubrow (2007), who has led a major national study of fostering interdisciplinary inquiry, concurs. Over the long arc of academic careers, Dubrow has found that "intellectual interests of faculty may extend far beyond the boundaries of a single discipline and/or take them into entirely new area of inquiry" ("Facilitating Intellectual Mobility," 2005). Each year, some perform work beyond their department homes, and some are awarded joint or adjunct appointments reflecting the evolution of their cross-disciplinary connections and commitments. As their teaching and research unfold over time, knowledge domains, realms of discovery, and constellations of collaboration may reach well beyond original disciplinary backgrounds and appointments.

Only a hologram could do justice to the changing trajectories of knowledge and education that Seabury and Dubrow observe. Chapter Two moves from the mapping of national drivers in this chapter to the organizational forms and practices they take on local campuses. In doing so, it addresses another pressing question in the minds of faculty and administrators: Where does interdisciplinarity fit? When Lynton Caldwell (1983) posed the question in environmental studies, he argued that the metaphor of fit prejudges the epistemological problem at stake in their emergence. Many fields arose because of a perceived misfit among need, experience, information, and the structuring of knowledge and curriculum embodied in disciplinary organization. If the structure of the academy must be changed to accommodate a new development, Caldwell admonished, then perhaps the structure itself is part of the problem. Caldwell is not alone in this view, though as we shall see in Chapter Four opinion differs on the best approach to institutionalization.

Chapter Two also deepens the conceptual framework of this book. Summing up key concepts of the framework introduced in this chapter, it is clear from the overview of science and technology, social sciences, and humanities that interdisciplinarity is a pluralistic idea. It is embodied in a heterogeneity of modes and forms of work that have fostered a distributed interdisciplinary intelligence and relational pluralism in the academy. Individual activities have discrete locations, but they also diffuse and intersect with other movements, adding to the greater hybridity of knowledge today, more frequent boundary crossing, and a growing multidisciplinary thrust of faculty work. Hybrid communities of practice range from trading zones where like-minded researchers and educators interact, to matrix structures of centers and programs, to emerging fields and, with sufficient critical mass, new paradigmatic fields. Hybrid discourses range from interim pidgin forms of communication to creoles that comprise a subculture or native language of a new domain. Local context results in added variability, manifested in differing degrees of in/visibility in the balance of overt and concealed interdisciplinarities across the surface and shadow structures of institutions. Creating a campus culture that is conducive to interdisciplinary research and education is a form of boundary work that requires identifying points of convergence, leveraging existing resources, building capacity and critical mass, platforming and scaffolding the architecture for a networked campus, benchmarking and adapting best practices, creating a resource bank, and institutional deep structuring of a robust portfolio of strategies aimed at programmatic strength and sustainability.

CHAPTER TWO

BRIDGING NATIONAL AND LOCAL MAPS

Chapters Two and Three bridge national developments and local contexts by defining the organizational forms and activities that interdisciplinary (ID) interests take on campuses and strategies for supporting them. Shared awareness reduces skepticism about ID change being too difficult to implement and anchors actions in informed decision-making about options. Chapter Two presents five snapshots of organizational forms and practices drawn from Klein and Newell's (1997) complex systems model of interdisciplinary studies (IDS); a Social Science Research Council study of IDS in liberal education (Rhoten, Boix-Mansilla, Chun, and Klein, 2006); Brint, Turk-Bicakci, Proctor, and Murphy's (2009) longitudinal study of IDS degree-granting programs from 1975 to 2000; the 2005 picture of multi/interdisciplinary studies from the National Center for Education Statistics and forthcoming 2010 Classification of Instructional Programs (http://nces.ed.gov/programs/digest/d05/tables/; http://nces.ed.gov/ipeds/cipcode/crosswalk.aspx?y=55); and the National Research Council's proposed new taxonomy for doctoral programs (Ostriker and Kuh, 2003; Ostriker, Holland, Kuh, and Voytuk, 2009). The chapter ends with a plan for local mapping and, transitioning to Chapter Three, the organizational variables for interdisciplinary change that need to be weighed.

INTERDISCIPLINARY MODES AND FORMS OF WORKS

When members of a campus community are asked, "What is interdisciplinarity?" they typically cite a particular development outlined in Chapter One or a particular activity such as team teaching, collaborative research, borrowing from another discipline, or creating a new field. They can be quite insistent, too, on what counts as genuine, asserting the necessity of teamwork over individual efforts, prioritizing problem solving, or dismissing approaches that combine existing approaches without critiquing the underlying structure of knowledge and education. Figure 2.1 is an overview of four major modes of interdisciplinary work that Rhoten and Pfirman (2007) identified. The examples on the right-hand side of the typology differ in both kind and scale, spanning amorphous cross-fertilizations, formal collaborations, topics that catalyze new fields, and problem-oriented research that reaches beyond the academy. (See also Calhoun and Rhoten, forthcoming.) Personal and institutional connections also differ, ranging on the left-hand column from intrapersonal to external interactions.

FIGURE 2.1. INTERDISCIPLINARY WAYS OF WORKING

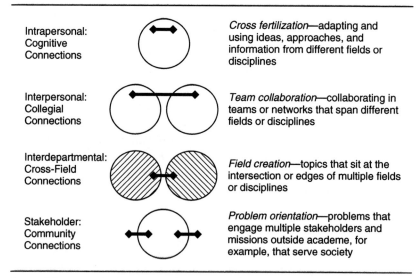

Intrapersonal: Cognitive Connections — *Cross fertilization*—adapting and using ideas, approaches, and information from different fields or disciplines

Interpersonal: Collegial Connections — *Team collaboration*—collaborating in teams or networks that span different fields or disciplines

Interdepartmental: Cross-Field Connections — *Field creation*—topics that sit at the intersection or edges of multiple fields or disciplines

Stakeholder: Community Connections — *Problem orientation*—problems that engage multiple stakeholders and missions outside academe, for example, that serve society

Source: Rhoten and Pfirman (2007). Reprinted with permission.

When pressed to cite the typical organizational forms and structures that ID ways of working assume, respondents tend to cite the most common institutional forms: programs, departments, and research centers. In order to answer the question more fully, Klein and Newell (1997) examined forms and structures over time. The comparison led them to conclude that higher education has been moving from a simple model to a complex one. The shift becomes apparent when comparing defining features of interdisciplinary research (IDR) and interdisciplinary studies (IDS) during the 1960s and 1970s—illustrated by features of the simple model in the left-hand column of Table 2.1—with the greater plurality of ID activities and forms today—illustrated by added features of the complex model in the right-hand column.

TABLE 2.1. FEATURES OF SIMPLE AND COMPLEX MODELS

Features of Simple Model	Added Features of Complex Model
Freestanding institutions	New ID approaches and trading zones
Autonomous colleges within universities	Changing disciplinary curricula
Centers and institutes	Learning communities and faculty networks
Departments and programs	Problem-focused research topics, projects
Majors, minors, concentrations	Shared facilities, databases, instruments
Self-designed majors	Subdisciplinary boundary crossing
Mainstream and alternative general education	Educational functions of centers
Individual courses within disciplines	Training for ID and collaborative modes
Tutorials and independent study	Collaborative research programs, projects
Travel study, internships, practicums	Intersectoral partnerships with government, industry, and communities

Source: Adapted from Klein and Newell (1997).

In the simple model, interdisciplinary work was often innovative, but its home was a familiar structure or format. The work was accommodated but did not challenge the existing structure of higher education. New forms and practices were typically added to the discipline-dominated structure of a campus. Simple systems may have multiple levels and connections in a hierarchy, but they operate according to a single set of rules. In contrast, complex systems are nonhierarchically structured. They obey multiple and conflicting logics and may exhibit a chaotic element. Simple structures still exist, but the current plurality of interdisciplinary activities adds to the complexity of the academy today. Moreover, Klein and Newell found (1997), interdisciplinary structures are no longer isolated or discrete. They may be interconnected in a shifting matrix, replete with feedback loops and unpredictable synergistic relationships.

Taken together, the increase in not only the number but also the kind of ID activities underscores the gap Burton Clark (1995) observed between simplified views and new operational realities that are transforming the way we think about knowledge and education. The gap is exposed by the academic ritual of introduction. The first question typically asked when meeting another faculty member for the first time is, "What department are you in?" or, alternately, "What is your discipline?" If the question changes to "What do you do?" the map of research and education on campus expands.

A member of an English department may be teaching courses in American literature while conducting research on narratives of the immigrant experience in the United States or coordinating an interdisciplinary program in film and media studies. A historian may be teaching a traditional survey course while conducting research on changing models of labor in the U.S. economy or collaborating with a feminist scholar on representations of women in early modern art. Faculty alliances also cross boundaries. A sociologist working on the rhetoric of science may talk more with linguists in the English department than with colleagues in the sociology department who are working on a new theory of urbanization. Members of a biology department will be involved in different networks and more formal communities of practice depending on whether their personal interests lie in molecular structures of DNA, cancer research, or the impact of climate change on human health. Titles are also deceptive. Most faculty engaged in women's studies, Sandra Coyner (1991) reported, identify with another community as a historian, literary critic, psychologist, or social worker. Naming tends to designate a position within a program—as a women's studies faculty, student, or director—more than the kind of work performed.

IDS programs are a primary benchmark of what is happening across campuses because they are the institutional home for many interdisciplinary interests in both education and research. The last authoritative directory of IDS programs in the United States appeared in 1996. Comparing his findings to the 1986 first edition of the directory, Alan Edwards Jr. reported that significant growth has occurred in areas where IDS was already strong, especially women's studies and general education. Honors also remains a prominent site, and despite downsizing and retrenchment, many programs had originated or been substantially revised since 1986. Most significant, the concept of interdisciplinarity has been diversifying. It now appears across general education, older and newer interdisciplinary fields, and the professions. The 410 programs listed in Edwards's directory were almost double the number in the 1986 edition of the directory.

More recent accounts, including the National Academy of Sciences (NAS) report, *Facilitating Interdisciplinary Research* (2004), add to the widespread sense that interdisciplinary programs are increasing. At Brown University, consistent growth in student interest has occurred, including student-designed concentrations and interdepartmental concentrations comprising about a third of standard programs. At Columbia University, the number of students majoring in interdepartmental or ID programs increased dramatically over a ten-year period ending in 2004. A 9.7 percent average annual increase in ID program majors and concentrations also outpaced interdepartmental program growth (6.7 percent) and departmental majors and concentrations (4.8 percent) from 1995 to 2002. At Harvard University, the number of undergraduate joint concentrations in chemistry and physics rose from fourteen to forty-five in a period spanning roughly 1989 to 2004. And at Stanford University, a multiyear decline in the number of students majoring in earth science was reversed when the major, based originally in geology, was reformulated into an ID program in earth systems.

Two recent studies provide a more broad-based empirical picture.

AN EMPIRICAL PICTURE

A national survey of IDS and liberal education and a longitudinal analysis of IDS programs add new data on what is happening on campuses. In 2006, the Social Science Research Council (SSRC) issued results of a national survey of 222 colleges and universities, a microstudy of eight selected institutions, and deliberations of a working group of invited experts and representatives of campuses in the microstudy. The SSRC sought to identify patterns of interdisciplinary education in liberal arts colleges and universities across public and private, small and large institutions. Respondents were asked to indicate which of five types of programs they offered and the estimated rate of student participation. ID majors received the highest percentage from the 109 respondents to a national survey, with 94.4 percent offering majors. Minors/certificates, at 85.2 percent, received the next highest report. In addition, 60.2 percent reported offering required ID courses with an estimated participation at 100 percent. Of the top ten majors in Table 2.2, more than half are in international and global or area studies, two follow a biology-plus model, and the most popular are in areas often considered advocacy/activism fields. Environmental studies and science, women's and gender studies, neuroscience and psychobiology, and American studies were the top-cited ID majors (Rhoten, Boix-Mansilla, Chun, and Klein, 2006).

No less striking, two-thirds of respondents to the SSRC national survey expected to increase ID offerings over the next five years. The most commonly cited motivation was research, based on a shared belief that the kinds of questions students and faculty are investigating today often require the expertise of scholars from more than one field. Other drivers are student demand and student outcomes. The prominent role of research is affirmed elsewhere. Elam and Ross (2000) described the Area One Program of Stanford University's revised general education requirement as

TABLE 2.2. TEN MOST FREQUENTLY OFFERED INTERDISCIPLINARY MAJORS

Majors	Percentage of Institutions Offering Major
Intercultural studies	13.08%
Latin American studies	16.82
African American and Africana studies	21.50
International relations, international studies	28.04
Asian and East Asian studies	31.78
Biochemistry and molecular biology	33.64
American studies	36.45
Neuroscience and psychobiology	36.45
Women's and gender studies	44.86
Environmental studies and science	63.55

Source: Rhoten, Boix-Mansilla, Chen, and Klein (2006).

a response, in significant part, to changes across the boundaries, theories, and definitions of humanities. The second of the two studies affirmed patterns identified by the SSRC group, though it conducted a more longitudinal examination of change from 1975 to 2000 in a wider range of institutional types.

The data for Table 2.3 came from Brint, Turk-Bicakci, Proctor, and Murphy's longitudinal analysis (2009) based on the College Catalogue Study (CCS). It represents a sample of 293 institutions for which complete microfiche were available from the Institutional Data Archive on American Higher Education. The research team considered four frameworks for understanding the institutionalization of new fields:

- Diffusion models, which explain change as a function of the efforts of organizations to improve stability and effectiveness
- Sociodemographic models, which view change as an outcome related to representation of new constituencies
- Organizational stratification models, which treat change as a function of unequal adoption of innovations due to inequalities in organizational resources, market power, or prestige

TABLE 2.3. FIELDS TYPICALLY ORGANIZED AS INTERDISCIPLINARY
PROGRAMS, 2000–2001

Program	Total	Number of Interdisciplinary Organizations (Percent)	Number of Department Organizations (Percent)
1. NON-WESTERN CULTURAL STUDIES	**324**		
Asian area studies	132	114 (86%)	18 (14%)
Latin American area studies	112	107 (96%)	5 (4%)
African area studies	51	42 (82%)	9 (18%)
Middle Eastern studies	19	19 (100%)	0 (0%)
2. RACE AND ETHNIC STUDIES	**250**		
African American studies	114	87 (76%)	27 (24%)
Ethnic and race studies	54	41 (76%)	13 (24%)
Chicano, Hispanic studies	41	27 (66%)	14 (33%)
American Indian studies	24	19 (79%)	5 (21%)
Asian American studies	17	14 (82%)	3 (18%)
3. WESTERN STUDIES	**227**		
European, North American studies	153	138 (90%)	15 (10%)
Western period history studies	70	68 (97%)	2 (3%)
European origin studies	2	2 (100%)	0 (0%)
Western studies	2	2 (100%)	0 (0%)
Canadian studies	2	2 (100%)	0 (0%)
4. ENVIRONMENTAL STUDIES	**215**	173 (80%)	42 (20%)
5. INTERNATIONAL AND GLOBAL STUDIES	**204**		
International relations, global	152	132 (87%)	20 (13%)
Peace, conflict studies	40	38 (95%)	2 (5%)
Political economy	12	10 (83%)	2 (17%)
6. CIVIC AND GOVERNMENT STUDIES	**194**		
Urban studies	99	87 (88%)	11 (12%)
Public affairs, public policy	48	37 (77%)	11 (23%)
Legal studies	47	38 (81%)	9 (19%)

(continued)

TABLE 2.3. CONTINUED

Program	Total	Number of Interdisciplinary Organizations (Percent)	Number of Department Organizations (Percent)
7. WOMEN'S STUDIES	**192**	173 (90%)	19 (10%)
8. AMERICAN STUDIES	**158**		
American culture or studies	142	123 (87%)	19 (13%)
U.S. regional studies	16	16 (100%)	0 (0%)
9. BRAIN AND BIOMEDICAL SCIENCE	**124**		
Cognitive, neuroscience	66	50 (76%)	15 (24%)
Biological psychology	21	17 (81%)	4 (19%)
Biomedical, biotechnology	19	18 (95%)	1 (5%)
Medical technology	18	12 (67%)	6 (33%)
10. OTHER	**387**		
Interdisciplinary studies[a]	106	98 (92%)	8 (8%)
Film studies	66	42 (64%)	24 (36%)
Liberal studies	57	50 (88%)	7 (12%)
Gerontology	43	39 (91%)	4 (9%)
Judaic studies	41	39 (95%)	2 (5%)
Science and society	22	19 (86%)	3 (14%)
Arts management	13	13 (100%)	0 (0%)
Health management	10	10 (100%)	0 (0%)
Folk studies	9	6 (67%)	3 (33%)
Ethics, values	5	5 (100%)	0 (0%)
Sexuality studies	5	5 (100%)	0 (0%)

[a]A small number of programs were listed twice in catalogues: as interdisciplinary programs and as departments.

Source: Data compiled from College Catalog Study Database. Brint, Turk-Bicakci, Proctor, and Murphy (2008). Original publication of the table, copyright held by publisher The Johns Hopkins University Press: Brint, S. G., Turk-Bicakci, L., Proctor, K., and Murphy, S. P. "Expanding the Social Frame of Knowledge: Interdisciplinary, Degree-Granting Fields in American Colleges and Universities, 1975–2000." *Review of Higher Education,* 2009, *32*(2), 155–183.

- Organizational ecology models, which explain change as the behavior of organizations adapting to the structure of an organizational field, factoring in both constraints and opportunities

The team chose to highlight ecological conditions created by the existing structure of an organization, factoring in the size of student enrollments, preexisting curricular emphases, and the proportion of arts and sciences to total degrees.

As Edwards did, Brint, Turk-Bicakci, Proctor, and Murphy restricted their selection to particular criteria for inclusion. Edwards's primary criteria were an explicit ID perspective, institutional recognition as an ID program, and persistence over time. Brint, Turk-Bicakci, Proctor, and Murphy selected degree-granting programs identified as interdisciplinary and having faculty from more than one department. They included both majors and minors, but excluded programs that offered courses without conferring degrees. They also excluded programs typically organized as departments in favor of programs typically organized as ID units during two-thirds or more of the period of their study (with the exception of film studies). They made this distinction in order to avoid overlap with managerial use of the "program" designation to maintain struggling fields without permanent resources or to provide a transitional location for upwardly mobile fields. They also adjusted their statistical analysis for programs that were eliminated, absorbed into departments, consolidated, or split into two. Programs that were eliminated or absorbed into departments were no longer included following the change in status. Consolidated programs were counted only once following their change in status, and programs that were divided were counted twice following the split.

This methodology has limits, prominent among them lack of measures for discriminating weak versus strong models (an index of interdisciplinarity examined more fully in Chapter Four). Yet the study provides evidence that significant growth has occurred over the twenty-five-year period in each of the nine areas in Table 2.3, even outstripping the rate of growth in student enrollments overall. The total number of ID fields in the sampled institutions grew by nearly 250 percent during the period spanning

1975 through 2000 and from 674 programs in 1975–1976 to 1,663 in 2000–2001. The order of frequency also bears a striking resemblance to the SSRC study, although Brint, Turk-Bicakci, Proctor, and Murphy's longitudinal approach revealed that rates of growth were unevenly distributed across fields. The number of ID units in international relations/global, race and ethnic, and women's studies, as well as brain and biomedical science, more than tripled. The number of programs in environmental studies nearly tripled, and the number of programs in non-Western cultural studies more than doubled. Western studies also showed strong growth, nearly doubling in count. Civic/governmental studies and American studies grew more slowly. U.S. and Western-oriented programs (American, Western, and civic/governmental studies) showed no signs of diffusing consistently across the twenty-five-year period.

Taxonomy

A taxonomy groups entities according to their common characteristics. Since the late nineteenth and early twentieth centuries, taxonomies of knowledge in the West have been dominated by the modern system of disciplinarity. Conventional taxonomies are being challenged, though, by the growth of interdisciplinary activities. Three recent reports yield quantitative data that will help campuses anchor the claim of increased activity in evidence about not only undergraduate education but also doctoral education and research in science and engineering. The most recent comprehensive picture is based on data published by the U.S. Department of Education's National Center for Education Statistics (NCES) in 2005. The NCES digest is a compilation of statistical information covering kindergarten through graduate school. At the level of postsecondary education, it provides a snapshot of college enrollment, faculty and staff, conferred degrees, educational attainment of the population, and expenditures. Of the total number of institutions reporting data on degrees conferred in 2003–2004, multi/interdisciplinary studies (MD/ID studies) was the seventeenth most popular of thirty-six categories at the bachelor's degree level (with 758 institutions reporting). At the master's degree level, it was fifteenth of thirty-three categories and at the doctoral degree level thirteen of thirty-two categories. Comparisons over time further validate the argument for increase (http://nces.ed.gov/programs/digest/d05/tables/):

- For bachelor's degrees, the baseline academic year 1970–1971 indicated that MD/ID studies was seventeenth of thirty-two categories. By 2003–2004, it was thirteen of thirty-three categories, with the total number increasing dramatically at two points. The tally in 1970–1971 was 6,346 degrees. In 1975–1976 it was 13,778. By 1993–1994 it was up to 15,652 and, with the exception of 2000–2001, rose steadily thereafter.
- For master's degrees in 1970–1972, MD/ID studies was ranked twenty-fourth of thirty-two categories. Here too the raw numbers grew over time, from 926 in 1970–1971 to 4,047 in 2003–2004.
- Stuart Henry's earlier analysis of statistics (2005) issued by the NCES in 2003 indicated that between 1991 and 2001, the number of enrolled students grew by 48 percent. Moreover, they were graduating from around 652 programs nationwide, with the possibility of entering 215 ID master's and 65 ID doctoral programs.

The argument for increase is reinforced when the complete set of categories in the NCES report is scrutinized. Two categories often associated with interdisciplinarity are treated separately from MD/ID studies: area, ethnic, cultural, and gender studies (a composite code) and biological/biomedical sciences (encompassing both disciplinary and interdisciplinary studies). Factoring in the first category alone raises the overall ranking and total numbers higher. The count rises even more when subcategories of Code 30 are considered. Code 30: Multidisciplinary/Interdisciplinary Studies includes not only the two categories just mentioned but areas reported within separate codes and in categories that capture cross-unit relationships, including the following examples:

- General synthesis of one or more biological and physical sciences as well as a general synthesis of mathematics and computer science

- Other recognized ID fields, including peace studies and conflict resolution, systems engineering and systems science and theory, information science and studies, gerontology, medieval and Renaissance studies, museology and museum studies, international and global studies, Holocaust and related studies, classical and ancient studies, Near Eastern studies and archaeology, intercultural and multicultural and diversity studies, and cognitive science, plus science, technology, and society
- Hybrid branches of psychology (biopsychology physiological psychology/psychobiology)
- Disciplines and professions cross-referenced with other codes, including psychology, history, social work, social sciences, and the specialty of adult health nursing

As this book was going to press, the U.S. Department of Education issued the updated version of its Classification of Instructional Programs (CIP). Starting in fall 2010, colleges and universities must use the new CIP when responding to the Integrated Postsecondary Education Data System Completions Survey (IPEDS). The 2010 IPEDS features 50 new four-digit codes for intermediate groupings, such as "anthropology," and 354 new six-digit codes for specific instructional programs, such as "cultural anthropology." A comparison of the 2000 and 2010 CIPs reveals other relevant changes. Among programs with a "multidisciplinary" descriptor, Child Abuse Pediatrics Residency Program has been added. Among programs with an "interdisciplinary" descriptor, new codes appear for Clinical Nurse Leader (working on an ID team), Cultural Studies/Critical Theory and Analysis, Ethnic Studies (now a distinct listing grouped under the older rubric of Ethnic, Cultural Minority, and Gender Studies), Human Biology, Human Computer Interaction, Pediatric Rehabilitation Medicine Residency Program, and Sustainability Studies. Of programs using the "Studies" name, Folklore, Disability, Deaf, Maritime, and Sports have been added, and new codes appear for Rhetoric and Composition/Writing Studies.

Relevant expansions within older categories also turn up. Besides Neuroscience, new entries appear, with the addition of subcategories noted in parentheses: Information Technology

(Infomatics), Chemical Engineering (Chemical and Biomolecular Engineering), Geological/Geophysical Engineering (Biochemical and Biosystems codes), Engineering/Industrial Management (Nanotechnology), Human/Medical Genetics (Genome Sciences/Genomics), and Bioinformatics (Computational Biology). Molecular Medicine and Neurobiology have new multiple designations as well, and Computational Science has been added to the CIP for 2010. The broad rubric of Anthropology has new codes for Sociology and Anthropology, Medical Anthropology, and Cultural Anthropology. Health and Wellness now appears as a category, and Digital Arts has been added to Visual and Performing Arts. The older category of Multi/Interdisciplinary Studies changed too. The prior designation specified programs that "provide a cross-cutting focus on a subject concentration that is not subsumed under a single discipline or occupational field." A new designation appears that distinguishes programs "integrated around a unifying theme or topic that cannot be subsumed under a single discipline or occupational field," citing a student-designated major as an example (http://nces.ed.gov/ipeds/cipcode/crosswalk.aspx?y=55).

A new taxonomy for graduate education affirms patterns in statistical tables and classification codes at the Department of Education while noting others. In 2005, a committee charged with examining the 1995 National Research Council's taxonomy of research-doctorate programs in the United States faulted the classification for outdated or inappropriate methodology that did not reflect the organization of programs in many universities. The subcommittee on taxonomy and interdisciplinarity recommended an overall increase in the number of recognized fields from forty-one to fifty-seven, including basic biomedical fields in medical schools and emerging fields of feminist, gender, and sexuality studies as well as nanoscience, bioinformatics, and computational biology. The category of global area studies, the subcommittee added, should include subfields of New Eastern, East Asian, South Asian, Latin American, African, and Slavic studies. "Biology" should be renamed "life sciences" and include agricultural sciences, the rapidly growing fields of communication and American studies should be recognized, and mathematics and physical sciences should be merged into a single category with engineering. The committee called attention to a widespread problem of naming as well. Old labels disguise new developments in disciplines and departments. Moreover, William Bechtel (1986) noted elsewhere, a field does not assume the same form everywhere. Biochemistry is a department in some places. In others it is combined with different disciplinary names and elsewhere is a subarea of molecular biology. Almost 40 percent of faculty in the pilot trials, the subcommittee also found, were involved in more than one program, leading to the recommendation that faculty teaching or supervising theses in more than one program be asked to name all of them (Ostriker and Kuh, 2003).

The final guide to methodology was being released as this book was going to press. It is most responsive to the category of Life Sciences and in the current version added an interdisciplinary field of Biology/Integrated Biology/Integrated Biomedical Sciences, with 120 programs. Most other changes to the 1995 study served to expand disciplines that were included, and programs were added in agricultural fields, public health, nursing, public administration, and communication. Appendix C of the 2009 methodology guide also includes the following "Emerging Fields": bioinformatics, biotechnology, computational engineering, criminology and criminal justice, feminist-gender-and-sexuality studies, film studies, information science, nanoscience and nanotechnology, nuclear engineering, race-ethnicity and postcolonial studies, rhetoric and composition, science and technology studies, systems biology, urban studies and planning (Ostriker, Holland, Kuh, and Voytuk, 2009).

Taxonomies of research are also being called into question. In 2008, the National Research Council commissioned the Panel on Modernizing the Infrastructure of the National Science Foundation's Federal Funds for R&D Survey. This survey, and the Survey of Federal Science and Engineering Support to Universities, Colleges, and Nonprofit Institutions, provides data on R&D spending and policy in the United States. Results of both surveys are cited in decisions about allotments of funding to particular fields and in public policy debate. Unlike the Classification of Instructional Programs developed by NCES in 1980 and periodically updated, the taxonomy for fields of science and engineering has not been updated since 1978. Since then, scientific research has become more multi- and interdisciplinary in character, yet the taxonomy does not capture those changes and related activities in the category of "not elsewhere classified" (NEC). NEC is a large and amorphous category that lumps together a plurality of developments, including new subfields, single-discipline projects for which a separate field has not been assigned, emergent fields, established ID fields, cross-cutting initiatives, problem-focus areas of research, and miscellaneous other. It also fails to discriminate multidisciplinary juxtapositions from integrative interdisciplinary approaches, as well as comprehensive transdisciplinary frameworks that posit a new conceptual synthesis or theoretical framework.

In its final report, *Data on Federal Research and Development Investments* (2009), the Panel on Modernizing the Infrastructure of the National Science Foundation's Federal Funds for R&D Survey presents a number of recommendations, including taking advantage of the affordances of new technologies in federating, navigating, and managing data. At present the Web is underused. Even when it is used, the full potential of the growing cyber-infrastructure of data is not tapped in a manner that is transparent and flexible for specific needs. The panel highlighted in particular the model of the National Institute of Health's Research Condition and Disease Classification (RCDC) database system. The RCDC demonstrates the potential of bottom-up comprehensive systems to incorporate taxonomic elements while permitting users to construct crosswalks with agency-relevant keywords (tags) used in projects and programs. Fields of science tags could be drawn from a prior taxonomy or be free text in cases where no existing tag fits, especially valuable for capturing newly emerging areas. Users could also query and build data tables based on their own interests and needs. A more open, flexible, dynamic, and transactional approach would depict research in a network representation that is more aligned with changing configurations of research. It would also take advantage of new techniques of semantic mapping, Web text mining, and controlled thesauri that are better able to capture the nature of the work itself and have been central to new mappings of knowledge domains (Panel on Modernizing, 2009).

Informative as these recent studies and taxonomies are, none of them factored in one of the fastest-growing sectors of IDS: general education. The growth of interdisciplinary and integrative approaches in this sector was so substantial from the 1980s forward that in 2000, the Association for Integrative Studies issued accreditation standards for interdisciplinary general education (examined more fully in Chapter Four). Interdisciplinarity also became a prominent interest in the work of the Association of American Colleges and Universities (AAC&U), an organization that provides national leadership and research on general and liberal education. The reasons for the growth intersect with all thirteen of the trend lines that Jerry Gaff (1999) identified in *General Education: The Changing Agenda.* As liberal arts and science subject matter are being updated, ID research is being incorporated and extended into professional and preprofessional programs. Synthesis and working with multiple forms of knowledge and information have become primary skills. The teaching of diversity and international themes, as well as moral and ethical issues, draws on new ID scholarship. First-year seminars are being organized around ID themes and problems, and senior capstone seminars afford opportunities to examine connections among majors, other disciplines, general education, and the "real world." Four-year programs foster progression from a multidisciplinary overview to higher-level synthesis. ID cores are replacing distribution models, courses are being clustered and linked in new combinations, and integrative learning communities have formed across the curriculum. ID outcomes are also receiving greater attention in assessment, and the needs of ID teaching are being recognized in faculty development programs, amplified by administrative support for curriculum planning, course development, and teaching core courses. Interdisciplinarity is increasingly endorsed in preprofessional and professional education as well.

A 2004 report of the AAC&U-sponsored Project on Accreditation and Assessment provides a panoramic view. The project compared targeted learning outcomes in business, engineering, nursing, education, and industry, as well as two regional accrediting agencies and AAC&U projects in liberal and general education. Interdisciplinarity is not a designated category. However, two of the ten categories are consistent with major learning outcomes associated with IDS in the SSRC study: integrative learning and breadth of knowledge. Imperatives in other categories also intersect with desired outcomes in many IDS programs and professional practice, foremost among them the capacity for finding and integrating multiple sources of knowledge and information, working collaboratively in teams, engaging in systems thinking, understanding contexts of practice, incorporating ethical and legal understanding, and using problem-solving and critical thinking skills. The engineering community's commitment is especially well documented in reports from ABET, the U.S. Accreditation Board for Engineering and Technology, and in a NAS report, *The Engineer of 2020* (2004). ABET calls explicitly for interdisciplinarity and integration while linking them to diversity, sustainability, community engagement, and international contexts (www.abet.org/).

LOCAL MAPPING

When asked what interdisciplinary programs are offered, most members of a campus cannot name them all. In some cases, multiple programs are clustered together in an office or center for IDS, but even then, it may not be a comprehensive grouping. A search on the campus website will not necessarily turn up all of the offerings either. Conducting an inventory is key to mapping what is happening locally:

- Identify current ID research and teaching interests, activities, and structures.
- Solicit information on both the overt and the concealed realities of interdisciplinarity, identifying both the visible, recognized surface structure and the less visible shadow structures.
- Include survey questions that solicit data and open-ended prompts for narrative experience.
- Collect all related official documents as well as unofficial reports and reflections.
- Use information from the inventory to create an institution-wide ID website.

The first principle of institutional change for facilitating interdisciplinarity, Klein and Newell (1997) urge, is "listening to the system" (p. 400). The inventory should be listening for not only overt interdisciplinarity and its surface structure. It should also capture the concealed reality, including the shadow structure of less visible activities, distributed interdisciplinary intelligence, ephemeral interests, and untapped points of convergence.

The importance of rendering the full extent of activities visible is underscored by a sidebar on Columbia University in *Facilitating Interdisciplinary Research* (2004). Columbia has been supportive of both interdisciplinary research and education, but officials admitted there were "almost no publicly accessible records of the administrative structures used to facilitate such work" (p. 20). There is no central record keeping for interdisciplinary units either. Lists were compiled for accreditation reviews in 1996 and 2001, and there was a new tally in 2004. Even with stepped-up accounting, though, officials caution that aggregate numbers cannot reflect their diversity and relations with other units.

The conventional approach to mapping is to tally up well-known educational programs and research centers, That is a good way to start. However, a broader inventory of activities and interests should be conducted. Table 2.4 depicts the range of structures and activities on campuses. Levels I and II are the most familiar. Level III is a bridge category, with differing degrees of formality in the interfaces. Levels IV and V recognize less visible examples, though they are often vital sites of intellectual energy and comprise an important part of the distributed interdisciplinary intelligence on a campus. The importance of level V is twofold. Some departments are already homes for interdisciplinary work, and the visibility of any one type may vary. Centers and institutes, for example, are well-recognized matrix structures that cross the boundaries of discipline-based departments. Some, such as the Beckman Institute at the University of Illinois at Urbana–Champaign, have a high profile, placing them squarely within the conventional location of level II. Others float in the shadow structure of their host institutions, reducing their importance.

Conducting the Inventory

The inventory should be conducted by a high-level administrative office charged with oversight for interdisciplinary initiatives.

TABLE 2.4. FRAMEWORK FOR AN INTERDISCIPLINARY INVENTORY

LEVEL I: INTERDISCIPLINARY INSTITUTIONS

Freestanding universities and colleges with an ID tradition or milieu

Freestanding universities and colleges with a new or heightened ID mission

LEVEL II: INTERDISCIPLINARY SITES

ID departments and programs

ID research centers and institutes

Hybrid disciplines

Integrative cores and courses in general education and in honors

Clustered and colinked courses, ID learning communities

Self-designed ID majors and graduate programs

ID training seminars and workshops

ID components of travel study, internships, practicums, and service-learning

LEVEL III: RECOGNIZED INTERFACES

Joint appointments of faculty

Cross-listed courses

Collaborative research and teaching teams

Shared facilities, databases, instrumentation

Alliances with government and industry for commercial knowledge production

Local, regional, national, and international programs and projects

Interinstitutional consortia

LEVEL IV: LESS FORMALLY RECOGNIZED PRACTICES

ID teaching and research of solo interdisciplinarians

Interactions around shared problem domain and topic interests of dispersed faculty

Borrowing of tools, methods, approaches, and concepts

Faculty interest groups

Migration of specialists across disciplinary boundaries

New subdisciplinary areas of expertise in ID research or teaching

Participation in national ID professional groups and networks

(continued)

TABLE 2.4. CONTINUED

LEVEL V: GRASSROOTS DISCIPLINARY PRESENCE

ID schools of thought and methods

Intersections with ID fields

New ID research interests

ID components and courses in the curriculum

Jobs for specialists in new ID subfields

The intellectual traffic between departments and ID centers and
   programs

Department-based conferences and other events featuring ID
   interests or speakers

ID knowledge production in individual scholarship

ID knowledge production in special journal issues, books, and reports

---

In the absence of such an office, a key administrator should oversee the process while working toward long-term central oversight. A single survey can be distributed to an entire campus, though variants for particular groups can also be devised, combining common questions with items tailored for faculty, administrators, program and center directors, or students. The most common format queries the nature and extent of current activities and interests, barriers, and incentives. At the University of Massachusetts–Lowell, a team was charged in 2005 with examining interdisciplinarity locally and making recommendations for institutionalizing support. As part of their research, the team sent a survey to the faculty (Archibald, 2009). At Wayne State University (WSU), the dean of the graduate school and vice president for research sent a survey to the entire faculty in conjunction with the Commission on Interdisciplinary Studies formed in 1991 (http://research.wayne.edu/idre/report_ids.htm). At Ohio State University (OSU), a task force for interdisciplinary research and graduate education appointed by the provost and dean in 1990 mailed questionnaires to two groups of graduate faculty: faculty whom chairs identified as involved in ID activity and a random sample of an equal number of other faculty.

Quantitative and qualitative methods should be combined in any survey, although formats differ. The ID-specific questions on the University of Massachusetts–Lowell survey used a Likert scale to determine the degree to which ID activities and interests were and should be occurring in research, teaching, and learning. The survey also sought perceptions of designated barriers and incentives, included an open-ended question of what respondents thought was "the biggest advantage of interdisciplinary work," and solicited feedback on the definition of interdisciplinarity. The highest percentage of responses to the question about definition identified collaboration of two or more departments or disciplines (89 percent), followed by problem solving, integration, and combinations of the prior connotations. The WSU survey solicited information about barriers, benefits, and incentives for ID instruction, research, service, and developing programs in rank order of factors from a predetermined list. Instead of the option of "NA" or "non" used in the Lowell survey, WSU added the possibility of "other" in each case. The Ohio State task force relied on two formats: circling yes or no (and in one case "doesn't apply") and rank ordering on Likert scales of agreement and degree of importance.

The cover letter for a survey should be clear about the purpose of the inventory and plans for follow-up. A minimal definition of interdisciplinarity is also important, without predetermining answers that exclude the spectrum of multidisciplinary and interdisciplinary degrees of integration, solo and collaborative modes of work, problem- and method-based foci, and emergent and established areas. The first page of the survey should gather identifying information: name, educational background, position, rank, years at institution, primary and other unit affiliations and joint appointments, areas of teaching and research, team teaching and research collaborations, principal investigator and co-principal investigator work, contributions and consultancies for projects and programs, cross-listed courses, and service activities in more than one field. Information about local designations can also be gathered, such as OSU's question about level of graduate faculty rank. WSU also requested rank ordering of up to four areas of teaching interests and research interests, a more open approach to self-identification that invites information beyond the overt reality of interdisciplinarity, while capturing emerging areas and more of the concealed reality.

Questions about education and research appear typically in separate parts of surveys, with some common questions repeating and others specific to the needs of research versus education. In both cases, the primary thrust is aimed at identifying the kinds of barriers and facilitating mechanisms delineated in Tables 3.1 and 3.2. Responses facilitate comparison of how the same issues are handled across units, while increasing the number of possible solutions. The importance of open-ended questions should not be overlooked. Inviting people to tell their stories gives them voice in the process and will reveal differing assumptions about the feasibility of local efforts. Respondents to the WSU and OSU surveys ranged from cynicism about positive change, to welcoming a new effort, to puzzlement over why changes were needed in what some already considered favorable environments. The WSU and OSU surveys also invited respondents to mention models and strategies used elsewhere. This request adds awareness of models around the country and can reveal external networking that might not be known otherwise.

In concert with the inventory, all pertinent documents should be collected, including reports and position papers tucked away in drawers and electronic files. Making them public is an important means of building trust. Document gathering is also a good means of countering negative folklore and errors of memory. On one campus, proponents of expanding interdisciplinarity were opposed by faculty who kept citing an earlier failure. After searching through the fog of institutional amnesia, an administrator new to campus learned that the program in question never actually existed. She also discovered a huge gulf in impressions. Opponents of interdisciplinary change contended that disciplines were the foundation stones of the university and should not be jeopardized. Proponents argued they were losing potential faculty, especially younger candidates, to universities that offer greater opportunities to do interdisciplinary work within both new fields and their own disciplines.

Documents related to the inventory exercise and related task forces should also be made publicly available. After years of being filed on the shelves in a small number of offices, the report of the 1993 commission on interdisciplinary studies at WSU was resurrected by an associate vice president in the division of research who was launching a new ID initiative. Gloria Heppner used the original set of recommendations to create a scorecard of what had changed by 2006 and made the original report available on a new interdisciplinary research and education website (http://research.wayne.edu/idre/index.php). The scorecard revealed changes in interests and activities, while affirming the need to continue addressing obstacles in the institutional culture. At the University of Massachusetts–Lowell, no official action has been taken yet on the team's recommendations. A new provost indicated strong support of interdisciplinarity by reinstating one course release time for the director of the gender studies program and giving the program a budget, the first in its thirty-plus year history. Yet the provost had not seen the team's report, and the website housing all of the transformation project materials has disappeared from the university website. The ID-specific questions in the Lowell survey do, though, appear in the appendix in Augsburg and Henry (2009a).

The inventory will also reveal a vital resource: points of convergence. Aldo Firpo (1999) and colleagues at the Medical Sciences Campus of the University of Puerto Rico call dynamic institutional activities and compartments "institutional points of multidisciplinary convergence." The concept of convergence derives from the natural sciences. In biology, it connotes the tendency for unrelated and distinct species to evolve toward similar structural or physiological characteristics under similar environmental conditions. In meteorology and oceanography, it designates meeting points or spaces of air flow and ocean currents. When Firpo sought points of convergence across the campus, he found them at all levels. Some were formally recognized, but others were not. They also appeared between individual students, faculty, and employees in varied mixes. Finding points of convergence, Firpo urges, is key to identifying sites and activities with a high capacity for promoting the formation and support of inter- and transdisciplinary work. They are also catalytic agents for a gradual and more systematic transformation into a more fully integrated operation.

An example from a team planning a new interdisciplinary general education program illustrates the potential that points of convergence embody. Its members were puzzled about how to involve the agriculture faculty, who were not only geographically separate from the main campus but also seemed distant from the program's mission. When the group realized that the agriculture faculty could make a valuable contribution to one of the projected themes of a new core curriculum, hunger, a separation became a point of convergence. This anecdote underscores the admonition of the American Studies Association to keep bridges in repair and be constantly looking for opportunities to build new ones with local faculty and staff, their counterparts on other campuses, and national professional organizations (www.theasa.net/publications/review_guide/guide_for _reviewing_american_studies_programs/). Otherwise programs might drift into isolation and risk the disdain of other units. This example also illustrates why sites off the main campus should be included in the inventory exercise, including satellite locations, research stations, laboratories, and partnerships within the community and all branches of government. Interinstitutional collaborations should be included too. The Five College Consortium in Massachusetts, for example, facilitates study in a number of areas by linking the University of Massachusetts–Amherst and Amherst, Hampshire, Mount Holyoke, and Smith colleges.

VARIABLES OF CHANGE

Before action is taken on results of the inventory, it is important to weigh the variables of organizational change that are generic to any kind of change and make them work for interdisciplinary purposes (Klein, 1996; Klein and Newell, 1997):

- Nature of the institution: size, organizational structure and policies, mission and type, and financial base
- Institutional culture: prior experience with interdisciplinarity, patterns of interaction among faculty and administration, nature of the academic community, local knowledge cultures, behavioral norms, and student population
- Nature and level of the desired change: institution-wide, program-wide, or a single course; general education, majors, programs, centers, and institutes; and cross-campus initiatives
- Requirements of the change: modification of existing structures or creation of new ones; small, limited, localized, and

incremental interventions or more global, comprehensive, or radical transformation
- Adequacy of material and human resources: internal feasibility, current faculty capabilities and interests, existing administrative personnel and support structures versus need for external consultation and funding
- Appropriate administrative structure, key administrative and faculty personnel

Size is a major variable. A faculty member at one university lamented, "This is a large ship to steer, and it doesn't turn quickly." In contrast, an administrator at a smaller university remarked, "You have to remember this is a small place. It's more nimble than a large institution." Large institutions are able to gather faculty in a range of fields and subfields. In their longitudinal study of IDS programs, Brint, Turk-Bicakci, Proctor, and Murphy (2009) affirmed this advantage. Their data indicated that capacity is related strongly to having a critical mass of faculty to support new fields and student interest. Size equates with a greater capacity to experiment and perhaps offer something for everyone. That said, universities such as Carnegie Mellon, Caltech, Brown, and Duke have enjoyed the advantage of smaller size in leveraging interdisciplinary initiatives (Sá, 2005).

Prior commitment to interdisciplinarity is another variable. Hampshire College and Evergreen State College were both founded as innovative interdisciplinary campuses. The University of Chicago has a long history of interdisciplinarity in both education and research, and it is also considered fundamental to the liberal arts mission of Albion College. Other institutions were strongly positioned for IDR from the start. Carnegie Mellon University was structured around nontraditional departments and views interdisciplinarity as a competitive advantage. Rockefeller University was founded as a research institution organized around laboratories rather than departments. It is less integrated than it was originally, but the flexible matrix structure of Rockefeller University is still less differentiated internally than other American universities. Stanford University's interdisciplinary signature has historical roots in provost Frederick Turner's slogan "steeples of excellence" and identification with a regional culture of interorganizational collaboration. At MIT, the commitment was anchored historically in industrial and military funding of multidisciplinary research laboratories. More recently, new cross-cutting units have been formed in engineering systems and computational and systems biology. Georgia Institute of Technology also has a history of supporting IDR that expanded in recent years with new initiatives in biotechnology, entrepreneurship, microelectronics, nanotechnology, and telecommunications (*Facilitating Interdisciplinary Research*, 2004; Caruso and Rhoten, 2001; Sá, 2005).

Knowing local history is another important strategy for change. Members of the Earlham College community contend that the most successful programs over the long term have tended to reflect the character and commitments of Earlham's Quaker heritage (Clark, Lacey, and Bingham, 1997). Lisa Lewis of Albion College urges a longitudinal sense of history. Even if an initiative does not pan out, it may morph into other forms that enhance the climate for interdisciplinarity on campus. Projected centers for interdisciplinary studies at Albion did not materialize, but a foundation for interdisciplinary study carries that mission forward in a coalesced and more manageable flexible design. When testing current activities, Lewis adds, it is important to reconsider extensions at a later date (personal communication, February 28, 2006).

In reconstructing the story of interdisciplinarity at the State University of New York (SUNY) at Potsdam, Sandra Sarkela (2001) demonstrated how traditional values can support innovation. Over time, SUNY–Potsdam evolved from a teacher training school into a teachers' college and then a liberal arts institution. Different initiatives emerged and faded through the years, from an early Freshman Forum to a two-semester learning community, an interdisciplinary humanities program, a School Within a School, a new version of the Freshman Forum called the Dean's Freshman Seminar, new learning communities and clusters of courses within the School of Arts and Sciences, and learning communities within the School of Education. Throughout this history, the heritage of education and music has been a powerful warrant for reform. A structure imposed without recognition of history and tradition, Sarkela advises, might be propped up with adequate funding but will not be sustained with enthusiasm and appeal to the institutional mission.

Brint, Turk-Bicakci, Proctor, and Murphy's longitudinal study of IDS (2009) also suggested that propensity is related to pre-existing curricular bases. New fields in the undergraduate curriculum grew primarily out of arts and sciences disciplines, not occupational-professional disciplines, suggesting that colleges and universities oriented to arts and sciences are more likely to attract faculty attuned to new movements in knowledge production. Geographical region was also a factor. Coastal areas tend to be more politically liberal, socially diverse, and closely connected to new economy industries that attract faculty and administrators receptive to programs for social and economic change. Forms of institutionalization vary by domain as well. In natural and applied sciences, graduate umbrella groups and ID research centers are primary vehicles of institutionalization. In contrast, new undergraduate curricula may play a comparatively larger role in arts, humanities, and social sciences. Large, wealthy arts and sciences-oriented universities on the East or West coasts appeared to be favorable environments for a greater variety of ID interests in general and, in particular, in internationally oriented fields and women's studies.

In working through the variables, a minimal understanding of the dynamics of organizational change is needed as well. Most faculty, planning committees, and even some administrators do not read the pertinent literature. Yet they should be aware of pitfalls and success factors that are generic to any type of change. Civian and colleagues (1997) offer opening caveats. Failure to anticipate implementation needs during the planning stage is a frequent stumbling block. So is trying to do everything at once and not allowing time for evaluating and revising a plan. The keys to effective change are an appropriate administrative structure, rewards and incentives, professional development, and an open participatory process. The texts and subtexts of an institution should also be recognized. The texts include obvious interests of the players. Subtexts, which are less readily known, can confound change. Hidden agendas of individuals and groups need to be understood in relation to local history and current circumstances. If not, they will reappear at a later date, deterring progress.

Trowler and Knight's studies of organizational change and innovation (2002) underscore the limits of the rational-purposive model of change reflected in many strategic planning processes and the commonsense understandings that many students and faculty have about the ways new knowledge and practices are implemented. In the logic of the model, change unfolds efficiently along a well-defined path flowing from top-down holders of power in pursuit of an explicit goal through directed energies, monitored outcomes, and rational decisions, including interdisciplinary priorities emanating from strategic plans. Their vision is encapsulated in formal policy statements and appropriate levers selected to ensure compliance through rewards, sanctions, and agreement on values and goals. In reality, however, policymaking and implementation processes are messy and even paradoxical. At the institutional level, they are more likely to result from negotiation, compromise, and conflict within social, political, economic, and psychological processes. Explicit front-stage goals also differ from organically developing objectives that have a creative nature and unanticipated consequences, including competing interdisciplinary interests emerging from the bottom up. Institutional cultures, in short, are protean and dynamic by nature. Viewed from an analytical telescope, differences in values, attitudes, assumptions, and taken-for-granted recurring practices look small. Viewed from an analytical microscope, they loom large, revealing a diversity of interests and affiliations (Trowler, 2002; Trowler and Knight, 2002).

Creso Sá (2005) paralleled Trowler and Knight's findings in bridging the literatures on organizational theory and interdisciplinary change. Individual predilections, preferences, and perceptions are powerful determinants of faculty behavior. Yet rational and opportunistic actors face cognitive constraints and information gaps that prevent optimal choices. Institutional elements such as actions, roles, and structures are resistant to change. They may be maintained for long periods of time without justification and are easily transmittable to new organizational members. The pursuit of legitimacy is a prime means of entrenching those elements for the sake of organizational survival and stable arrangements. They contribute to a rationalized myth that perpetuates perceived benefits of prevailing arrangements in academic structures, such as the quality control vested in disciplines and departments. The inertia of actors in the system is strengthened by taken-for-granted assumptions and unquestioned practices that have a normative status presumed to be natural. Operating in combination, institutional environments thus limit options that individual and groups envision as possible alternatives for organizational change, such as interdisciplinary research and studies.

Lasting improvement of a curriculum, Jerry Gaff (1991) admonished, requires a "more pervasive, deeper, and supportive structure" (p. 156). The same is true of the research profile of a campus. Showcase models and ad hoc measures do not substitute for a systemic approach. The next chapter presents a framework for platforming interdisciplinarity through actions aimed at capacity building and creating an institutional deep structure. These actions will continue to require bridging the national and local maps. When the interdisciplinary programs team at the University of Massachusetts–Lowell was charged with making data-driven decisions, they combined their local survey with a literature review, benchmarking of programs at other institutions, and interviewing administrators of those other programs to learn about barriers and how they overcame them. They also contacted the Association for Integrative Studies and sought board members' assistance at various stages throughout the process. In this manner, they were able to draw on the national picture while reading the local institutional culture (Archibald, 2009). The same process of learning, adapting, and implementing outstanding practices is needed when platforming as well.

CHAPTER THREE

PLATFORMING INTERDISCIPLINARITY

In the world of computing, the term *platform* refers to hardware architecture or software frameworks that allow software to run. A campus is neither hardware nor a software framework, but creating a favorable campus culture requires establishing the architecture for a networked operating system. John Unsworth's description (2008) of the shift from Web 1.0 to Web 2.0 suggests an analogy. Emphasis shifted with Web 2.0 from the computer as platform to the network as platform. Put in terms of institutional cultures, the network of interactions and synergies becomes the platform, not simply the hardware structures and software strategies that facilitate them.

The key to a strong platform for interdisciplinary change is crafting a robust portfolio of strategies rather than adopting a single initiative or model. The concept of robustness is familiar to engineers. Robust design is not absolute. It depends on multiple factors. Making a building more earthquake proof, for example, depends on whether it is in an earthquake-prone zone, the materials being used, and the function the building will have (Nowotny, Scott, and Gibbons, 2001). A robust portfolio for a local campus will take into account both structure and behavior in a systemic approach described in this chapter. Transformative and incremental approaches should be combined, as well as strategic targeting and a general loosening of barriers. Top-down and middle-level strategies should also be combined, along with interests that arise bottom up from faculty work. The chapter closes with discussions of central oversight, leadership, and an interdisciplinary endowment that goes beyond allotted budgets to a portfolio of resources encompassing funding, space, and equipment.

STRATEGIES FOR CHANGE

Toombs and Tierney (1991) identified three major approaches to curriculum change that are also applicable to institutional change. The first model, modification, adds new knowledge, techniques, and practices to existing disciplines and professional fields. Connections and meta-reflections on the disciplines are fostered but are often limited to special programs. Accretion may eventually result in significant change, and using existing courses and pilot projects as launching points is a sound strategy. Yet existing compartmentalizations are preserved. More content, topics and themes, concepts, and theories are introduced, but the structure, purpose, and characteristics of an institution do not change. The second model, integration, provides a sense of unity, larger scope of study, and connections among disciplines and throughout the curriculum. Its impact, though, is often partial, and interdisciplinary programs are only suffered to exist. The third model, transformation, moves beyond while encompassing elements of modification and integration. It recognizes the need to address new issues, such as gender equity, ethnicity, multiculturalism, globalism, ethics, the environment, health, and educational policy. These issues pose questions and make demands that are only partly engaged at present.

A transformative model is more likely to foster what Wátzlawick, Weakland, and Fisch (1974) called "second-order change," shifting the paradigm of understanding while allowing space for new thought and action. In contrast, first-order change simply moves the furniture around. However, Cathy Davidson argues, seemingly small changes allow both major interdisciplinary flexibility at the institutional level and significant faculty development at the individual level (personal communication, June 6, 2008). Davidson, who served eight years at Duke University as the first vice provost for interdisciplinary studies in the country, describes the process as a form of handicraft. Long-term sustainability depends on creating human and institutional infrastructures in support of big ideas. The initial steps in designing a new global interstructure at Duke included forming an association for executive directors of interdisciplinary research and teaching centers, formalizing review processes for centers, and changing rules for how tenure files would be judged. The hard work of change, Davidson concluded, lies in working out complex arrangements that sustain ideas over time.

Others concur. Drawing on his experience as associate dean of the Office of Interdisciplinary Studies at the University of Alberta, Rick Szostak (2009) advises others to "be prepared to build a new program through time" (p. 226). In that vein, the National Academy of Sciences (NAS) report, *Facilitating Interdisciplinary Research* (2004), offers recommendations for both transformative change and incremental steps. Transformative change requires rapid and discontinuous approaches to existing structure and practice, but significant change can result from simple steps. More generally, Sá (2005) observed, comprehensive root-and-branch reforms are not typical. Change in the academic world tends to occur slowly and incrementally through iterative processes. Howard Gardner (2004) arrived at a similar conclusion based on case studies in a variety of settings. Change results most often from a slow and even almost unidentifiable shift of viewpoints instead of a single argument or sudden epiphany. Changes that seem to erupt dramatically often mask more subtle processes that gel over a longer period of time. It is also more difficult to replace a simple way of thinking about a matter with a more complex one. "Simpler mind changes," Gardner advises, "tend to trump more complex ones" (p. 92). At both Duke and the University of Southern California (USC), interdisciplinary change was nurtured over long periods of time with multiple self-assessment exercises and planning cycles. Duke began in 1988 and USC in 1994 (Sá, 2005). Likewise, Portland State University's effort to create a new general education curriculum with increased interdisciplinary (ID) opportunities was the result of a lengthy planning process and multiyear implementation schedule (Reardon and Ramaley, 1997).

Just as transformative and incremental approaches should be taken into account, strategic targeting and general loosening of barriers should be combined. Strategic targeting promotes selected initiatives, often dressed in transformative rhetoric. General loosening of barriers contributes to longer-term organizational flexibility and cultural change that improve the climate for both incremental steps and targeted priorities. In his study of research-intensive universities, Creso Sá (2005) identified basic approaches to reducing perceived costs and risks of doing interdisciplinary research (IDR). Institutionalizing new formal and informal norms endorses and legitimates IDR within the system of policies, practices, routines, structures, and cultures. Continuous interventions create or adapt organizational structures with new administrative units and ORUs (organized research units such as centers or institutes). Continuous interventions also align financial incentives to ID goals, stimulating faculty opportunism with grants from the central administration or ORUs.

A significant number of interdisciplinary strategic targets in recent years have been tied to state-level initiatives in knowledge-based industries, in a partnership that offers states economic development while providing universities with revenue at a time of declining state appropriations. In analyzing strategic planning documents, Sá (2005) found that targeted initiatives were often designated as priorities at the federal level, echoing the logic of strategic planning and management aimed at matching organizational strengths with opportunities in the environment. Prime target areas include biotechnology, computer and information science, computational biology, environmental studies, genomics, materials science, and nanoscience and engineering, though initiatives were underway in ethnic and regional studies, gerontology, urban studies, and children, youth, and family studies as well. Broad themes of sustainability and globalization are also being prioritized, as are regional imperatives such as forestry and economic recovery (abstract from "Interdisciplinary Teaching and Research at Northwestern University," www.northwestern.edu/provost/highestorder/self-study-hoe2 appendix.pdf).

Strategic targeting is the result of both top-down and bottom-up stimuli. Two examples illustrate how organized faculty efforts can gain institutional backing and harness sizable investments and long-term commitments. The Genomics Initiative at Cornell University was one of three "strategic enabling research areas" (Sá, 2005). It evolved from a task force into a permanent body with new faculty affiliations and, in 2002, a life science initiative with plans for new faculty, a building, and a graduate fellowship program. The task force also urged changes in the way that Cornell makes faculty appointments in biological science to order to encourage ID collaboration, cross-departmental hiring in focus areas, and investments in space and infrastructure (www.genomics.cornell .edu/). In 1993, a faculty task force at Rice University defined a nanotechnology initiative building on existing ID strengths in science and engineering. By 1997, several new faculty had been hired, a new lab completed, and the Center for Nanoscale Science and Technology opened. The center's infrastructure played a key role throughout the transition from basic research to developing and commercializing nanotube technologies. The diversity of applications for fullerene-based molecules also laid the foundation for extensive ID collaboration among scientists at Rice (http://cohesion.rice.edu/centersandinst/cnst/index.cfm; *Facilitating Interdisciplinary Research*, 2004).

General loosening of barriers is a more amorphous task than strategic targeting. When respondents to data-gathering surveys for the NAS report ranked top impediments to IDR, individuals gave the highest percentages to promotion criteria, budget control, indirect cost return, and incompatibility with strategic plans. Provosts gave highest rankings to promotion criteria, special allocation, budget control, and unit reporting. Table 3.1 is a composite of barriers and disincentives that appear in the literature. In the aggregate, to echo the NAS report, their combined effect exacerbates the "accumulation of disadvantage" *(Facilitating Interdisciplinary Research,* 2004), marginalizing units that do not enjoy priority and conferring second-class citizenship on their members.

The title of the University of Washington's internal report on facilitating interdisciplinary research and education sums up what it takes to facilitate ID research and education: "Seeding, Supporting, and Sustaining Interdisciplinary Initiatives at the University of Washington" (www.grad.washington.edu/acad/inter disc_network/InterdisNetwork.htm). Seeding, supporting, and sustaining is a multitiered process that does not rely on single actions. Single actions, in fact, run counter to long-term change in organizational culture. Table 3.2 groups the facilitating strategies

TABLE 3.1. BARRIERS AND DISINCENTIVES TO INTERDISCIPLINARITY

ORGANIZATIONAL STRUCTURE AND ADMINISTRATION

Rigid one-size-fits-all model of organizational structure

Discipline- and department-based silos of budgetary and administrative categories

Territoriality and turf battles over budget, ownership of curriculum and research

Ambiguous status of ID programs, centers, and institutes

Piecemeal approaches

Lack of experienced leaders

Resistance to innovation and risk

Dispersed infrastructure

No clear and authoritative report lines for ID units

PROCEDURES AND POLICIES

Inflexible guidelines that inhibit approval of new programs and courses

Rigid and exclusionary degree requirements

Lack of guidelines for ID hiring, tenure and promotion, and salary

Inadequate guidelines for grants management and research collaboration

Unfavorable policies for allocation of workload credit in ID teaching

Unfavorable research policies for sharing indirect cost recovery from external grants and allocating intellectual property

RESOURCES AND INFRASTRUCTURE

Inadequate funding and ongoing support for ID units

Inadequate number of faculty lines for interdisciplinary studies (IDS) and IDR

Restricted access to internal incentives and seed funds for ID research and curriculum development

Competition for funds and faculty between departments and ID units

Inadequate or no ID student assistantships and fellowships

Inadequate space and equipment and inflexible allotments of use

Weak or no faculty development system

Ignorance of ID literature and resources in national networks

---

(continued)

TABLE 3.1. CONTINUED

Insufficient time for planning and implementing program and project infrastructure

Insufficient time to learn the language and culture of another discipline

Insufficient time to develop collaborative relationships in team teaching and research

RECOGNITION, REWARD, AND INCENTIVES

Invisibility and marginality of ID research, teaching, service, advising, and mentoring

Reliance on volunteerism and overload

Weak networking channels and communication forums

Ineligibility of ID work for awards, honors, incentives, and faculty development programs

Lack of support at department, college, or university levels

Negative bias against ID work

TABLE 3.2. FACILITATING STRATEGIES AND MECHANISMS FOR INTERDISCIPLINARITY

ORGANIZATIONAL STRUCTURE, ADMINISTRATION, AND POLICIES

Alternative administrative structures

Program-level control of budget and infrastructure

Report lines with designated responsibilities

Procedures for course and program approval, research management

Policies for hiring, tenure and promotion, salary, and merit

Policies for research and teaching evaluation, program review, learning assessment

Openness to innovation and tolerance for risk

Alignment of interdisciplinarity with strategic plan themes

Timely interface between new research developments and the entire curriculum

Inventory of activities, structures, and interests

LEADERSHIP, ADVOCACY, AND STEWARDSHIP

Top administrative support at the level of president, provost, and deans

Central oversight body for ID research and education

A central ID website

(continued)

Table 3.2. Continued

Annual forum for directors of programs, centers, and institutes

Strong and experienced leaders

Unit-level advisory boards of internal and external stakeholders

FUNDING

Baseline funding for IDS and IDR units

Dedicated tenure-track faculty lines and stable appointments in programs and centers

Cross-department budgeting mechanisms

Flexible resources at the department level

Seed funding through internal special initiatives and regular programs

Systematic identification of external sources

Equitable credit allocations for team teaching, indirect cost recovery on external grants

Alignment of interdisciplinarity with capital campaigns at both campus and unit levels

INFRASTRUCTURE SUPPORT

Dedicated space for IDS and IDR units

Pooling and sharing of space, facilities, and equipment

ID design principles for new buildings and remodeling projects

Communication system for collaboration and information flow

Release time for program and project development in teaching and research

Faculty development programming (including graduate students and postdoctoral fellows)

Resource banking of ID resources and literatures

RECOGNITION

Visibility on central ID website

Visibility in the public face of a campus (for example, materials, advising, and recruiting system)

Counting service for committee work, mentoring, and thesis and dissertation advising

Awards and honors in existing system and new ID-specific competitions

Inclusion of interdisciplinarity in all annual and unit reports

ID unit-level publications: online newsletter, journal

and mechanisms that will be discussed throughout the rest of this book into five major categories.

CENTRAL OVERSIGHT

Central oversight is crucial to a systemic approach, although it should not be confused with a monolithic superstructure. Nor is the purpose of oversight to micromanage programs. It is aimed at moving beyond the adhocracy of a case-by-case basis to a more comprehensive and coordinated approach to fostering and sustaining interdisciplinarity. Five actions are key:

- Establish a high-level interdisciplinary oversight body.
- Appoint or assign an administrator with oversight responsibility.
- Form an institution-wide steering council or oversight committee.
- Identify supportive administrators, faculty, and staff at all levels.
- Create a central website for interdisciplinary research and education.

The top-down argument runs counter to a widespread belief that the best interdisciplinarity percolates up from faculty interests. Yet both are needed. Neil Sullivan, former vice provost for research at the University of Southern California, advises that "ideas can bubble up from the bottom, but they need to be embraced by the top" (cited in *Facilitating Interdisciplinary Research*, 2004, p. 102). In reviewing the literature on organizational management, Trowler (2002) also found that the "implementation staircase" goes both down and up, combining structure and the agency of actors in a system (p. 12). Indicative of this general finding, Sá (2005) reports that the most ambitious initiatives seem to thrive where serious faculty buy-in and senior administrative backing are combined. At the same time, the middle tier must not be neglected. In adapting Huy and Mintzberg's (2003) triangle of change to the academic environment, Diana Rhoten (2004) emphasized that interdisciplinarity is not suffering from simply lack of extrinsic attention at the top by funding agencies and research leadership or intrinsic motivation at the bottom by faculty and students. Systemic implementation is lacking in the middle tier of academic management structures.

There is a temporal imperative as well to working across top, middle, and bottom levels, one that will reappear in Chapter Five in the discussion of tenure and promotion. This imperative is affirmed in an action research project aimed at building a knowledge base for ID policies and practices. Launched in 2007, the Consortium on Fostering Interdisciplinary Inquiry is composed of ten leading universities that have made significant investments in ID initiatives. The study targeted eight major categories: academic administration and faculty governance, collaborative technology, development and fundraising, education and training, equity and diversity, finance and budget, research, and space planning and allocation. Using a collaboratively developed assessment tool and local surveys, a representative group of campus leaders conducted self-studies and then shared preliminary results at a fall 2008 conference. Although the final report has not appeared yet, Gail Dubrow, director of the consortium, commented that the picture emerging from the data underscored the temporal imperative. Leadership in higher education comes and goes. Even the most powerful set of interdisciplinary strategic initiatives introduced by a committed leadership may diminish with the arrival of a new administration seeking to establish its own signature priorities. Or it may respond to perceptions of excessive centralization in funding targeted priorities with a counterphilosophy of decentralization that indirectly weakens central capacity to mount intercollegiate and ID initiatives. Similarly, leadership at the grassroots level of particular interdisciplinary initiatives waxes and wanes (personal communication, July 13, 2009).

The challenge, then, Dubrow emphasizes, is to build institutional structures that sustain interdisciplinary activity beyond individuals at any level. Oversight structures such as the Network of Interdisciplinary Initiatives at the University of Minnesota, conceived by Dubrow, can have continuing organizational, advocacy, and policy capacity beyond the more individualistic model of leadership. Sustainability, Dubrow concludes, requires not only connecting top and bottom leadership but building a collaborative model of leadership that vests power, authority, and agency in larger groups and infuses the mandate throughout the functional responsibilities of the entire organization. Top-down mandates provide momentum, but the experience of working with systems based on collegiate and departmental models of resource flows lies in the bottom up—in details that are not necessarily apparent in research administration, finance and budget, development, and other areas (personal communication, May 20, 2009, and July 13, 2009; www.myu.umn.edu/metadot/index.pl?id=1562406).

The strongest oversight structure is a central office for both IDR and IDS. The reluctance to open a new office or unit is understandable in a time of strained finances. Gains in external funding and greater efficiencies in the institution at large, though, can offset the added expenditure. Campuses operating on decentralized models resist central oversight, but it is not in conflict with dispersed and entrepreneurial approaches. Central monitoring will make good on the rhetoric of endorsement by providing coordinated management and a stable anchor that weathers changes in personnel and finances. It can also increase the competitive posture of a campus by demonstrating that interdisciplinarity is taken seriously. Coupled with a central website dedicated to interdisciplinarity, central oversight provides greater visibility, legitimacy, and access to internal and external resources, forestalling the loss of opportunity and frustration that occurs when initiatives fall through the cracks. It should not be the work of one person alone. The leader of a designated body should work in concert with a council or committee with wide representation across campus. Directors of programs, centers, and major projects are crucial members, as are liaisons to governance bodies and administrative offices. A central unit is also well positioned to network findings and recommendations of prior task forces and study groups. Short executive summaries for particular constituencies can be combined with focus group meetings to discuss next steps. In the absence of prior studies, a central unit is an ideal body for such a study and follow-up. It is also keenly poised to engage in resource banking, discussed in the Resources section at the end of the book, and can serve as a communications hub for both IDR and IDS.

The idea of an oversight body is not new. Georgia Institute of Technology established an Office of Interdisciplinary Programs in 1973 to foster and coordinate ORUs. Virginia Tech established the Office of Interdisciplinary Programs in 1995, and Pennsylvania State University, the University of California–Davis, and Stony Brook University have had similar units under the office of a provost or a vice president for research. North Carolina State University opened an Office of Publications and Proposal

Development to improve the quantity and quality of interdisciplinary work (Sá, 2005). And despite the mixed track record of sustaining IDS programs at San Francisco State University, Raymond Miller (2009) credits establishment of the University Interdisciplinary Council with broad representation for the continuing facilitation and review of proposals and programs. The most common locations for central offices are divisions of the provost or vice president for research or education. The graduate school is also a major location, and on smaller campuses, administrative offices are charged with oversight of the curriculum.

At the University of Alberta, the Faculty of Arts created the Office of Interdisciplinary Studies (OIS) in 2003. An earlier effort to provide an administrative structure collapsed due to objections from department chairs. In the wake of that failure, Szostak (2009) recalls, women's studies and East Asian studies managed to attain departmental status. A program in Middle Eastern and African studies (MEAS) survived without official support due to the dedication of a small group of faculty, and a graduate program in humanities computing (HuCo) was created. When OIS opened, it was responsible for seven programs: the MEAS; HuCo; a new individualized major; a new science, technology, and society program; an international studies minor; religious studies; and comparative literature. Film studies chose to join the English department, and religious studies selected ID status in the new OIS. So did comparative literature. The OIS benefited from transfer of budgets. Its broad-based governance structure also resulted in a dispersed body of supporters, greater potential for collaboration across units in some courses, and the combined intellectual and organizational strength that comes from a diversity of insights. When OIS was established, it was impossible to govern a graduate degree outside departmental structures. The Faculty of Graduate Studies and Research, though, was amenable to changing its rules. Religious studies and comparative literature graduate programs were transferred into OIS. The structure of HuCO also changed. The OIS today is a potential home for any ID programs in the faculty of arts. A new certificate in peace and conflict studies has been added, though the office has not absorbed all programs. Women's studies, East Asian studies, and Spanish and Latin American studies remain within departments.

As the University of Alberta example suggests, central structures can provide an organizational home for dispersed programs, thereby reducing their isolation. At the University of Massachusetts–Lowell, the interdisciplinary programs team proposed a central hub for interdisciplinary and integrative activities. The goal of a hub is to bring groups together across units while providing specialized support and opportunities to acquire new skills while addressing common barriers ("Final Report," 2007). The Center for Interdisciplinary Studies at Webster University uses a variant of a hub model to group multiple programs, including ancient studies, ethics, general studies, international human rights, international studies, environmental studies, liberal arts, multicultural studies, women's studies, and a self-designed ID major. The common structure provides a single visible place where students can find information about majors, minors, and certificates (www.webster.edu/depts/artsci/d_interdisciplinary.htmWebster).

At Edgewood College in Madison, Wisconsin, the School of Integrative Studies launched in 2006 is providing not only a home for dispersed programs but, founding administrator Dean Pribbenow reports, is also nurturing and embedding best practices in integrative and interdisciplinary learning across campus. The six programs clustered together in the school are human issues studies, environmental studies, women's and gender studies, the center for multicultural education/ethnic studies, the center for global education, and the honors program. The oldest and largest of them, human issues, is a required component of general education requirements for all undergraduates, to be completed during the junior or senior year through supervised independent study or an approved course that integrates interdisciplinary study with experiential learning and ethical deliberation. In addition, the school is involved with new integrative studies minors and majors, a first-year experience and new common reading program, efforts to integrate classroom and community-based learning more fully, and links with majors and professional schools. More comprehensive changes are also envisioned. One of the most promising is a revised general education program that calls explicitly for integrative, inquiry-based, relevant learning experiences that prepare students for taking creative action on contemporary social issues. Central to the new program is a three-level integrative core curriculum that moves developmentally from first through senior years. Members of the school are providing leadership in implementation of the core, which will integrate the major with general education, experiential learning with the classroom, and formal knowledge with skills and values that promote public participation (personal communication, May 11, 2009).

Study teams and workshops are also good catalysts for campus-wide efforts. In alignment with a new strategic plan, the University of Idaho embarked on a plan to create a more supportive institutional culture. Idaho already had several strong ID programs, including newly funded strategic initiatives such as Water of the West and Sustainable Idaho. These precedents were assets for recruiting and retaining new students and faculty. Yet existing areas still needed to be strengthened and new ones developed in order to support strategic planning themes, the research and land-grant missions of the institution, and important graduate and professional programs. A strategic planning subteam developed a two-day workshop held in March 2007 on the life cycle of projects in academic programs, research institutes, and strategic initiatives. The five stages highlighted at Idaho were building an ID team; acquiring funding and administrative support; determining an effective structure and organization; assessing progress, merit, and future potential of the work; and building sustainability or sunsetting programs. The actions targeted for immediate attention included identifying clear definitions of interdisciplinary activities so that assessment tools will be valid and appropriate; defining clear expectations and rewards in hiring, tenure, and promotion; and providing a workshop for department chairs so that they can start designing a clear structure for recognition and credit for ID activities (www.uidaho.edu/provost/strategicactionplan/goal2/interdisciplinaryworkshop.aspx).

At the University of Washington (UW), organizers of the Network of Interdisciplinary Initiatives used the NAS report, *Facilitating Interdisciplinary Research* (2004), as a framework for an effort aimed at creating institution-wide change, though they expanded their focus to include teaching and student experiences across a wider array of fields. The network has functioned as an interdisciplinary advocacy group composed of faculty, staff, and students from three UW campuses. It evolved from conversations with the staff of seventeen ID degree and certificate programs housed in the graduate school. During the first half of the 2004–2005 academic year, Gail Dubrow, who was associate dean of the graduate school at the time, and Jennifer Harris, a postdoctoral research associate, met with directors and staff of each of the seventeen programs in semistructured interviews focused on identifying structural barriers and supports. Their preliminary findings, presented to participants at the first meeting of the network in February 2005, addressed five major themes: administrative organization, faculty participation, building intellectual community, finance-funding-budgeting, and stewardship-leadership-advocacy. Focus groups of faculty and students from the pool of programs followed, along with separate surveys of graduate students and faculty affiliated with the programs. A smaller working group also formed to guide future activities of the network. The year ended with an event that included briefing papers.

The following year, another meeting of the work group and another event took place, as well as follow-up activities with the provost's office, to advance key policy recommendations. The final top three priorities that emerged in the recommendations were faculty appointments, promotion, and tenure; allocation of resources from indirect cost recovery; and allocation of resources through development and outreach. (Focus group questions, surveys, and documents appear in appendixes to the Dubrow and Harris report; www.grad.washington.edu/acad/interdisc_network/InterdisNetwork.htm).

A Central Interdisciplinary Website

A centralized ID website offers three advantages: visibility, legitimacy, and resource banking. Visibility and legitimacy go hand in hand. Information from the inventory can be used to remap the campus while creating links to all ID units and activities with their materials and resources, as well as information submitted by respondents to the survey, periodic updating, and new entries. Any site will have a local signature.

At the University of Michigan, the site was designed in conjunction with a faculty development program in the Graduate

School (www.rackham.umich.edu / academic_information /rii/).
At Wisconsin–Madison, the Cluster Hire initiative is the major
locus, and at the University of Washington, the Network for
Interdisciplinary Initiatives. At Wayne State University, the
emphasis is on finding and supporting research collaborators.
After the original site was designed, a new questionnaire was
added on particular types of collaborators, ID education programs that respondents are contemplating, a fuller description
of their research interests, and service on external review
panels that could help others who are preparing applications
(www.research.wayne.edu/idre). Even with a local stamp, though,
a number of common features belong on a central ID website:

- A homepage previewing the sections
- A regularly updated news and ID events calendar (including
  both central and unit-level activities, as well as interdisciplinary
  traffic across programs, center, and departments)
- A regular e-newsletter and special bulletins for publicizing
  events and successes (coordinated and cross-referenced with an
  ID with column in other campus publications)
- Links devoted to IDS programs, IDR centers and institutes, and
  other projects and activities
- Links to on-campus support services, such as offices of teaching
  and learning, grants and fundraising, and library collections
- Continuously updated information on internal and external
  funding opportunities, followed by targeted bulletins to individ-
  ual units and personnel
- A collaborators' database and interest inventory
- A beginning bibliography of literature on IDR and IDS, with an
  archive of selected readings
- Links to national organizations and networks
- Links to and copies of state-of-the-art national reports
- A blog connected with an ID listserv or wiki

Two sites—at Duke and the University of Minnesota—have a
high percentage of ideal features and were created in conjunction
with central oversight bodies. Oversight at Duke was established
in 1998 and has continued to provide leadership through the

new Office of Interdisciplinary Program Management. An inter-disciplinary administrators working group meets each semester to enhance networking opportunities to facilitate a community of support and ID practice. The office works collaboratively with deans and department chairs to overcome obstacles and create supportive structural changes, including policies on hiring, appointments, promotion, and tenure guidelines. It also provides information about programs to internal and external organizations, and careful attention has been paid to the needs of extradepartmental research units, with guidelines for creating, managing, reviewing, and renewing school-based centers. The current updated version of the Duke ID website has five sections: homepage (with short descriptions, news, and events), education (with links to programs), university institutes (with links and information on faculty hiring initiatives), school-based centers (with links to more than sixty centers across Duke's nine schools, plus guidelines), and administration (with information on the Offices of the Vice Provost and of Interdisciplinary Program Management, plus an archive of news and stories) (www.interdisciplinary.duke.edu).

Launched in 2006–2007, the University of Minnesota's website is the public face of a coordinated institution-wide effort to heighten the profile of IDR and IDS (www.interdisciplinary .umn.edu/). An inventory identified more than three hundred IDR centers at the university spanning both emerging and mature fields. The website evolved from a 2004 strategic positioning process that prioritized substantial central investment with state support that targeted complex intellectual, scientific, and social problems. Incentives for cross-college collaboration were also provided and new centers that foster collaboration, including advanced study, the environment, translational neurosciences, informatics, and science and engineering. Like Duke, Minnesota has made changes in policies to ensure that interdisciplinary work is valued in tenure and promotion, along with changes in policies for equitable distribution of indirect cost recovery. In addition, it has developed an ID advocacy network among faculty, students, staff, and postdoctoral fellows, and it added support for collaborative and interdisciplinary skills development.

The latest version of the website combines dynamic graphics on the homepage with four sections:

- *Background:* explanations of the initiative and central administrative support
- *Administration:* further information and links to administrative supports, policies on creating and evaluating centers, sharing indirect cost recovery, promotion and tenure
- *Interdisciplinary initiatives:* a searchable database of center and institutes, major interdisciplinary initiatives, all-university centers and institutes
- *News and events:* a calendar of events and links for selected institutes and libraries

The provost's interdisciplinary team worked collaboratively with the assistant vice provost for interdisciplinarity to foster system-wide planning, development, implementation, and monitoring of major ID initiatives. The team was also charged with conducting reviews of major existing initiatives, encouraging affiliations to foster new programs, developing institutional policies and procedures, establishing priorities for fundraising, and monitoring central investments in interdisciplinary activities. Four leaders on the team spanned components of research and education across campus: an office for collaborative research services under the vice president for research, an office of ID initiatives under the dean of the graduate school, the vice provost and dean for undergraduate education, the vice provost for faculty and academic affairs, and leadership for changes in procedures for promotion and tenure.

Building a central website is an occasion for cross-checking and updating all print materials for inclusion of ID units, especially as they are being moved into electronic formats. In the words of the interdisciplinary programs team at the University of Massachusetts–Lowell, they should be "looped in," not separated and accessible only through multiple links ("Final Report," 2007). They should appear along with department-based programs and have a counterpart inclusion in the catalogue so students know what they are looking for and can move easily across sections. Programs should appear inside their college sections with the same type and size of headings and formatting as departments have, the same alphabetical listing, and indications of whether they are degree granting, minor, or certificate programs. If they cross college boundaries, programs should be listed in all pertinent colleges, though complete information may appear in only one place. So too, policies for program creation and course approval should mirror the process in place for departments. They should have parallel program course prefixes, report tools and databases for monitoring student progress, course information including cross-listings, contact information, and directories. A corresponding inclusion should occur in open house and new student orientations, plus recruitment, advising, and career placement. Finally, coordinated networking should be instituted with offices of admissions, registration, and marketing. These actions, the University of Massachusetts–Lowell team emphasized, are simple, low-cost and even free means of increasing visibility and inclusiveness.

LEADERSHIP

Leadership belongs in any discussion of oversight. Support at top levels of the president, provost, deans, and heads of the graduate school and undergraduate curriculum is crucial to nurturing and sustaining supportive cultures. At Duke, provost Peter Lange has been a major agent in fostering interdisciplinary change, and President Michael Crow has been a powerful driver of change at Arizona State University. At Northwestern University, senior leadership has provided strong support in recent years for cooperation across schools and financial and logistical structures. Authors of a 2004 report on interdisciplinary research and teaching described the prior philosophy at Northwestern as "catch-as-catch-can," a familiar posture on many campuses (Abstract, 7, www.northwestern.edu/provost/highestorder/self-study-hoe2 appendix.pdf). At Albion College, interdisciplinarity was also a top presidential priority for former president Peter Mitchell, and the commitment is shared by the board of trustees, which reaffirmed IDS at its February 2006 retreat as the key component in the college "value" statement and a logical driving force to differentiate Albion from its peer institutions. The new president, Donna Randall, also believes strongly that an interdisciplinary approach to undergraduate education is essential to solving complex problems and "to become architects of social change in the 21st century" (Lisa Lewis, personal communication, August 14, 2008).

In a series of state-of-the-art reports on administration of interdisciplinary programs, Beth Casey (1994, 2002, forthcoming) defined five major principles of good practice: administrative oversight, structural flexibility, organizational culture, program protection, and administrative leadership. In 1994, she situated the principles within four major structures: IDS programs, general education, ID schools, and ID colleges. In each case, she urged administrators to examine their institutional and college mission statements, asking how they might serve current knowledge needs. She also endorsed a program of faculty development and a new culture of evidence in assessment. The trends Casey noted in 1994 continue, though in 2002 she placed greater emphasis on the role of new scholarship and two additional needs that are catalyzing structural reform: support of boundary crossing that addresses the urgent problems and challenges of our time and restructuring of undergraduate liberal education through learning communities. More generally, the trend toward fusion has also resulted in an increase in the number of support structures that resolve traditional problems of staffing and budget while introducing collaborative work modes and administrative supports, including tenure protection.

Recently Casey (forthcoming) reaffirmed her earlier recommendations while calling for a new social contract for the university, greater attention to changing demographics, and William Tierney's (1999) concept of devolvement from an older hierarchical authority to a flexible, flat, heterarchal level for decision making. Administering ID units of any type, Casey notes, requires entrepreneurial leadership, the ability to build networks and form collaborative partnerships, and knowledge of best processes of scholarship, curricular design, pedagogy, and assessment. She advocates a cross-campus structure to coordinate and connect all programs, centers, and institutes. At program and center levels, Casey suggests monthly meetings of a council chaired by an associate dean of a college. Directors should sit on the dean's council with department chairs, and their contracts should be equitable in administrative versus research and teaching time. If they do not have direct access through a position on such a council, they need clear report lines to someone who sits on one. Deans and directors should also have institution-wide policies for dual appointments and mechanisms for releasing faculty to participate, and should be knowledgeable about interdisciplinarity. For their part, faculty and other staff should ask direct questions about capacity and willingness to support ID programs in job interviews.

One of the underappreciated forms of leadership is switch-boarding, Ellwyn Stoddard's term (1992) for a person who is an exchange point for information and support. Karen Peterson of the Fred Hutchinson Cancer Research Center began facilitating faculty team development for large IDR grants in January 2004 (*Facilitating Interdisciplinary Research*, 2004). She identified calls for proposals of interest to faculty and then alerted the center and its division directors. On identifying pertinent faculty, she invited them to participate and then had them develop their proposals. At Stony Brook University, the associate vice president for research, Martin Schoonen, played a similar role by bringing together teams to respond to requests for applications and broad announcements that invite a multi- or interdisciplinary approach. His position was split fifty-fifty between a three-year vice-presidential appointment and a professorship in geoscience. Schoonen did not organize seminars because he believes that faculty are not seeking more talks. They will attend a meeting, though, if it is about a funding opportunity. After a team was assembled, Schoonen guided them through proposal paperwork, deadlines, and planning phases, while also creating an electronic home for file sharing. These efforts have resulted in not only financial gains but also community building, including subsets of team members working together on a smaller scale—for instance, an economist working with a nutritionist, a materials scientist with a microbiologist, and an environmental scientist with a virologist.

Echoing Firpo's (1999) points of convergence in Chapter Two, switchboarding brings together like-minded faculty and staff, brokering resources and guiding the mutual learning that is crucial to collaborative work. As director for research collaborations, Nancy Christ of Wayne State University has combined efforts to help faculty find collaborators with a mechanism for broadcasting searches for equipment, building a database of ID research groups, and publicizing faculty commons meetings for exchanging ideas and building collaborations. Christ also stresses the importance of connecting individuals with knowledge of grant seeking with applicants, including faculty who have served as reviewers on judging panels. They possess a form of wisdom that often goes unnoticed. An even less visible but vital point of convergence lies in the buried wisdom of knowing how to navigate policies and procedures to get things done. The conversation ends all too often with, "You can't do that here." Yet in many cases, someone does know how to do it. This kind of information typically lies in the heads of individuals. When they leave an institution, it is lost, underscoring the importance of central tracking and record keeping. Christ adds that she kept track of the money generated by external grants she helped nurture, demonstrating how central roles and units can generate funding to meet institution-wide needs through overhead cost-recovery (personal communication, August 28, 2008).

Senior academics, principal investigators, and heads of teaching teams also play key roles. The two top recommendations for principal investigators among respondents to the preliminary NAS survey were increasing leadership and team-forming activities and building networks with researchers in other disciplines (*Facilitating Interdisciplinary Research,* 2004). Senior academic scientists were influential figures in proposing major initiatives and ORUs such as the Bio-X program at Stanford that fosters IDR in medicine and biology and the Stanford Institute for the Environment, the Penn State Huck Institutes for the Life Sciences and Materials Research Institute, and Arizona State University's Institute for Computing and Information Science and Engineering (Sá, 2005). The NAS report also recommends rewarding leaders who initiate ID programs and providing incentives for departments aimed at sharing indirect costs and revenues, seed money, course credit assignments, intellectual property, space, personnel, and other resources. Beyond the usual managerial skills, respondents to the survey also called for leaders with a clear vision, effective skills of communication and team building, and the ability to grapple with turf issues. Collaborators need to be brought together early to work toward agreement on key issues such as methods, goals, and time lines. A leader should catalyze the integration of knowledge and skills in multiple disciplines, not simply engage in "stapling" them together.

Influential allies are also important points of convergence. Innovation studies indicate that the best route into an organization is through opinion leaders, whose advice others seek. The readiness of individual actors in the system differs, however. In his groundbreaking work on strategies for change, Jack Lindquist (1997) identified five major types that appear in all organizations or communities:

- Innovators—a few who will be eager to try out new things and are typically uncomfortable with the status quo
- Early adopters, a somewhat larger group, although rarely more than 12 to 15 percent of an organization
- An early majority, consisting of roughly a third of the population, who are cautious followers who can be engaged.
- The late majority, a skeptical group that typically awaits evidence that a new practice is feasible, effective, and likely to be rewarded
- Laggards, the final 15 percent, who resist changes until everyone else has moved on

Generally the typical time frame for adopting new behaviors is several years, and more radical ideas may take even decades.

AN INTERDISCIPLINARY ENDOWMENT

The Network for Interdisciplinary Initiatives at the University of Washington summed up the typical approach to financing interdisciplinary programs and projects: "Most interdisciplinary initiatives are forced to cobble together funding from multiple sources on an annual basis and lack institutional venues for securing sustained funding, even when they have demonstrated success on an on-going basis." At Washington and elsewhere, "Institutional investments in interdisciplinary initiatives have waxed and waned, with seed money and patchwork supports more readily available than sustained funding for proven enterprises" (Dubrow and Harris, 2006, p. 54). Relying solely on official budget allocations or a single pot of money shortchanges the innovation horizon for programs. Table 3.3 presents a range of strategies and tactics for building an interdisciplinary endowment that leverages existing resources while generating new ones, both large and small. Interdisciplinarity has a reputation for being

TABLE 3.3.   STRATEGIES FOR BUILDING AN INTERDISCIPLINARY ENDOWMENT

Build a diversified financial portfolio of multiple sources.

Target interdisciplinarity and strategic plan themes in capital campaigns at both institution-wide and unit levels.

Align campus agendas with state and federal funding agendas.

Coordinate with development and alumni offices to channel both unspecified and specified donor gifts.

Place some discretionary resources under central oversight.

Redirect existing resources to support internal incentive and seed grants.

Fund a designated number of proposals for programs that advance interdisciplinary excellence in strategic planning themes with prospects for external funding.

Identify internal and external funding sources for pilot courses and programs.

Channel indirect costs and overhead from external grants to innovations and local seed grants.

Establish seed grants for curriculum development, teaching, and research using existing competitions and discretionary money.

Implement a flexible accounting system that assigns proportional credits and revenue.

expensive. Collaborative research and team teaching do require more funding. Yet, the interdisciplinary studies team at the University of Massachusetts–Lowell stresses that many no-cost and low-cost changes can significantly enhance program effectiveness ID programs ("Final Report," 2007; see also Archibald, 2009).

Facilitating Interdisciplinary Research (2004) presents a wide range of recommendations for funding of both team building and integration, opportunities for formal training and learning in other fields, mechanisms for interinstitutional cooperation, and sharing of buildings, equipment, and organizations. The report urges funding organizations, in particular, to take an active role in facilitating IDR by creating special programs, providing seed funding, and instituting longer-term programs. They can also promote equal leadership status with multiple principal investigators; remove barriers to partnerships among universities, industry, and federal labs; and create in-house criteria to ensure that proposals are integrative and cross organizational boundaries. Within academic institutions, most of the budget is fixed in recurring categories. Flexible funds tend to be assigned to departments and colleges, leaving administrators with scant central fiscal resources for initiating or sustaining ID programs and projects. One of the top recommendations for campuses is to develop more flexible and equitable budget and cost-sharing policies across department and school lines, while streamlining procedures to allocate targeted resources to individual units.

Making money flow sideways is key to budget reform in a vertical funding system. Christina Gonzalez of the University of California–Davis called the process a "highly customized engineering work that must take the individual characteristics of each campus into account" (*Facilitating Interdisciplinary Research*, 2004, p. 108). UC–Davis experimented with two approaches: distributing funds from a central office to ID programs without going through deans and matching funds from a central office such as the graduate school to support a program. Over time, emphasis shifted to matching funds, and the budget formula was updated to stipulate that deans supply future matches from their own budgets.

Other institutions, including Duke University and the University of Michigan, moved to more flexible budget models for managing interdisciplinary work (*Facilitating Interdisciplinary Research*, 2004). At Duke, the central office for ID research and education works with the development office to create strategies for program fundraising, and the new provost's common fund small grants began in fall 2008. At Michigan, the older value-centered incremental model of budgeting was replaced by a system that allows mixing activity-based and discretionary budgeting. Within the activity-based part of the mix, revenues move preferentially toward units credited with larger revenue generation. By introducing a model that balances activity-based and discretionary budgeting, the provost and the president were able to retain significant discretion in funding initiatives at school, college, or research-unit levels independent of revenue-generating capacity. Flexible resources can be reserved for reallocation across units.

Academic reorganization is another strategy, though it is controversial. The units being moved are not always sanguine about the change. Yet reorganization can foster budget savings and greater flexibility for interdisciplinary work. Elizabeth Capaldi (2009) recounted one such change. In 2007, Arizona State University (ASU) implemented a new "faculties" model that separates graduate education from department control, making it a university-wide function. Individuals qualified to supervise graduate work in given fields can be members of several "faculties" at the same time. The change supplemented disciplinary doctorates with new interdisciplinary Ph.D. programs in sustainability, biological design, neurosciences, media arts and sciences, social science and health, social science and the environment, and applied linguistics. Changes occurred in undergraduate education as well. The School of Life Sciences, for instance, created six faculties from five departments. The merger produced eleven degree offerings. Faculty needed for particular courses are spread across the school, and each year the associate director for undergraduate programs meets with faculty leaders to discuss the teaching portfolios of more than one hundred faculty in the school, then tries to even out teaching loads, address curricular needs, and plan for enrollment. The money follows the person teaching the course, regardless of topic, and interdisciplinary and disciplinary teaching are treated the same. More recently, Arizona State has created new units that resulted in cost savings when smaller colleges and their recurring costs were eliminated. Eleven schools, one institute, and three colleges were formed from former departments, schools, and colleges. The new units are headed by a school director or dean who has the same responsibility department chairs had for faculty hiring, evaluation, and workload assignments. Each individual belongs to a primary and a second "faculty" to avoid creating new silos, and every year the school evaluates the viability of groupings. New groupings have led to new intellectual synergies, degree programs, organizational units, and research projects. The question of interdisciplinary rigor, though, is not addressed.

SEEDING CHANGE

Seed grants play a prominent role. Over half the institutions in the preliminary survey for the NAS report indicated they were supplying "venture capital" (*Facilitating Interdisciplinary Research*, 2004).

Amounts ranged from $1,000 to $1 million, though centered at $10,000 to $50,000, and were typically one- to two-year awards. Indirect cost recovery from external grants plays a key role in incentive funding, and Columbia University has used resources from licensing intellectual property. Stirred by a strategic plan calling for undergraduate research programs focused on IDS, the University of Southern California (USC) introduced an incentive fund for projects involving faculty in more than two schools and fellowships with release time from teaching. USC's former Center for Interdisciplinary Research also awarded competitive annual fellowships, and recipients participated in a fellows program to discuss their work and issues surrounding interdisciplinarity. Washington State University's initiation of collaboration program provided small sums up to five thousand dollars in support of meetings and retreats where faculty could interact and develop ideas for ID programs. When the University of California at Berkeley launched a new ideas initiative in 2001, 120 preproposals were received and winnowed to ten clustered themes, and the following year, a call for full proposals resulted in selections with new faculty positions in computational biology, regional and metropolitan studies, nanosciences, and new media. The University of California at Davis, Duke, and Harvard have implemented similar initiatives (*Facilitating Interdisciplinary Research*, 2004; Sá, 2005).

Just as incremental strategies play an important role in stimulating change, small- and medium-sized funding can make a difference. Reflecting on his experience at Duke University, provost Peter Lange (2006) commented that "active leadership needs to have active money." Lange did not have a lot of flexible money when he embarked on a culture shift on campus. Yet, he found, "it doesn't take a lot of discretionary money to make a lot of impact. I can get the deans and chairs to buy in with this discretionary money." New funding opportunities were created, including the provost's common fund, which started in the fall of 2008. It is important, Lange added, to have a stream of funds that resists budget cutting and other pressures. Barry Gold of the David and Lucile Packard Foundation also endorses the value of small pots of money to support meetings, bring people together, travel, learn how to work together, and train for teamwork. Sometimes, Creso Sá (2005) noted, modest investments are expected to lead to large grants. Yet returns on investment can be difficult to track. Sá warns against looking only for immediate success in the form of sizable external funding. The work that groups start may mature and produce rewards that reinvest in long-term changes in structure and behavior, including complex and diffuse benefits such as establishing leadership in new areas. Returns on investments for large ID facilities are also difficult to evaluate, and some have expressed skepticism about whether momentum can be sustained.

The development office is an essential partner. Interdisciplinarity can be given a priority in institutional fundraising, and a development officer can be charged with ongoing oversight for ID fundraising. The case can also be advanced with foundations. The Fred Kavh Foundation was formed to support the fields of cosmology, neuroscience, and nanoscience. It funded nine institutions in universities as well as four professorships, and research prizes (*Facilitating Interdisciplinary Research*, 2004). Local foundations play a role too. At Albion College, the Foundation for Interdisciplinary Studies supported faculty efforts to integrate interdisciplinary study into their courses and pedagogy with grants of five thousand dollars (interview with Lisa Lewis and Beth Lincoln, Feb. 28, 2006). Resources from both restricted and unrestricted donations can also be funneled to faculty and program development, student training, faculty chairs, and cross-unit appointments. At Johnson C. Smith University, both dedicated and unrestricted funds were used to build two new houses that became nurturing environments for faculty development and ID initiatives. Investing in the grant writing process is another strategy. Ohio State University's Large Interdisciplinary Grants Development Program has awarded up to $250,000 for research groups to prepare proposals for NSF and NIH grants, with the expectation that successful proposals would pay back initial investment through indirect cost recoveries. At Case Western University, a $150 million fund to simulate ID research and to nurture centers was established, and a commission on research and graduate education recommended hiring a proposal development staff to help faculty with ID grant writing, as well as funding to simulate ID research and nurture centers (Sá, 2005). Central units can also sponsor faculty visits to funding agencies and other universities, while encouraging senior faculty to mentor junior faculty in proposal writing.

Before the recent global economic crisis, Dubrow observes, private institutions worried less about centralized fundraising because they were not subject to the scrutiny faced by public institutions. They could staff up central enterprises, including support for strategic priorities that cut across colleges. Public institutions, in contrast, tended to concentrate capital campaigns in individual colleges. As a result, they have had less experience in framing complex multicollege themes. When colleges share a common thread in strategic priorities, attempts are made to coordinate multiple deans and development officers. Yet a decentralized model complicates and may even undermine fundraising for very large interdisciplinary initiatives, including "transformative gifts," which might appeal to donors (personal communication, July 13, 2009).

Space and equipment should be considered an essential part of an endowment profile. The inventory exercise should gather information on existing space and equipment with the aim of enhancing the sharing and underwriting of centralized equipment and instrument facilities for use by multiple disciplines, programs, and projects. A percentage of indirect costs from projects could be credited to support shared infrastructure and space, especially when large investments are required. *Facilitating Interdisciplinary Research* (2004) calls space a fungible asset that can be repurposed or renovated. For instance, MIT's Building 20, constructed during World War II and initially the home of the Radiation Laboratory, was torn down to create a place for a complex of buildings housing activities in computer, information, and intelligence systems. Even a small space can make a difference. At Bemidji State University, a large room next to the honors program was transformed into a common meeting place where brown-bag lunches were coupled with a faculty development program.

New building designs are also fostering interdisciplinarity. At Albion College, notes Lisa Lewis, some collaborative work occurred prior to building a new science complex. However, much of it went unfinished because of the physical separation in different buildings across campus. Even when buildings were close, the physical barrier of having to walk down stairs, cross a corridor between buildings, and climb another flight of steps was enough to curb collaboration. One of the motivations for developing the new science complex was to facilitate and foster interdisciplinary teaching and research collaborations among science departments. The four science buildings are physically connected on all floors, and an open and inviting atrium serves as a gathering space for students and faculty from all disciplines (no small factor in northern winters). The traditional science departments were placed within the complex with the deliberate intent of supporting key synergies. Analytical and physical chemistry, for example, is around the corner from the spaces occupied by physics. Molecular biology is located near the spaces for biological and organic chemistry. Geology and biology are adjacent to each other, and math and computer science are located between the four sciences. Within the first few weeks after the building opened, faculty were already talking about piloting a new upper-level interdisciplinary seminar focused on science as portrayed in film (personal communication, August 28, 2006).

Other facilities are nationally recognized models. Stanford University's James H. Clark Center houses the Bio-X program. Proposals and decisions about space assignments are initiated by faculty. The architectural design of the Janelia Farm Research Campus of Howard Hughes Medical Institute combines research laboratories with support areas, a conference center, and housing for visitors. Scientific programs and space combine to foster collaboration and flexibility for small teams in two primary areas: the interface of emerging technologies and application to biomedical problems, and project-oriented space for visitors to come together and use new technology for problem solving. Other benchmark facilities include the University of Michigan's Life Sciences Institute, the Center for Biotechnology and Interdisciplinary Studies at Rensselaer Polytechnic Institute, the Cal IT–California Institute for the Telecommunication and Information Technology on the UC-San Diego and Irvine campuses, the University of Chicago's Interdivisional Research Building, and new facilities at Duke's French Sciences Center, the Cornell Life Sciences Technology Building, and the University of Wisconsin–Madison's Wisconsin Institute for Discoveries (Sá, 2005; *Facilitating Interdisciplinary Research*, 2004).

The final topic of this chapter—space—is not just a physical location. It is also a metaphor for an intellectual and organizational place, raising the topic of institutionalization. Once again, differences in the way interdisciplinarity is constructed frame the discussion. Klein and Newell (1997) contended that interdisciplinarity will not be a matter of agreement on campuses—conceptually, practically, or politically. It is a complex concept, and attitudes are shaped by differences of disciplinary worldview, training, and educational philosophy. Even the same keyword, such as *innovation,* has different connotations. In science and medicine, it is aligned with discovery and product invention. In American studies, it is linked with educational experimentation and alternative paradigms. Mark Kann (1979) came to a similar conclusion in a study of forms of interdisciplinary explanation. He identified three major political positions. Conservative elites align interdisciplinarity with solving social and economic problems, without concern for epistemological questions. Liberal academics demand accommodation but maintain a base in the middle ground of the existing structure. And radical dissidents challenge the existing structure of knowledge, demanding that interdisciplinarity respond to the needs and problems of oppressed and marginalized groups in order to achieve greater equality. These and other differences, as we shall see in the next chapter, shape views of whether interdisciplinarity should be institutionalized, and how.

CHAPTER FOUR

FOSTERING PROGRAMMATIC STRENGTH AND SUSTAINABILITY

This chapter looks more closely at conditions for programmatic strength and sustainability. The chapter begins by defining arguments in the debate about whether interdisciplinarity (ID) should be institutionalized. This topic is a matter of considerable dispute. The debate is not an idle theoretical exercise, since differences will appear in local efforts to create sustainable change. Being familiar with the arguments is a crucial form of know-how in furthering the principle of platforming introduced in Chapter Three. After defining critical mass factors for strong programs, this chapter defines five principles for program review: interdisciplinarity, antecedent conditions, benchmarking, balance, and partnership. It closes with lessons on the political economy of interdisciplinary studies (IDS) programs from a new collection of case studies that illustrate the five principles and other lessons about programmatic strength and sustainability applicable across all program types.

INSTITUTIONALIZATION

The spectrum of debate ranges from the belief that regularizing ID practices in conventional structures undermines their raison d'être to the belief that a common definition and criteria of institutional strength are mandatory for survival. The former pole of debate is reflected in Stanley Fish's argument (1989) that any strategy which calls into question the foundations of disciplines theoretically negates itself if it becomes institutionalized. The latter pole is the argument for professionalization of IDS as a kind of überdiscipline that sets standards for all modes of interdisciplinary work, regardless of type. Two questions for thinking about programmatic strength follow from the debate. First, what is the relationship of disciplinarity and interdisciplinarity? And, second, how necessary is institutionalization for the development and sustainability of ID fields and projects?

A discipline is a field of inquiry into a particular aspect of the world. Disciplines specify the objects we study, the methods and concepts we use, criteria for validity and truth, and the economies of value that structure our professional lives (Messer-Davidow, Shumway, and Sylvan, 1993). In this respect, a discipline is a system of power with control over resources, identities, and patterns of research and education. Disciplines constitute economies of value that are encoded in canons of work and the professional apparatus of publication and conferences. Studies of disciplinarity, though, reveal conflicting models. Standard models connote stability, normality, and unity, signified in images of a structure, a foundation, and a territory. Other models accentuate historical change and dynamism, and heterogeneous practices, signified in images of a network or a web. All disciplines, moreover, are not identical. Although they share a common process of disciplining knowledge, their outcomes differ. Lumping all specialized inquiry into a polyglot category ignores crucial differences in their institutional formations and their degrees of openness to the kinds of interdisciplinary developments portrayed in Chapter One. The differences come to a head in the proposition that a successful interdisciplinary field becomes "just another discipline," with all of the attendant intellectual and organizational technologies that delimit domains of inquiry. This too is an oversimplification of the plurality of forms and practices of interdisciplinary work.

In addressing the question of institutionalization, Fish (1989) contended that normalizing practices undermines the very meaning of interdisciplinarity. He took particular aim at the logic of new interdisciplinarity in humanities in left culturalist theory, deconstruction, Marxism, feminism, radical neopragmatism, and new historicism. They were all critical of two kinds of boundary making: the social structures by which lines of political authority are maintained and the institutional structures by which disciplines establish and extend their territorial claims. Yet, Fish charged, the multitude of studies and projects do not transgress boundaries through radical actions. They center on straightforward tasks requiring information and techniques from other disciplines. Or they expand imperialistically into other territories. Or they establish a new discipline staffed by a new breed of counterprofessionals. In responding to Fish, Alan Liu (2008) offered an apologia for interdisciplinarity that accepts the epistemological critique of its ideological and imperialist operations and the illusion of a complete freedom of mind unimpeded by boundaries. However, he argues, the epistemological critique does not offer terms of analysis for the pragmatics of interdisciplinarity. Liu is critical of certain practices, including the ambition of pantextualism in humanities and, more so, the current corporate form of ID teamwork allied with big science. The threat of a new uniformity of interdisciplinarity in team science, though, differs from other protocols, practices, and conventions. They produce their own closures, but they also make available new areas of formulations of knowledge barred by previous configurations. Ultimately, Liu proposes, interdisciplinary knowledge is a rhetoric, and the essence of that rhetoric is to reconfigure closures to make them answer to current urgencies.

The conception of interdisciplinarity as an architectonic art lies at the heart of Richard McKeon's earlier essay, "The Uses of Rhetoric in a Technological Age" (1979). McKeon retraced the long historical connection of rhetoric with the development of theory, practice, and methods to create alternative forms and outcomes of knowledge production. Subject-matters, he wrote, are not ready-made to respond to all of the questions and issues we encounter: "We make subject-matters to fit the examination and resolution of problems, and the solution of problems brings to our attention further, consequent problems, which frequently require the setting up and examination of new fields" (p. 18). The productive art of constructing new interdisciplinary fields challenges conventional priorities. Although the political economy of the academy forces them to play the traditional power game of seeking resources and securing institutional space, Stanley Katz (1996) contends that the formation of such fields marks the possibility of a more flexible design.

The second question follows from conceiving of interdisciplinarity as an architectonic art that reorganizes existing categories by exploring new topics and developing new subject matters. How necessary is institutionalization for the pragmatics of reconfiguring conventional closures and, in doing so, developing the ground for new designs? Ethan Kleinberg (2008) argued in a recent essay, "Interdisciplinary Studies at a Crossroads," that institutionalization is a "Faustian bargain." Success, in other words, comes at a price. Echoing Fish, Kleinberg contends that the academic structure and place of the majority of ID programs, departments, and centers are not substantially different from the units they were designed to reimagine and to challenge. As a result, they affirm Bill Readings's dystopic vision of *The University in Ruins* (1997). Liberal arts education and the university in general, Readings argued, have been transformed into a corporate-style service industry selling the notion of "excellence." IDS has generated new competitive specializations for niche markets, but in the process has also further fragmented the university with new disciplines anchored by the familiar professional apparatus of learned societies, annual meetings, publication venues, and canonical bodies of work. In the process of making a "pact with the devil," Kleinberg laments, IDS lost the flexibility, spontaneity, and open-minded approach that characterized its development in the first place, beckoning "the end of real interdisciplinarity."

Kleinberg is wise to warn against isolation and the myopia of self-legitimation. In its place, he favors the kinds of dialogue, exchange, and new ideas that occur when traditional disciplines are brought into contact. Yet his solution stops short at citing two models—theme-based colloquia in Wesleyan University's College of Letters and issue-based programs such as Science and Society or Feminist, Gender, and Sexuality Studies—and urging "internal self-restraint" in order to avoid producing "ersatz disciplines." Making the right choices, he maintains, means adopting a posture of generosity that nurtures pathways, intersections, and intellectual exchanges. But, Kleinberg essentializes a "real interdisciplinarity," while reinscribing the dichotomy of disciplinarity and interdisciplinarity. He allows that critical mass factors are "essential requirements," but insists that "the beauty and utility of interdisciplinary studies reside not in their institutional strength but their protean nature and their ability to build bridges and make connections among the disciplines, across departments, and throughout the university" (p. 10). The coupling of beauty and utility captures a vital quality of interdisciplinarity, but it ignores the need for institutional space to develop ID epistemology, methodology, and influence. It also minimizes threats highlighted in a contrasting view of interdisciplinarity at a crossroads.

Stuart Henry (2005) grounds the contrasting answer to the question of institutionalizing interdisciplinarity in the power of disciplinary hegemony, drawing on Cindi Katz (2001) and, more particularly, Rodgers, Booth, and Eveline's application (2003) of Plumwood's five denunciation strategies of "otherization" (1993):

- *Backgrounding,* which reinforces the distinction between disciplines and interdisciplines, normalizing the priority of the former over the latter
- *Incorporation,* which defines the other in relation to the master in a hierarchy, obscuring the independence of interdisciplinary method
- *Instrumentation,* which maintains disciplinary advantage by appropriating interdisciplinarity as a complementary resource and an instrumental appendage, further denying its autonomy
- *Radical exclusion,* which separates ID work discursively as fundamentally different from and outside disciplinary work
- *Homogenization,* which labels and stereotypes the other, pitting "us" against the black box category of an interdisciplinary "them"

Rodgers, Booth, and Eveline (2003) admit that counter tactics can never overthrow disciplinary hegemony. They argue instead for "getting around the rules of constraining space" by controlling boundaries, defining separate criteria for ID work, developing an independent method, establishing methodological and theoretical rigor, formulating recommendations for practice, and creating a self-regulating guild. The future of interdisciplinarity as a practical project, they contend, lies in negotiating the material and representational economy in which it is deployed. Negotiation requires moving within the existing disciplinary structure in order to transcend it—in short, playing the political game of "making a difference."

One of the most frequent questions that arises in negotiating how to make a difference is whether to be a program or a department. Programs offer greater flexibility for team teaching, multi- and interdisciplinary collaborations, and community projects. Yet even if they offer majors and minors, many programs do not confer degrees and tend to rely on joint appointments, interdepartmental cooperation, and coordinators, directors, or committees lacking the authority of departmental chairs. For these reasons, the National Council of Black Studies endorses the departmental structure. Departments, it argues, offer a direct and stable connection to the power structure of an institution and greater autonomy over curriculum, budget, and staffing. They are also equated with tenure-track faculty who can devote time to developing and sustaining a particular area, and they contribute to unit power through increased representation on institute-wide committees (Alkalimat, 2001). A similar position is shared in women's studies.

Diane Elam (1990, 2002) defines the space of women's studies as both a "discipline of difference" and an "interdisciplinary discipline." She contends that departmental location does not deprive women's studies of radical politics. Rather, it harnesses funds and tenure lines for that purpose. Mindful of the small number of full-time appointments in the field, Robyn Warhol (2002) urges using departmental spaces to focus on the changing character of disciplines. The modeling of interdisciplinary research (IDR) and IDS is expanded at more sites, and new faculty and tenure lines are inclusive of women's studies. The "both-and model" does not dichotomize disciplinarity and interdisciplinarity. In order to change the disciplines, one program coordinator remarked, women's studies had to be "of them, in them, and about them" (cited in Boxer, 1982, pp. 671, 693). The field offers intellectual community and an institutional site for feminists who do most of their work in disciplines, legitimating gender as a category of analysis at those sites (Addelson and Potter, 1991). "Creolized disciplines" such as women's studies, Cornwell and Stoddard (2001) also point out, are not necessarily confined to a single purpose or effect. They can be alternative, resistant, or emergent. The field may be viewed as an emergent discipline with its own canons, methods, and issues. At the same time, it is an alternative or is resistant to traditional discursive practices of disciplines.

CRITICAL MASS

The concept of critical mass derives from physics, where it means the minimum quantity of nuclear fuel required for a chain reaction to start. The national status of interdisciplinary fields is a strong factor in the legitimation of local initiatives. Strength is measured by the number and scale of research and teaching programs and the development of an infrastructure for communication, a scholarly body of knowledge, and a self-defined shared epistemology. The realities of critical mass, though, differ at the campus level. The local political economy of academic power, administrative fit, economic incentives, and community pressures are strong determinants. Units range from an augmented form of specialization, to a program or center, to an autonomous department, school, or college. More programs carry the name than grant a degree, few offer all undergraduate and graduate degrees, and many turn out to be multidisciplinary combinations of departmental courses coordinated by a faculty member and housed in a traditional department or other program. Status also varies. On one campus, faculty enjoy the freedom to pursue their interests with all the perks. On another, they struggle to survive and find their interdisciplinary work discounted in the reward system (Klein, 1996, 2005).

Some programs survive on little or no administrative support. However, sustainability is diminished by a weak infrastructure, isolation, and burnout. Moreover, Diana Archibald (2009) warns, new programs have to reinvent the wheel because they are not part of a "community of ID practice" with pertinent know-how signaled by the critical mass indicators in Table 4.1 and the characteristics of strong models identified in Augsburg and Henry's (2009a) new collection of case studies of IDS programs. Weak models have inadequate or no dedicated faculty, relying solely on borrowed faculty from other units. They lack core courses, relying on a multidisciplinary mix of existing disciplinary courses. The mix adds breadth and available knowledge, information, and

Table 4.1. Critical Mass Indicators for Sustainability

A free-standing, autonomous unit

A voice in unit policies and procedures

A visible and secure location in the organizational hierarchy of a campus

Structural coherence

A spine of core ID courses

A clearly defined ID mission

A shared intellectual agenda

Adequate personnel, including dedicated and full-time faculty and staff

Strong and experienced leaders

A sense of community and shared experiences

Faculty development

Incorporation of "best practices" and pertinent literatures

Proactive attention to integrative and collaborative processes

Adequate financial resources and control of budget

Adequate common space and equipment

Appropriate criteria of evaluation and assessment

Equal access to the institutional reward system and incentives

Affiliations with other units and external communities

Source: Adapted and updated from Rich and Warren (1980), Caldwell (1983), Klein (1996), and Klein and Newell (1997).

methods. Yet disciplines are arrayed in an encyclopedic alignment that Ellen Messer-Davidow dubbed a "multidisciplinary mélange" (2002). They also lack a clear interdisciplinary intellectual agenda, programmatic infrastructure, and partnerships.

In contrast, strong models have a core faculty with full-time appointments located entirely or partly within a program. When faculty from other units are involved, the program's leader has leverage to obtain their participation and a formal affiliation or joint appointment. Programs have a clear report line to an upper-level administrator. Their leaders and faculty have a voice in policy, curriculum, budget, program evaluation, and personnel matters. Programs are anchored in best practices and an understanding of interdisciplinarity communicated to all parties. When other units play a role, they have shared governance, and all support staff and advisors are knowledgeable about the program. The curriculum also has a spine of required core courses, ensuring that attention is paid to interdisciplinary theory, concepts, and methods. At a minimum, the core should include an introductory seminar and a culminating experience such as a thesis, project, or seminar, though Stuart Henry recommends that strong models have at least twenty credit hours of required ID courses (personal communication, August 9, 2006). The larger institutional culture supports the program as well, with equitable policies for participation in workload assignments and the reward system. The faculty development system also supports the program, and appropriate criteria of evaluation and learning assessment are used (Augsburg and Henry, 2009b, 2009c; R. Miller, 2009; Augsburg, Henry, Newell, and Szostak, 2009).

A popular reform initiative illustrates the difference between multi- and interdisciplinary forms. Learning communities have appeared across campuses in recent years. The simplest models to implement are linked courses that typically focus on a theme. "Approached seriously," Valerie Bystrom (2002) advises, "linked classes can open interdisciplinary spaces and nurture what sprouts there" (p. 75), increasing the likelihood of embedding new structural models and pedagogies into a campus culture. Interest groups, sometimes called a colloquy model, are typically multidisciplinary. A small cohort of students takes two or three courses that may be aligned in a thematic cluster but are not modified. In contrast, integrated links, coordinated programs, and team-taught programs make a more conscious effort to achieve interdisciplinarity. The coordinated studies model may constitute a student's or a faculty member's full load, though it typically runs one or two quarters. Integrative studies present a unified theme and are often accompanied by a writing component. Team teaching may also occur. (For models, see O'Connor, 2003; Spear, 2003; Washington Center for Improving the Quality of Undergraduate Education, www.evergreen.edu/washcenter/home.asp.)

The interdisciplinary arts and sciences (IAS) program at the University of Washington, Bothell campus, illustrates how evolution toward separate degrees can occur without sacrificing a common commitment to interdisciplinarity. In autumn 1990, the liberal studies program at the newly opened campus began teaching classes with twelve faculty. Program options were grouped under a single bachelor of arts in liberal studies degree. When the program changed its name to interdisciplinary arts and sciences in 1998, the B.A. degree title switched to interdisciplinary studies. Over time, new study options were added in American studies; community psychology; culture, literature, and the arts; environmental science (B.S.); environmental studies; global studies; interdisciplinary arts; science, technology, and society; and society, ethics, and human behavior. In April 2009, IAS petitioned to convert all of these options to majors. The interdisciplinary studies B.A. continues to house an individualized studies option and serve as a platform to pilot new options. The conversion was designed to raise the visibility of options to potential students, provide better recognition of graduates' achievements, and consolidate a twenty-year program-building process. Bruce Burgett, professor and director of interdisciplinary arts and sciences, describes the proposal as a response to changing needs and interests, as well as internal self-study and an external review that recommended IAS differentiate its curricular offerings while enhancing an emphasis on interdisciplinarity. Doing so is in keeping with the institutional mission of Bothell, which opened with a strong commitment to pedagogical innovation, collaboration, and interdisciplinary education. Within this framework, IAS developed a culture centered on integrative values and portfolio-based assessment student learning. All IAS degrees meet four core learning objectives: critical thinking, collaboration and shared leadership, interdisciplinary research, and writing and presentation. The integrative model of degree delivery, Burgett emphasizes, gives IAS flexibility in allocating teaching across different areas and working with a faculty spanning the arts and sciences. The "undepartmentalized" structure gives faculty and staff greater ability to adapt quickly to fluctuations in student interest and resources than is customary in traditional departmental structures (personal communication, July 20, 2009).

Interdisciplinary research is no stranger to lack of sustainability either. Not all of the National Science Foundation's Engineering Research Centers, for example, achieved self-sufficiency after external funding ended. Some matured into stable organizations, but others disintegrated (Sá, 2005). Starting a new center or program may also mean closing or reducing another area. Mindful of this problem, provisions for sunsetting a center after a certain period of time have become more common (*Facilitating Interdisciplinary Research*, 2004). Innovative campuses such as the University of Wisconsin–Green Bay, the University of California–Santa Cruz, and Evergreen State College have also had to accommodate to disciplinary, market, and demographic pressures. They retain interdisciplinary features, but the original radical spirit has been dampened. As the final section of this chapter demonstrates, strong programs have also been subjected to involuntary reduction, starved of budgetary and faculty resources, and confronted with larger class sizes. In the dwindling and declawing of ID initiatives, full-time faculty return to departments, programs are staffed increasingly by adjuncts, and experiments disappear for lack of leadership, faculty, and students (Henry, 2005; Spear, 2003).

The stunting of both IDR and IDS is hastened by budget crises, the departure of a supportive administrator, the arrival of a new president or provost with a different agenda, and the escalating opposition of influential opinion leaders on campus. Interdisciplinarity is not the only victim. In the current economy, traditional departments with low numbers are being eliminated. Yet ID programs are typically the first to be called into question, faulted for lacking rigor, being redundant, and, the ultimate trump card, being expendable frills.

PROGRAM REVIEW

The cornerstone of traditional thinking about program review is progress toward clear and agreed-on goals. Yet interdisciplinarity presents several complications that make a standard model inappropriate. More than one discipline, profession, or interdisciplinary field is involved, with sometimes conflicting assumptions about what to evaluate and how to do it. Context and content differ by knowledge field and institutional location. Innovative approaches often call for new ways of assessing quality, and collaboration introduces complication. The challenge of ID evaluation is compounded in new fields and areas of high innovation and risk taking, especially where the knowledge domain is still being charted and consensus on validation criteria is lacking. Novelty of the boundary-crossing kind, Dan Sperber emphasized in an international virtual seminar on interdisciplinarity, may also intentionally undermine current understanding in disciplines ("Rethinking Interdisciplinarity," 2003–2004).

In the past, the topic of ID evaluation did not constitute an identifiable literature. Accounts were scattered across multiple forums and were usually longer on anecdotal and normative views than on empirical, longitudinal, and large-scale studies. In the absence of clear guidelines, discipline-based standards were often applied. Moreover, institution-wide evaluation forms often lack criteria that address the distinctive features of interdisciplinary programs. Therefore, it is crucial to define those features and appropriate ways to evaluate them. Otherwise others may likely supply default answers that are inappropriate. The better developed a field, the more likely that guidelines or best practice models are available. Women's studies, for example, has published recommendations for evaluating feminist scholarship and learning assessment (National Women's Studies Association, 2000; Musil, 1992). The American Studies Association (ASA) has also issued a guide to program review, and the Association for Integrative Studies (AIS) has guidelines for accreditation in ID general education.

The discussion that follows integrates insights from the ASA and AIS documents. The AIS *Accreditation Standards for Interdisciplinary General Education* (2002) represent state-of-the-art counsel intended for use in both general education and IDS programs. The accreditation task force drew on the Association of American Colleges' model for program review and educational quality in the major in formulating six categories of recommendation: goals, curriculum, teaching and learning, faculty, administration, and assessment (www.units.muohio.edu/aisorg/PUBS/reports/genedaccred.html). The *ASA Guide for Reviewing American Studies Programs* (1997–1998) is a step-by-step guide through initial preparation, self-study, external review, and follow-up. The appendixes include a checklist of documents for the self-study (www.theasa.net/publications/review_guide/guide_for_reviewing_american_studies_programs/).

Program review is typically driven by institution-wide schedules, but ID programs are not necessarily part of regular five-year review cycles. They may also be mandated when financial concerns arise or changes are proposed, such as moving from a minor to a major, adding a graduate program, or restructuring to respond to new goals, student populations, and research missions. Program review usually entails a standard set of questions about the history of a unit, structure and requirements, student numbers, rates of retention and graduation, faculty qualifications and performance, curricular and research strengths and weaknesses, resources, and areas for change. Some of the data needed for documentation may be available through central data gathering but, if not, must be compiled. Additional explanation may also be required for special interdisciplinary awards and other accomplishments unfamiliar to those outside ID programs and departments. A strategy of preparedness, or what ASA calls constructive diligence, is the best investment in the integrity of the ID program review process. As one ASA member remarked, "The best way to prepare for a program review is to constantly prepare for it." Review should not be an isolated exercise but part of "the lived daily experience" of a program, embedded within its culture or structure of feeling. Diligence means creating "an intentional culture of evidence," not a regime of surveillance.

Five interdisciplinary-specific and overlapping principles should be incorporated into the review process when responding to standard questions and, as needed, adding supplementary explanation and documentation.

PRINCIPLE 1: INTERDISCIPLINARITY

ASA and AIS raise the same fundamental question: How central is an interdisciplinary focus to a program? Both organizations call for a clear working definition of interdisciplinarity, proactive attention to integration, and systematic comparison of disciplinary approaches to determine their strengths and limits. In an AIS forum aptly titled "Apollo Meets Dionysius" (Newell and others, 2003), participants disagreed on how detailed the comparison should be. Some argued that the concept and method of interdisciplinarity belongs at the heart of study. Others favored broader theme- and problem-based study, a view that also emerged in the SSRC study of IDS programs. Moreover, Lisa Lattuca (2001) found, in fields that prioritize critique of knowledge, the premise of integration is disputed along with the view that disciplinary grounding is the necessary basis for ID work. Yet integration is widely viewed as the litmus test of interdisciplinarity (Klein, 2008b).

Principle 2: Antecedent Conditions of Critical Mass and Programmatic Strength

In synthesizing lessons about and defining a model for evaluating Transdisciplinary Tobacco Research Centers, Stokols et al. (2003) defined the antecedent conditions that produce collaborative readiness for team science. They include the presence of institutional supports; the breadth of disciplines, departments, and institutions encompassed by a center; the degree to which team members have worked together on prior projects; the proximal location of offices and laboratories; and the availability of electronic linkages. The more contextual factors that are aligned at the outset, the greater the prospects for success. The same principle applies to IDS, and the critical mass factors and indicators of strong programs above provide a counterpart checklist of antecedent conditions for ID program review.

Principle 3: Benchmarking

Benchmarking aligns local programs with national trends, models, requirements, and goals. Alignment does not obviate a local signature highlighting unique features of a program, such as excellence in particular areas of research and teaching, community links, or local strategic planning priorities. It situates the local, though, within a larger national context that incorporates tested assumptions about quality and best practices. Guidelines and accreditation reports from pertinent professional organizations should be used. Counterparts in peer programs and leaders in national organizations are also good sources of appropriate criteria and models, as well as potential external reviewers.

Principle 4: Balance

Interdisciplinarity is not the only variable in many ID programs. They typically span four major goals that need to be balanced in a logical sequence of requirements, including core ID and discipline-based courses, electives, and other experiences such as independent study or internships. A working balance of multidisciplinary breadth, disciplinary depth, and integrative synthesis is key to both intellectual and organizational coherence:

- Generic competencies: written and oral communication, numeracy, critical thinking, and computer and information literacy
- Discipline- and profession-specific content and skills, methods, tools, concepts, and theories
- Multidisciplinary breadth of knowledge: overview of multiple disciplines and fields
- Interdisciplinary-specific content and capacities: the knowledge produced in specific fields and integrative skills

PRINCIPLE 5: PARTNERSHIP

Partnerships span other parts of a campus and communities at local, regional, and national levels. The ASA cautions against confusing independence with isolation. Many American studies programs, for example, enjoy autonomy, but the majority also depend on other units for courses, faculty contributions, and opportunities for teaching assistants. Moreover, contributions are often reciprocal, since core faculty teach courses and perform services for other departments, such as English and history, and have overlapping interests with other interdisciplinary fields, such as women's, ethnic, and media studies. If protocols for relationships are not in place, ASA recommends establishing them rather than leaving ties to informal channels and the goodwill of others. Advisory committees composed of representatives from several departments can build and maintain healthy bridges while lending political muscle in negotiations for resources.

THE POLITICAL ECONOMY OF IDS

A new collection of case studies affirms the five principles while adding other lessons about strength and sustainability. Augsburg and Henry's compilation, *The Politics of Interdisciplinary Studies* (2009a), was prompted by a sense that undergraduate IDS degree programs were under attack. The editors and several authors were especially concerned about generic or generalized units in the form of a broad-based curriculum or clusters of disciplines, often called a cluster college, college within a college, or a stand-alone program. The broad variant focuses typically on an overview of humanities, social sciences, and science and technology, coupled with capstone experiences. The cluster variant focuses on particular areas, such as social sciences, humanities, or science. The authors contrast the generic/generalized type to content-based and subject-focused majors that were prominent in major studies of IDS by the Social Science Research Council and Brint, Turk-Bicakci, Proctor, and Murphy (2009) examined in Chapter Two, though some chapters in the book deal with those types. (Insights from Rick Szostak's and Diana Archibald's chapters including those types appeared earlier in this book.)

Many generic/generalized programs were founded as telic institutions in Grant and Riesman's sense of purposive reforms (1979) that promote a different conception of undergraduate education. They shared a commitment to student-centered education, innovative pedagogies, collaborative curriculum design and teaching, and flexible administrative structure. The golden age of telic institutions, Martin Trow (1984–1985) found in studying their histories, usually lies in the early years, steeped in "the romantic, evangelical and utopian ideologies" of their founders. The transition from birth to maturity brought problems. Routinization, conflict, privatization, and withdrawal resulted in diminished levels of spontaneity, creativity, community, and involvement. The programs that survived the longest, Trow found, typically moved from experimentation to regularization and complementary niches. The composite picture that emerges from the Augsburg and Henry (2009a) collection is mixed. Some programs survived through adaptation. Others were weakened, and some were terminated. The case studies are complex so should be read in their entirety to follow all the twists and turns over time. The key lessons, though, may be extracted, since they illustrate the five principles for program review and other lessons of strength and sustainability applicable to IDS programs of all types.

The Interdisciplinary Studies Program (INTS) at the University of Texas at Arlington combines all five of the principles. The INTS began thirty years ago as an open enrollment experiment in theme-based, student-designed combinations of courses guided by advisors. Director Allen Repko (2009) called the original format a multidisciplinary retention program that fostered lingering perceptions of INTS as a refuge for students who could not succeed elsewhere. He attributes transformation into a sustainable mainstream program to a combination of generic and ID-specific strategies. The generic strategies included alignment of the program to the institutional mission, creation of a student database, effective marketing, and persuasive report writing. The ID-specific strategies included anchoring a new three-course core curriculum in an authoritative definition of interdisciplinarity, forming an alliance with a benchmarking professional organization (AIS), placing integration and ID learning outcomes at the heart of the program, and pairing a definition of interdisciplinarity with a statement of the program's distinctive mission. Repko also attributes the successful transformation to forging partnerships with other units.

When the program was moved to the School of Urban and Public Affairs, the school gained a significant increase in enrollment and stronger competitive position for campus resources. INTS, in turn, gained an increased budget, additional tenure-track lines, greater freedom in program development, and a supportive dean. The strategy of "turfing out" from the core also continues to build partnerships with other units in the form of new courses. Yet a surge in enrollment, coupled with limited resources, requires developing more efficient approaches to advising and teaching that will not diminish the ID mission, undermine antecedent conditions that have been established, or tilt the balance toward reductive service components.

Repko's caveat echoes in Rick Hendra's account (2009) of the devolution of the individualized University Without Walls (UWW) program at the University of Massachusetts–Amherst. The University Without Walls innovation emerged in the progressive college movement of the 1920s and 1930s. The defining characteristic is individual students' roles in helping to design a program. Hendra cautions against confusing individualized degrees with ID degrees. They often lead to interdisciplinary programs but may be narrower in scope, broader, or problem focused. Admitting its first students in 1971, UWW at Amherst developed multiple factors needed for interdisciplinary strength in individualized programs: one-on-one meetings with an advisor, a UWW handbook with definitions and guidelines, and a six-credit introductory seminar designed to provide intellectual substance for the program planning process. Over time, however, streamlining measures diminished those strengths. Curriculum goals were deemphasized in writing the degree plan, a split developed in how to teach the degree development course, the founding director and several veteran staff left, and a series of financial cutbacks ultimately resulted in moving UWW from a state-funded to a self-sustaining program. Today the degree is standardized in professional track programs assembled out of previous course work and experience. The seminars, which gained more credit hours at one point, have been consolidated into a single course. The format is also shifting to all online and blended formats, a faculty sponsor is no longer required, and the advisor's role has been scaled back. Most students are simply choosing a multidisciplinary degree instead of designing an interdisciplinary one guided by strong advising, course work, and a comprehensive handbook.

The principle of interdisciplinarity is a prominent theme in Raymond Miller's personal saga (2009) of IDS at San Francisco State University. Miller sorts through a long and complex series of changes that began in 1945, marked over the years by integrative segments in general education, subject-focused IDS programs such as ethnic studies and women's studies, generic IDS departments, and other innovations. The institutional culture has been support-ive of interdisciplinary education, and a number of programs are still thriving, including criminal justice, international relations, human sexuality studies, public administration, and urban stud-ies. However, some are gone, as is the umbrella structure of the Center for Interdisciplinary Programs. The generic departments, in particular, illustrate the difference between weak and strong programs. San Francisco State had four such departments: creative arts, humanities, science, and social science. All four developed their own ID majors at undergraduate and graduate levels, and they were responsible for the academic preparation of teachers. By 2008, though, only the humanities program remained. Human-ities was the only one of the four generic departments to follow a self-contained curriculum strategy for its majors. The other three followed a core-satellite model, which meant that most courses students took in their respective majors were likely to be in other departments. Since the self-contained approach requires a larger cadre of faculty, it gave humanities more political protection, but only as long as layoffs did not threaten the faculty core.

During the recession of 2000–2001, budgetary cutbacks resulted in major closures. Of the eleven programs proposed for discontinuance, ten were interdisciplinary. One of them was the social science department, charged with being too expensive, out-of-date, and its mission duplicated in other units. Miller (2009) refutes all three charges, though the last one merits elaboration since it is heard more widely today in the midst of financial cutbacks. The charge of duplication rested on the premise that interdisciplinarity had become a pervasive value throughout the parent College of Behavioral and Social Sciences. Yet IDS at San Francisco State and other institutions spans a continuum of weak and strong programs. One of the distinguishing claims of generic/generalized programs is their proactive attention to the integrative process of weighing multiple perspectives and implications for knowledge production and transmission. Miller goes so far as to call this focus an "academic specialization of its own" and casts doubt on whether faculty in other "ostensibly" ID fields engage in such rigor. Wentworth and Carp (2009) agree to the extent they call commitment to wholeness and interrelatedness the subject matter of generic/generalized "transdiscipline" programs. All agree, though, that the loss of such programs means that a campus likely loses this critical mass factor. "Weak interdisciplinarity prevails," Miller (2009) laments, "while strong interdisciplinarity withers away" (p. 128).

The Politics of Interdisciplinary Studies (Augsburg and Henry, 2009a) is skewed toward one institution, with three full chapters devoted to San Francisco State. Yet the other two chapters furnish parallel lessons. Helen Goldsmith (2009) retraced the history of the liberal studies major at San Francisco State from its beginning in 1972 as a response to California's preparation standards for future school teachers. Liberal studies had always been housed in the Division of Undergraduate Studies and relied heavily on faculty in traditional departments. Program leaders considered the major to be multidisciplinary because it lacked a curriculum requirement or a significant student experience that fosters integrated interdisciplinary connections. The program consisted of forty-six semester units structured around four discipline-based areas providing breadth across disciplinary clusters. It was initially a self-designed major, allowing students to explore an overarching theme and choose courses from four areas to address it. Like counterpart individualized programs, though, it was not well understood or anchored. In the late 1980s, a common twenty-five-unit core of eight courses, with two in each subject area, was developed to provide greater cohesion. In addition, students chose an area of emphasis that was subsequently increased to twelve units. Changes to the curriculum helped to alleviate some problems with depth and strength of courses, thematic planning, and common experiences. However, program leaders persuaded the provost to support hiring their own core faculty, a move that both Miller and James W. Davis, below, consider crucial to reduce vulnerability. The five new tenure-track assistant professors who joined liberal studies in fall 2007 are viewed as a means of reinvigorating interdisciplinarity on campus. They have already created new gateway and capstone courses in the major. However, three challenges face the program now: integrating them into the larger institutional culture while not overloading them with multiple obligations, keeping the program an all-university endeavor with its own faculty, and surviving drastic budget cuts in California.

Davis (2009) traced the history of San Francisco State's Inter-Arts Center (IAC) from its founding in 1954 through final closure in 2001. The IAC offered programs focused on experimental and ID expression in the arts, allowing investigation of emerging fields that combined and synthesized separate areas and even new forms of expression. The major in interdisciplinary studies was more multidisciplinary than interdisciplinary since there were no synthesis courses designed to develop integrative ideas, understanding, or creative methodologies. Between 1985 and 1989, the unit gained five tenure and tenure-track positions. Between 1992 and 2003, efforts were also made to design and require synthesis courses, and an associates program was developed to add faculty from other departments in the college.

Davis drew five lessons from the history of the IAC. First, a dean's understanding and support of interdisciplinarity is crucial and should be an explicit topic in job interviewing. Second, given general lack of understanding of interdisciplinary versus multidisciplinary approaches, frequent dialogue and collaborative efforts with faculty in related fields are mandatory. Third, the relationship between an ID program and affiliated departments and programs needs to be reinforced at intersecting points such as cross-listed courses, shared symposia, and shared visiting artists and lecturers. Fourth, saddling a program with responsibilities beyond its primary mission reduces it to a service organization—in the case of IAC, a group of nondegree college-wide special programs. Fifth, it is wiser to place ID programs within an academic unit that is equivalent to a department, and preferably independent of a traditional discipline where its distinctive mission may be lost.

The INTS at Arlington, UWW at Amherst, and IDS programs at San Francisco State illustrate another important lesson: not all ID programs are born strong. This lesson echoes in Peter Wakefield's description (2009) of the current effort to strengthen Emory University's undergraduate IDS major in American studies and in interdisciplinary studies in culture and society. In contrast to hostile or neutral environments, Emory University is a hospitable institutional culture for the undergraduate IDS major, located in the administrative home of the nationally respected Graduate Institute of Liberal Arts (ILA). The undergraduate IDS major has consisted of a student-designed and advisor-guided plan of twelve courses: seven self-designed concentration courses selected from departments and five ID frame courses, with two additional courses focused on preparation and writing of a senior research project. A new planned spine will replace the former frame courses.

- IDS 200: Foundations Toward Interdisciplinary Study: a team-taught, lecture-style course addressing the question, "What is evidence?" across disciplines, with visits by faculty outside ILA
- IDS 201 Special Problems in Interdisciplinary Studies: smaller, problem-based expansions of "What is evidence?" applied to faculty and graduate student instructors' research problems
- IDS 300/700-level theme-based courses reflective at an advanced level on faculty's research interests; frequently team-taught and involving both undergraduate and graduate students
- IDS 400: Capstone Seminar, possibly in conjunction with the American studies senior seminar, involving a substantial writing component that will replace the independent senior project

These structural changes are meant to provide a shared conception of interdisciplinarity anchored in a new foundation that engages significant texts, collaborative conversation with visiting faculty from across campus, a critical organizing problem, and traditions of engagement that are part of the defining fabric of ILA. It was the original administrative home of African American studies at Emory, and several faculty hold joint appointments. Emory's Center for the Study of Public Scholarship was also founded by an ILA faculty member and has opened the campus to a wider range of knowledge forms.

Paul Burkhardt (2006), who wrote elsewhere about dismantling Arizona International College (AIC), echoes the principle of strategic engagement, though in a more dire case. AIC opened in 1996 as a campus featuring innovative problem-based ID learning communities. By October 2001, however, the president of the main University of Arizona campus decided to close AIC to protect more traditional units while moving toward a plan of focused excellence on the home campus. Burkhardt (2006, 2009) advocates staking claims to critical mass factors because they create and protect a space for difference that enjoys stability, self-governance, and equitable inclusion. Yet, he recommends doing so in a complementary fashion to avoid the dichotomy of "us" versus "them." The process of strategic engagement, he warns, is slower than revolutionary actions. It takes a long time to lay the groundwork for conceptualization of a shared project and a shared institution. Strategic engagement requires discursive integration of both internal and external groups. William Newell's account (2009) of the Western College Program at Miami University affirms Burkhardt's recommendation in the form of structural integration urged by the American Studies Association.

Faculty of the Western College Program crafted myriad individual ties, Newell (2009) reports, but did not integrate the program into the rest of the institution in a manner that would allow both distinctive features and cooperation. The program was founded in 1973 as a four-year interdisciplinary, living-learning, experimental cluster college. Its curriculum spanned the familiar triad of disciplinary clusters, senior projects, and opportunities for self-designed concentrations. Like their counterparts in other telic programs, newly appointed faculty immersed themselves in designing and teaching multisection core courses. The work was a powerful bonding experience, but it fostered an "us" versus "them" mentality that reinforced the boundary between the larger institution and the program. Western College eventually became a national exemplar of IDS programs, gained the local status of a full-fledged permanent division of the university with a guaranteed seat on a number of committees, and changed its name to the School of Interdisciplinary Studies. Yet the school was still perceived as a program for slackers, remedial students, or the opposite image of an honors program for eccentrics, or a haven for radical activists. Three decades after its inception, Western became caught in the squeeze of falling enrollment and an institutional budget crisis, with added charges of insularity, lack of innovation, and problems mentoring junior faculty. Today the faculty are being dispersed to disciplinary home departments, though a few might be selected for a new program that could incorporate yet undetermined elements of the Western model into other programs.

If remnants of the Western model survive, it will be in a place of increasing resort for stand-alone programs: a college of liberal arts and sciences. The move has been enriching for some but crippling for others. The move offers new connections and opportunities for program development, but some founding faculty and administrators are bitter about the trade-off. Frequent movement is also problematic, sapping energy to adjust and to justify the interdisciplinary mission anew. Over the course of its thirty-four-year history, the Interdisciplinary Studies Program at Wayne State University was moved across three colleges, two of them terminated in the course of the program's lifetime and its status shifted from program to department back to program. Within a shorter lifetime, the bachelor of interdisciplinary studies at Arizona State University has been an undergraduate program housed in the Graduate School, a program in the Division of Undergraduate Services, a school with a University College, and a program in a School of Letters and Sciences within a University College (Augsburg, Henry, Newell, and Szostak, 2009).

Janette Kenner Muir's chronicle (2009) of New Century College (NCC) at George Mason University sends another message shared by Wentworth and Carp (2009): expect disruptions. NCC was formed as an independent college in the mid-1990s in response to national dialogue about the quality of the under-graduate experience. More than fifteen years later, it offers an integrative studies major with concentrations, four ID minors, a first-year experience, a living and learning residential program, and experiential and service-learning programs. Like counterpart programs elsewhere, the integrative studies major started with an open model of options that was trimmed to twelve areas, though students can still propose their own degrees. Each concentration integrates learning communities and experiential learning. Students may also specialize through minors, and a final capstone course provides space for reflection and assessment of learning experiences. In 2000, NCC was moved to a college-within-a-college model under the auspices of the College of Arts and Sciences (CAS). NCC was to maintain its own graduation requirements, but faculty and others worried about lack of autonomy under the new structure and the impact on resources. The move also occurred under a dean who had earlier recommended closing the college. Some, Muir recalls, considered it a "shotgun wedding."

Greater curriculum oversight by the CAS resulted in NCC faculty having to provide more justification for innovative teaching methods, variable credit for experiences outside the classroom, and problem- and competency-based learning. Its budget was also reduced by more than 50 percent, resulting in loss of faculty positions and increased workloads for the remaining faculty and staff. Financial incentives for disciplinary departments to teach in NCC learning communities were reduced as well, along with opportunities for exchanges with other programs that nurtured new pedagogical methods and team teaching. In addition, the bachelor of individualized studies was moved to a stand-alone unit within the larger college and grew increasingly isolated from NCC.

Another structural change was also to follow, though Muir is optimistic about the latest phase. When CAS was restructured into two separate colleges—the College of Science and the College of Humanities and Social Sciences (CHSS)—NCC remained in the CHSS, along with most other ID programs with a humanities or social science focus. Muir highlights four benefits. First, internal selection of a dean familiar with ID learning and programs in the CHSS helped position NCC in a manner that required less explanation and justification. Second, the dean created a structure that grouped all eleven ID programs in the college in a way that provided greater synergy and support. Third, governance structures created for the new college provided greater transparency and accountability, and NCC faculty moved to the forefront of leadership in the College of Humanities and Social Sciences. Fourth, a new associate dean for NCC appointed after a nationwide search was instrumental in elevating NCC to greater strength. Programs continue to grow, and new full-time faculty with lines in NCC have joined the college, but fewer faculty from around the university are participating. In the end, Muir cautions, "There is never time for complacency in interdisciplinary learning" (p. 192).

In telling the story of interdisciplinary studies at Appalachian State University, Jay Wentworth and Richard Carp (2009) underscore tensions between the need for normalization to gain strength and sustainability and a mission for insurgency aimed at unsettling those practices. After thirty-seven years, eighteen of them as a department, interdisciplinary studies was relocated in 2008 to a new university college overseen by a vice provost for undergraduate education. The IDS degree will become a home for self-designed majors and remaining concentrations, and all tenure-line faculty have been relocated in disciplinary departments and reassigned in whole or in part to ID programs. The change was driven by a new administration's emphasis on economic accountability. In tracing the history of the department, Wentworth and Carp demonstrate how discipline-like normalization strategies were used to move from the periphery toward the core of campus. Yet, they caution, those strategies do not guarantee success. The department served students well, developing expertise in ID theory and practice. Yet, echoing Newell (2009), it allowed much of the interdisciplinary activity on campus to be isolated. Several programs, including women's studies, sustainable development, global studies, and Appalachian studies, also matured to the point that they wanted independent degree status. (The ILA at Emory has also been an incubator for ID interests that now have their own departments.)

In drawing lessons from this history, Wentworth and Carp (2009) join Muir (2009) in stressing the importance of regular and excellent assessment to provide continual and persuasive evidence of effectiveness. It is also crucial to avoid isolation, gather support from alumni, raise money, and gain strong backing from upper administration. IDS will never fit within a hegemonic discipline-driven culture, but Wentworth and Carp urge taking "fits" if they are offered. (Tellingly, the title of their chapter is "Phoenix.") Co-location in the new UC structure was not a voluntary move. But it will bring greater visibility, support, access, and fruitful interaction, despite lack of resident faculty for programs. The new college clusters together the IDS major with five other ID degree programs, a residential learning community once affiliated with the department, a new ID general education program, honors, and academic advising beyond the department level (http://universitycollege.appstate.edu/).

For others, the involuntary option is termination. The Department of Interdisciplinary Studies at Wayne State University began in 1973 when the University Studies/Weekend College Program (USWCP) opened on the ashes of the celebrated telic experiment, Monteith College (Furtado and others, 2009). Styled as a Monteith for working adult students, the new USWCP had an open admissions policy and the familiar theme-based triadic curriculum plus competencies and capstone experiences. Over time, the student population shifted from predominantly male workers in the auto industry to a more diverse group of students from Detroit-area corporations and a majority of African American women. The original package of integrated modules of weekly workshops, telecourses, and weekend courses eroded with a growing number of transfer students. The program also added nonprofit sector studies, a master's degree, and online courses. The USWCP gained department status, became an externally respected national model, and secured a name change reflecting its interdisciplinary mission. Yet despite being a strong model with many critical mass factors, high revenue, and student numbers, the department was closed suddenly in late 2007 with no due process or discussion of alternatives.

Under the guise of a budget cut and false charges of duplicating courses elsewhere in the university, the board of governors closed the department even though the anticipated state shortfall was reinstated within a month. The university also granted new lines to some traditional departments, elevated the multidisciplinary honors program to college status, and invested substantial funds in a new initiative to build clinical and translational science. Supporters of the department deployed tactics of prevention and response to threats: mobilizing students, alumni, campus allies, and political groups; engaging in letter writing and a media campaign; creating a Web-based "situation room"; and soliciting public testimony. In the end, however, they were overwhelmed by a perfect storm of political, ideological, academic, and economic arguments, even in the face of counterevidence.

"Sustainability," Repko (2009) reminds readers, means "the capacity to function indefinitely" (p. 145). However, as he and others demonstrated in Augsburg and Henry (2009a), indefinite is not necessarily forever. Newell (2009) concluded that IDS programs "are *always* at political risk"; running against the grain makes them "low-hanging fruit." The interdisciplinary studies team at the University of Massachusetts–Lowell adds a collective voice from the planning stage. A representative group of faculty worked two years building what Archibald (2009) called an airtight case for what the campus should do to institutionalize support for interdisciplinarity. They provided a data-driven 117-page report that anticipated every conceivable objection, accounted for every contingency, and presented a flexible and multifaceted plan. Yet the document sits on a shelf. Top-down leadership will be crucial. But, Archibald concludes, leaders at both administrative and faculty levels must work together.

Lest war stories lead to the conclusion that interdisciplinarity is pragmatically impossible, the Augsburg and Henry volume (2009a) demonstrates that while some programs are closing, others are being born, sometimes even in the same institution. Augsburg and Henry are joined in the concluding chapter by Newell and Szostak. Together they make a case for professionalizing the field of IDS, in essence disciplining interdisciplinarity with an integrative methodology associated with the generic/generalized type. One niche cannot professionalize a field for all program types, and there are periodic slippages throughout the book between generic and subject-based IDS majors. More dialogue is needed among proponents of all types. Guidelines on program review and integration from the American Studies Association and the National Women's Studies Association, to name just two examples, are missing from the book. At the same time, other organizations and counterparts in other fields would benefit from the literature and arguments in Augsburg and Henry (2009a). So too would those who believe that interdisciplinarity is everywhere—in the "air we breathe," a claim used in support of discontinuing one program with no clear understanding, criteria, or proof to back it. This erroneous assertion is also belied by impediments in the career life cycle addressed in the final chapter.

CHAPTER FIVE

MONITORING THE INTERDISCIPLINARY CAREER LIFE CYCLE

Amid ringing endorsements of interdisciplinarity, two initiatives mark the limits of institutionalization. In 2007 ten leading universities formed the Consortium for Fostering Interdisciplinary Research, with the aim of identifying barriers and sharing strategies. In framing the project, Gail Dubrow commented, "We don't yet have the solutions. But we know what the problems are" (2007, p. 1). That same year, the Council of Environmental Deans and Directors (CEDD) issued *Interdisciplinary Hiring, Tenure and Promotion: Guidance for Individuals and Institutions* (Pfirman and others, 2007). Described as the first comprehensive approach to the entire pre- and post-tenure experience, the *Guidance* document originated in environmental studies but is intended for use in other fields as well. The actions of both the consortium and the council are timely. Even slight deterrents, the National Academy of Sciences (NAS) report, *Facilitating Interdisciplinary Research* (2004), warned, retard progress toward career milestones such as completing degrees, gaining academic positions, raising funding, securing tenure, publishing results, and sustaining long-term research portfolios. In the aggregate, the "accumulation of disadvantage" can become not only substantial but "onerous" (p. 93).

One respondent to a campus-wide survey about interdisciplinarity put the matter succinctly: "The University will receive what it rewards" (*Report of the Commission on Interdisciplinary Studies*, 1993, p. 21). Few institutions have taken a comprehensive approach to the interdisciplinary career life cycle. As a result,

Pfirman and Martin (forthcoming) found, interdisciplinary scholars must often negotiate their own process and structure at the same time they are trying to navigate them. Nevertheless, the composite body of strategies being used across campuses today yields guidelines for greater intentionality and protection. Some tactics have been covered in earlier chapters, including central oversight, visibility, and coordination. This chapter considers hiring, tenure and promotion, and faculty development. Like the CEDD's *Guidance* document, it does not regard phases of the career cycle as isolated steps. Defining and implementing an interdisciplinary career model requires attention to needs that begin well before hiring, continue with career rewards, and take deeper root through ongoing faculty development.

HIRING

When interviewing new faculty for Albion College, former president Peter Mitchell found that the consistent theme among candidates has been interest in interdisciplinarity. In recent years Albion has made three tenure-track appointments to faculty educated in the fields of international studies, ethnic studies, and women's and gender studies. In addition, department-based hiring supported an institute for environmental study, and a projected increase of roughly forty-two new tenure-track faculty was underway, with other affiliations anticipated. This many new faculty in a small college will have a major impact (Lisa Lewis, personal communication, Aug. 14, 2008). In larger institutions new interdisciplinary hiring is also in place or planned using both familiar mechanisms, such as joint appointments and faculty lines for ID programs, and newer tactics, such as cluster hiring, cohiring, funding schemes that make the transition over time from central resources to greater departmental matching, and selectively pooling funds for faculty lines and start-up costs. In addition, the post of at-large university professorship can ease movement between departments, as well as courtesy appointments that recognize interactions and collaborations without the formality of joint appointments (*Facilitating Interdisciplinary Research*, 2004).

The targeting of new interdisciplinary faculty has garnered a lot of attention recently and in some cases has served as a test bed for more comprehensive changes in institutional policies. An interdisciplinary faculty hiring initiative at Northeastern University was expanded recently beyond the original three-year commitment to appoint thirty faculty at associate and professor levels. Initial hiring added strengths in network science, neuroimaging, biophysics and biomedical optics, criminal justice, African American literature and history, race and gender inequities in health care, and bridging economics and business. In conjunction with a new academic plan, the initiative moved beyond existing work in fields such as nanotechnology, biotechnology, sensing and imaging, and urban policy to include appointments in economics, law and business, biology, and civil and environmental engineering (*Facilitating Interdisciplinary Research*, 2004; www.northeastern.edu/distinguishedfaculty/learnmore.html).

Cohiring is a collaborative model. The Beckman Institute for Advanced Science and Technology at the University of Illinois at Urbana–Champaign has helped to hire fifty new faculty, supplying 50 percent of starting salaries and 50 percent of start-up costs. In 1996, Pennsylvania State University devoted $5 million to hiring new faculty for a life sciences initiative while creating an ID graduate program and building shared technical resources. To fund the initiative, the provost charged all departments with making a 10 percent reduction in their budgets, and savings were recycled to the university. The resulting Huck Institutes of the Life Sciences is a virtual organization comprising seven colleges. Huck Institutes does not have its own faculty lines or internal research programs but has collaborated with colleges and departments for cohiring. It provides academic and technical support, as well as funding to promote excellence in life sciences in and between units on the University Park and Hershey campuses. Faculty appointments reside in departments of participating colleges within the university, though the Institutes is administered by the infrastructure of the Intercollege Research Programs and its own oversight body (www.huck.psu.edu/).

The University of Washington's Program on the Environment (PoE) does not have its own faculty lines either. Launched in 1997, it was established as a partnering agent that brings together faculty and students to augment existing programs and offer integrated educational programs that cross disciplinary boundaries. To facilitate the plan, the president created a budget that the program used to hire faculty in collaboration with departments and schools. PoE paid part of start-up costs and salary for the initial three to five years, and then departments became fully responsible. Colleges and departments were also encouraged to donate faculty time for teaching environmental studies courses, with student hours credited to the faculty member's home department. In addition, PoE could use its budget to compensate departments for faculty teaching within the program in the form of release time. Budget cuts in the state of Washington have presented a serious challenge to the entire campus, though a new College of the Environment (CoE) opened in fall 2009. POE is now affiliated with the new CoE, as well as four other academic programs: Forest Resources, Marine Affairs, Atmospheric Sciences, and Earth and Space Sciences. The Joint Institute for the Study of the Atmosphere and Ocean has been part of the College since July 2008, and the new combined structure also incorporates an Environmental Institute and a Program on Climate Change (*Facilitating Interdisciplinary Research*, 2004; http://depts.washington.edu/poeweb/; http://depts.washington.edu/poeweb/about/index.html; www/cnbc.cmu.edu/).

Cluster hiring has generated a lot of interest. This approach links multiple positions in separate units around a designated theme or initiative. A hiring line resides within a department while an individual is employed on campus but reverts to centralized control if vacated, typically the office of the provost. Cluster hiring is being used in multiple institutions, including Purdue and Michigan. When the University of Michigan announced a new initiative in 2007 to create one hundred new tenure-track faculty positions, it targeted junior faculty with ID research and teaching interests focused on significant questions or addressing complex problems. Positions cannot be budgeted as joint appointments, but a secondary appointment in another area would be acceptable. In addition to salary and benefits, a start-up package may be requested consisting of equipment and renovations, and the proposing school or college must commit space, added elements of a start-up package, and merit pay. To date, two years of cluster appointments have been authorized (www.provost.umich.edu/faculty/jrfacultyinitiative.pdf).

One of the most prominent cluster hiring programs emanated from a strategic planning process at the University of Wisconsin–Madison in the mid-1990s. Five phases of hiring occurred before funding ended, resulting in forty-nine clusters with 137 faculty lines. Schools and colleges also matched six additional cluster positions. The provost's office worked with a lead dean to oversee searches and monitored policies involving home department placement, start-up packages, tenure and promotion, and interface with other units. A cluster coordinator serves as the lead faculty member in charge of a particular cluster (*Facilitating Interdisciplinary Research*, 2004; www.clusters.wisc.edu/). The Wisconsin initiative received positive responses, though faculty raised concerns about tenure review, salary equity, and support for infrastructure. A review showed no difference in prospects for tenure among cluster faculty. Variations across clusters, though, suggested that attention needs to be paid to the unique character of a particular area and merit processes involving multiple units. Responding to concern about infrastructure, the provost also created a campus-wide competition for additional support for graduate students, program assistants, lab assistance, and other expenses. The website for Wisconsin's program is a model for this approach, with beautifully designed materials on the clusters and sections on leadership, policies, an annual conference, and the enhancement grants. Peyton Smith, assistant vice chancellor for extended programs, recalled that some clusters did not work out, but the program has succeeded overall in fostering a new energy on campus (personal communication, March 14, 2007). Some departments were not receptive initially, but one chair commented that the scheme is changing the way the department looks at new faculty.

Increasing the number of joint appointments is one of the top recommendations for hiring in the National Academy of Sciences report on interdisciplinary research (IDR), between two departments or between a department and an interdisciplinary (ID) program or center (*Facilitating Interdisciplinary Research*, 2004). The ease of making such appointments, however, varies by campus and even on the same campus. Split appointments are often touted as a value-added organizational approach. Yet units may not have equal resources or the authority to originate a request for a joint appointment, let alone the same criteria of evaluation. Unequal resources can be offset with centralized funding support for salary, merit pay, and infrastructure costs. Even so, positions carry burden-added personal costs in the form of face time in two locations, split loyalties, a fragmented sense of home, and higher networking costs. Put simply, two halves do not add up to only a single or necessarily integrated whole, and faculty may wind up "serving two masters and satisfying neither." The CEDD's *Guidance* document (Pfirman and others, 2007) suggests allocations of sixty-forty or seventy-thirty for joint appointments, with the higher percentage going to a designated home department. Regardless of percentage, expectations in both units should be specified at the outset, and academic responsibilities should match fiscal responsibility. Programs that draw heavily on faculty from discipline-based departments might also create a budget line to pay for ID advancement, teaching, and development costs.

Pfirman and others (2007) cite several models, including the joint appointment checklist at the University of Southern California and "Guidelines on Interdisciplinary Faculty Appointments in the College of Arts and Sciences" at Ohio University. The Ohio guidelines are consistent with the faculty handbook, which locates tenure within a designated home department. The coordinator of an ID program may also qualify for an ID appointment. The expected home unit must be designated, a summary description of the ID appointment must be included, and the search committee must ensure representation from all relevant units. Appointments are still treated as single job assignments, with the assumption that departments and programs will cooperate in good faith. The home department normally carries full budgetary responsibility for base salary and benefits, though special circumstances may allow a secondary unit to share budgetary responsibility. Any special terms and conditions must be outlined in the summary description, which specifies a term of duration not to exceed five years, with the possibility of renewal, modification, or dissolution in the final year. The summary description also delineates expected efforts in teaching, research, service, and advising, plus any added administrative responsibilities, apportioned time in primary and secondary units, and related matters of budget, space, and secretarial and travel support (http://ncseonline.org/CEDD/cms.cfm?id=2042; www.cas.ohiou.edu/facultystaff/guidelines/InterdisciplinaryFac Appt.pdf).

The CEDD *Guidance* document admonishes campuses not to plunge immediately into the search and hiring process. Stage 1 is the time for engaging in holistic conception of the career life cycle and self-conscious consideration of local departmental and disciplinary structures and cultures. Expectations need to be clarified, impediments analyzed, and high-level structures established to "oversee and champion interdisciplinary activities." Likewise, two recommendations for stage 2 will guide searching and hiring at stage 3. First, all relevant institutional components crucial to the ongoing success of a new faculty member should be involved as early as possible, including disciplinary and interdisciplinary faculty, research scientists, senior administrators, representatives of tenure and promotion committees, and pertinent institutes or centers. Second, a memorandum of understanding should be drafted that clarifies expectations about scholarship, teaching, mentoring, voting rights and responsibilities, service, budget, space, and departmental and community participation. Tenure and promotion criteria should also be articulated in the memorandum of understanding and, for joint appointments, the home unit and apportionment of responsibilities. In addition, the job advertisement and interview should indicate that the institutional culture supports interdisciplinarity.

The CEDD recommends that the composition of the search committee replicate the anticipated committee structure for pretenure and tenure review as much as possible and that the selection be stipulated in the memorandum of understanding (MOU). The committee should reflect both the nature of the person sought and possible institutional homes. Because members of a hybrid committee will not be accustomed to working together, some attention should be paid to differences between their disciplines or between those disciplines and the interdisciplinary focus of the search. More extensive networking, logistical, and financial investment may be needed as well. Units have different forums for candidate presentations, styles of presentation such as reading papers versus Power Point slides, and days and times for gathering. Exhibit 5.1 is a sample checklist.

EXHIBIT 5.1 INTERDISCIPLINARY MOU CHECKLIST

Strategic Issues

- Managing expectations
- Maintaining flexibility and contingencies

Home

- Department(s)/program(s)/center(s)
- Space
- Budget (amount and split)
  - Salary
  - Start-up

Promotion/Tenure Committee Research/Teaching Community

- Balance

Disciplinary/Interdisciplinary

- Balance

Mentoring and Advising Departmental/External Formal/Informal Research

- Basic/applied/theoretical/descriptive
- Publications
  - Number
  - Journals
  - Citations
  - Style: synthesis, analysis

Public Scholarship

- Outreach
- Engagement
- Stakeholder involvement

Teaching

- Departments
  - Classes
- Team teaching
- Advising
  - Undergraduate
  - Academic
  - Research
  - Graduate

Campus Participation Department/Program Meetings

Committees

Campus Programming

- Presentations
  - Annual meetings of professional societies
  - Workshops
  - Invited versus volunteer
  - On campus
- Support
  - Funding sources
  - Amounts

Committees

- National
- International
- Leadership

Approvals:
Department(s):
Program(s)/Center(s):
Dean/Provost:

Source: Pfirman and others (2007).

TENURE AND PROMOTION

When respondents to the National Academy of Sciences (NAS) survey, *Facilitating Interdisciplinary Research* (2004), were asked to rank the top five impediments to IDR on their campuses, tenure and promotion criteria received the highest percentage, followed by budget issues, strategic plans, and space. In a recent speech to the American Conference of Academic Deans, Cathy Trower likened interdisciplinary faculty seeking tenure to Alice in Wonderland (cited in Powers, 2008). In Trower's account, Alice fails to get tenure. Richard Carp (2008), however, has a more apt literary parallel: Blanche DuBois in Tennessee Williams's *A Streetcar Named Desire*. In Lewis Carroll's novel, Alice awoke from her dream unscathed. In Williams's play, Blanche was raped by her sister Stella's husband and driven mad by Stella's unwillingness to accept her account of the rape. In a review of the CEDD's *Guidance* document (Pfirman and others, 2007), Carp applauded the overview of policies, procedures, and documents. However, borrowing from the language of Williams's play, Carp cautioned that interdisciplinary scholars must often rely on "the kindness of strangers." Drafting the memorandum of understanding at an early stage fosters greater intentionality, but there is no guarantee it will be effective.

The key actions in discussions of interdisciplinary tenure and promotion include rewriting guidelines, establishing committee structures for pretenure and tenure review, defining appropriate criteria, and paying careful attention to dossier preparation. Two academic leaders offered further insight at the Quality Assessment in Interdisciplinary Research and Education meeting in February 2006. Peter Lange (2006), provost of Duke University, and C. Judson King (2006), a former provost and senior vice president for academic affairs of the University of California, underscore the importance of a comprehensive approach to change. If an institution wants to promote excellence in interdisciplinarity, Lange urges, the process for evaluation must be clear and well articulated. Creating such a process may require significant emendation to policies not only for tenure and promotion but appointments as well. Put another way, King urged, interdisciplinary scholarship and its evaluation must become "part of the cultural fabric of the broader institution."

Lange (2006) shares the CEDD's recommendation that pretenure and tenure reviews replicate the committee structure and procedures for tenure recommendations in concert with the letter of appointment. Most respondents to the CEDD survey reported using joint committees from more than one department. At Iowa State University, representation on a joint committee is roughly proportional to the percentage of the candidate's appointment per unit. Assessments from the committee are submitted to the head of the primary unit, who ensures that all units have identical copies of the record (www.clas.uiowa.edu/faculty/promotion_tenure/tenure_jointly_appointed.shtml).

Even with a strong memorandum in place, however, Blanche may still be dependent on the kindness of strangers. The average tenure of deans and provosts, Carp (2008) points out, is roughly five years, but the tenure clock runs for six years. Departmental faculties and personnel committees also change, increasing the odds that the people who will ultimately decide on tenure and promotion were not involved in the hiring process. They may not even have been at the institution at the time of hire and may have their own agendas. In the context of a supportive institutional environment, an MOU will go far to ensure equity in all academic personnel evaluations. Yet good faith and a general institutional commitment are not sufficient to guarantee fair treatment.

At a minimum, the CEDD recommends, the chair or director of other units in which a faculty member holds an appointment should be consulted. At Duke, Lange (2006) reports, a letter from the ID unit must be in a candidate's file, and the dean must comment explicitly on interdisciplinary elements. When there is doubt about departmental narrowness, Duke allows the option of creating an ad hoc committee to reexamine a candidacy. The University of Southern California (USC) stipulates that the primary department handles tenure, promotion, and merit by regular procedures within a unit. Yet the guidelines also indicate that a department or school must take care to evaluate interdisciplinary scholarship properly. If a candidate's work does not match department priorities but furthers policies of the university, explanation is required. Ohio University's guidelines require that the home department administer all peer evaluations, probationary reappointment, and promotion and tenure progress evaluations and recommendations. However, any peer evaluation committee must include at least one voting representative from the secondary unit, with additional membership specified in the summary description. Each peer evaluation committee is also expected to produce a single written evaluation, though members representing the secondary unit may append a statement if desired. Standard procedures then follow within the home department, using the statement and any appended statements from additional members of the committee. After that, the material is forwarded to the dean together with material from the home department's chair.

King (2006) cautions that "departmentalism" is involved as much as "disciplinism." If direct representation is not in place, individuals in comparable positions or experience in making evaluations of interdisciplinary work should be allowed to write a letter. At the very least, more than one person with a similar title and set of job responsibilities should be involved—someone who will understand the challenges of working in an ID field even if she or he is in an unrelated area. The University of Michigan urges training department chairs and division directors to deal with the complications of hiring, reviewing, and promoting ID faculty. The dean plays a pivotal role in the process too, standing between the department and provost levels in a position to adjudicate differing assessments. The dean's role should not be a single moment in the life of a candidate but part of a systematic approach to managing interdisciplinarity on campus. Lange (2006) stresses the importance of having a system that propagates down to the department level and has built-in backups at the dean's level nurtured when hiring deans. Steve Hyman (2006), provost of Harvard University, concurs. Hyman crafted understandings with incoming deans that nurture discipline-based work while protecting against rigid silos. In devising criteria for an incoming dean of engineering, for example, he added stipulations such as counting joint appointments (*Facilitating Interdisciplinary Research,* 2004).

Pfirman and colleagues (2007) suggest enclosing a list of frequently asked questions (FAQs) to help internal and external evaluators. One of the questions should describe appropriate publication venues and typical genres of scholarship. Synthesis papers are not uncommon in ID fields and should be distinguished from simpler reviews that might be discounted for lack of originality. Finding outlets can be challenging. Yet Ann MacNeal and Frederick Weaver (2001) concluded from the experience of faculty at Hampshire College that the expansion of interdisciplinary associations has opened up venues for scholarship on feminist issues, the Third World, race and ethnicity, cultural studies, environment, AIDS, cognitive science, college teaching, and other forums of heterodox scholarship. Some journals open to interdisciplinary work, such as *Science* and *Nature,* are large and prestigious. Most, however, are small. Interdisciplinary journals also serve several functions. *Comparative Studies in Society and History, Philosophy and Public Affairs,* and *Les Annales* bridge traditional disciplines. The *Journal of Peace Research* and the *Journal of Conflict Resolution* cover problem-focused fields, while the *Journal of Historical Geography* and the *Journal of Psycholinguistic Research* advance hybrid fields (Dogan and Pahre, 1990). David Hollinger (1997) also cites the "transdisciplinary 'professional'" journal. This genre of scholarship exhibits a blend of scholarly and essayistic styles that differs from disciplinary journals and journalistic periodicals read by the wider public. Leading examples in humanities and social sciences are *Critical Inquiry, American Quarterly, Public Culture, Modernism/Modernity, Raritan, Common Knowledge, Representations, Salmagundi, Social Text,* and *Theory and Society.*

Dossier preparation takes on a greater burden for interdisciplinary candidates. Readers of the dossier need to be educated on two levels: the local campus committee and writers of external letters. Some individuals on college and university committees are likely to lack expertise in the candidate's area. Moreover, they and external reviewers may know one part of a candidate's profile well but not necessarily the entire range. In addition to a curriculum vitae, a copy of the guidelines used for internal review should be included in the packet sent to external evaluators, as well as the position announcement, the letter of appointment, and the memorandum of understanding. Some institutions solicit more than the usual number of letter writers for interdisciplinary scholars to account for their broader range. Increased numbers, though, can have a negative effect. At Macalester College, candidates are asked to indicate any red flags that reviewers should be aware of. A list of FAQs can also include explanations of the nature and significance of the area of scholarship, individuals' contributions to multiauthored projects and publications, the added time required for securing grants and preparing for ID research and teaching, co-principal investigator status, and the absence of familiar honors and awards. Exhibit 5.2 is the CEDD checklist for annotating an interdisciplinary curriculum vitae (Pfirman and others, 2007).

Any discussion of tenure and promotion raises the larger question of appropriate criteria for evaluating interdisciplinary research and teaching. Generally, Lange advises (2006), the direction of dossier preparation should flow away from conventional disciplinary measures and proxy criteria. The two default biases operate in tandem. In highly innovative work, he adds, criteria are more difficult to devise, especially when it has a dynamic element that may be changing the nature of departmental work.

EXHIBIT 5.2 CHECKLIST FOR ANNOTATING AN INTERDISCIPLINARY
CURRICULUM VITAE

Annotation of a CV is intended to provide clarity on background and creative contributions that are either unexpected or not obvious to a reader who is unfamiliar with the candidate and with their area of expertise. Since cultures vary from institution to institution and field to field, here are some ideas on what might be included in the annotations.

Educational Background

- Note interdisciplinary issues, for example, PhD committee spanning several departments

Related Experience

- Note any interdisciplinary aspects of positions, including joint appointments

Scholarship and Other Professional Contributions

- Identify fields of endeavor and include a statement of scholarly goals
- Annotate publication list with:
  - Your specific contribution
  - Significance and potential impact of the work
  - Type of work, for example, meta-analysis/synthesis
  - Journal standing
  - Why this publication venue was selected (i.e., invited paper, or journal read by policymakers/stakeholders)
  - If citations and other quantitative metrics are important at your institution, perhaps include the number of citations from a "cited reference" search for non-Web of Science journals, and perhaps also conduct a subject category analysis . . .

Public/Stakeholder Engagement

- Note professional contributions to business/public good, include assessment of impact

Grant Support

- Note contribution to activity, explain your role and responsibility as principal investigator or co-principal investigator
- If the funding source is unusual, note reason for using this source, perhaps also note success rate within this program area
- Note any issues related to interdisciplinary implementation that are important for reviewers to know

Awards and Recognition

- Include leadership of interdisciplinary committees

Teaching and Advising

- Note co-teaching where relevant, and indicate how work was shared
- Note "extra" advising or mentoring of students that is due to interdisciplinary nature of position

Service

- Separate out "extra" service that is related to the interdisciplinary nature of the position, for example, serving on the search committee of another department

Source: Pfirman and others (2007). Reprinted with permission.

The simplest answer to the question of appropriate criteria is that judgment about ID work should not differ from disciplinary work: seek evidence of a substantial contribution that advances knowledge in a field and a substantial impact on scholarship and teaching. Yet, Lange raises two related questions. What constitutes the field, and is there a scholarly community with shared standards of evaluation? The pivotal consideration in determining quality, he exhorts, is "getting the procedures right." Doing so requires understanding the core intellectual problem or challenge of a field, identifying members of its expert community, using relevant literature as a guide, and identifying ways that a candidate's work has influenced others. Identifying experts who fit the problem space is easier in recognized fields such as women's studies and American studies, which have established epistemic communities with qualified peers. The task is more difficult in emerging fields where criteria of excellence have not been developed yet, the community and literature is less well defined, and the pool of qualified experts is smaller. "The more underdeveloped the interdisciplinary field," Lange cautions, "the greater is the likelihood of error of judgment." At Duke and USC, candidates are asked to indicate appropriate peers. This process is not uncommon in disciplines too. Yet Lange considers it "more insistent" with interdisciplinary candidates.

The CEDD's *Guidance* document urges reviewers to shift emphasis toward intellectual achievement and leadership, not traditional metrics. If members of a committee do not know much about a field, they tend to count proxy forms of validation. Leading bibliometricians, though, do not endorse substituting secondary data for direct reading of research (Feller, 2006). Conventional metrics are usually prioritized, such as numbers of patents, publications, and citations; rankings; and peer reviews. Yet when the interdisciplinary studies research team at Harvard University interviewed researchers and educators, they found that such measures sidestep "warranted interdisciplinary knowledge" (Boix-Mansilla, 2006). More primary or epistemic forms of evaluation are needed that address the substance and constitution of the work, such as experimental rigor, aesthetic quality, fit between framework and data, and the power to address previously unsolved questions in a discipline (Boix-Mansilla, 2006; Boix-Mansilla, Feller, and Gardner, 2006; Klein, 2008a).

The Harvard team's findings are part of an emergent literature on ID evaluation and assessment that identifies expanded indicators. New conceptual models and explanatory power provide feedback to and outcomes in multiple disciplines and fields. New integrative frameworks, methodological and empirical analysis, and research hypotheses enhance the study of particular problems. The scope and conceptualization of research topics also broaden, and levels of analysis are bridged. Individuals' capabilities expand as they develop new expertise and research methods, work in more than one discipline or field, and collaborate in ID projects and programs. Their changing career trajectories are evident in new appointments and affiliations in other areas, co-mentoring of students in other departments, recognition outside their original disciplines, and service on multidisciplinary advisory or review groups. Publication criteria have expanded as well, to include counting contributions to multiauthored works and work in new journals. In the public and private arenas, outcomes include public and policy brokering, new treatment protocols, and disseminating research results through position papers and expert testimony. And long-term impacts and unforeseen consequences register the impact of ID approaches, though they are missed by short-term and linear models of evaluation (Klein, 2008a).

The need for expanded indicators is affirmed in a recent literature review commissioned by the National Science Foundation (NSF). The review was prompted by the same imperative that led to the National Research Council's task force on modernizing NSF's Federal Funds Survey discussed in Chapter Two: increasing interdisciplinary research (IDR). In this case, NSF asked SRI International's Science and Technology Policy Program to identify modes and measures for output and possible additions to the National Science Board's *Science and Engineering Indicators* (SEI). A number of recommendations emerged. A single model of evaluation is not adequate to account for differences in types of IDR, modes of integration, and variances by units of analysis, discipline, field, or country. *Measurement* is also too narrow a term for the task. *Evaluation* encompasses a wider range of assessment, and the task force called for expanding beyond publications in selected journals and conventional bibliometrics. Network measures, dynamic models, heuristics, or a combination of them are needed. Short-, middle-, and long-term impacts need to be considered as well, and the problem of taxonomy resurfaces. Subject classification codes are determined by database managers or other experts. Yet different classification systems produce different results for the same measure of IDR. Scopus and Elsevier's new SciVal offer wider databases of journals, though the SRI task force joined the National Research Council's task force in calling for greater use of new technologies. Recent developments in algorithms can standardize analysis and map underlying dynamics of relationships among disciplines and specialties, complemented by advances in animation and visualization (Wagner, Roessner, and Bobb, 2009).

FACULTY DEVELOPMENT

Faculty development means more than keeping up with one discipline. In the curriculum, Jan Civian and colleagues (1997) report, it may also mean serving in general education, developing ID courses and programs, and teaching themes across the curriculum such as ethics, globalization, and diversity. Faculty are also incorporating new discoveries into the curriculum. They are cultivating skills for teaching theme- and problem-based courses, projects, and theses. And they are contributing to interdisciplinary majors such as environmental science and women's and gender studies. Research profiles are changing too, requiring continuing education in new knowledge areas, conceptual approaches, methodologies, skill sets, and instrumentation. When Lisa Lattuca (2001) interviewed faculty engaged in interdisciplinary research and teaching, she found that they were more willing to make changes if their disciplines were moving in certain new directions. Even then, however, there is no guarantee. A strong program of faculty development is crucial to supporting interdisciplinary professional development at all stages of the career life cycle.

Not surprisingly, interdisciplinarity is on the programming schedule of many teaching and learning centers, and divisions of research and graduate schools are offering seminars in new knowledge areas. A central oversight body, though, still has an important role to play in coordinating efforts across campus, offering new opportunities, and ensuring that best practices and the literature are used. Table 5.1 is a composite of strategies for faculty development that spans formal and informal mechanisms.

Many familiar mechanisms have been adapted for interdisciplinary purposes. Faculty workshops and seminars are crucial forums for conveying information about the nature of interdisciplinary studies, supplemented by individual and small-group follow-up for curriculum and syllabus design, models and guidelines for ID research, interdisciplinary learning assessment, team teaching and integrative pedagogies such as collaborative and

Table 5.1. Strategies for Interdisciplinary Faculty Development

---

Workshops and seminars on IDS and IDR, including integration and collaboration

Minicourses and training sessions in new content areas, instrumentation, and skill sets

Forums for internal teaching and research presentations

Coordinated scheduling and forums for external speakers

Half- and full-day retreats, program and project workdays

Campus conferences and discussion of events streamed from other campuses

Resource banking in alignment with central oversight and a website

Sabbatical leaves and summer immersion experiences

Leaves and release time for continuing education and program development

Travel support for conferences and visits to other programs, centers, departments, and projects

Financial support through internal grants and seed money for curriculum and research development, internships, and fellowships

Mentoring and working with external consultants

Immersion through on-the-job participation in interdisciplinary work, including team teaching and research collaboration

Social gatherings and opportunities for informal sharing

Common spaces

---

experiential learning, learning and living-and-learning communities, and inquiry- and discovery-based learning. Campus-wide meetings are also effective means of examining barriers and facilitating mechanisms, along the lines of internal conferences at the Universities of Wisconsin and Minnesota. Seminar series target a wide range of particular interests, including the topics of nanoscience, life sciences, global change, and cultural diversity. Shorter training sessions are effective forums for disseminating information about new research areas, scholarly approaches, instrumentation, and analytical techniques of other disciplines. Events may be offered to a general audience at a central site or targeted for particular groups in their locations, including laboratories and off-campus sites. Interactive video facilities are good venues for broadcasting national events and meetings with personnel at distant locations. Discussion forums and learning modules can be structured around them and broadcasts captured for future viewing. Speaker series can be coordinated too. State-of-the-art speakers in many disciplines contribute insights from new interdisciplinary developments and emerging fields. Events that are streamed live or recorded can be placed on the central website in viewable or downloadable form, adding to the resource bank described in the Resources section of this book.

IDS and IDR place a greater burden on continuing education. Over half the respondents to the NAS committee survey reported having sought training in additional fields through a postdoctoral fellowship, another advanced degree, or daily interaction in projects. The importance of time repeats. It takes time to gain new knowledge and skills, develop relationships with colleagues in other disciplines, and learn their language, cultures, knowledge, and evaluation methods. Concrete strategies include course release time for curriculum development and travel to professional conferences and distant facilities. Special fellowships also foster learning. The Center for Interdisciplinary Research at the University of Southern California has awarded competitive fellowships providing up to fifty thousand dollars for research expenditures. The position freed fellows from teaching and service duties, and they meet biweekly to discuss their research and issues surrounding interdisciplinarity. The expected outcome was a proposal for a large grant or a book (Sá, 2005). With the support of a five-year National Science Foundation grant, Harvard's Kennedy School of Government conducted a program aimed at bringing together a critical mass of younger scholars to foster collaboration on problems linking science and policy with global environmental problems. Year-long training experiences included discussions of key papers, research presentations, and exposure to ID methodological and professional approaches and perspectives (*Facilitating Interdisciplinary Research*, 2004).

Two additional mechanisms loom large: postdoctoral fellowships and summer immersion experiences. Postdocs afford time for deeper training in a new discipline, though the shortage of interdisciplinary fellowships is a continuing impediment.

Facilitating Interdisciplinary Research (2004) offered two recommendations. Potential fellows should explore both formal and informal ways of gaining ID experience by networking with potential collaborators in other disciplines and by doing internships in industrial and nonacademic settings. They should also identify institutions favorable to ID work, with strong profiles, mentoring, support technologies, and facilities. Postdoctoral fellowships include a variety of supports. The Interdisciplinary Research and Training Initiative of the Fred Hutchinson Cancer Center included a dual-mentor program, a joint degree program, a pilot project fund, and an interdisciplinary club. The Burroughs Wellcome Fund's Career Awards at the Scientific Interface has supported young researchers working at the interfaces of biology and other disciplines. The awards supported two years of advanced postdoc training as well as transition into a tenure-track position for three years.

Summer immersion experiences afford intensive time free of regular duties (*Facilitating Interdisciplinary Research,* 2004). In addition to well-known visitor programs at the Woods Hole Marine Biological Laboratory, the Shingobee Headwaters Aquatic Ecosystems Projects in Minnesota has offered summer ID immersion in hydrology and provided instrumentation support for similar sites in other states. The University of Michigan's Biological Research Station has hosted summer ID immersion for both resident and short-term researchers. Originally developed by biologists, the site also drew the interest of atmospheric scientists, who saw the value of instrumentation at the research station for their work. The station provided additional learning support through weekly talks inspired by the biosphere atmosphere research and training model, as well as the Integrative Graduate Education and Research Traineeship Program (IGERT) and a multidisciplinary doctoral training program.

Participation in team teaching is another form of immersion training. Sitting in on a course the semester before teaching it is one of the best means of getting a sense of what IDS entails. The faculty development plan in the learning communities program at Temple University evolved as academic-year sessions were replaced with two-day stipend-supported summer workshops for faculty teaching in the fall. Teaching teams become learning communities themselves, developing themes and pedagogies collaboratively supported by a faculty handbook (Laufgraben, 2003). At the University of North Carolina, Asheville, faculty in the required ID general education humanities program formed teaching circles. This kind of informal, small, cooperative workshop is also used on other campuses to allow faculty to present their points of view and refine practices (Downes, 2000). At Indiana University–Purdue University Indianapolis, regular informal meetings of faculty teaching teams, dubbed "pods," foster collegial interactions and wider audiences (Evenbeck, Jackson, and McGrew, 1999). Creating course and program portfolios also provides a longitudinal picture of a curriculum, aiding revision and evaluation, and bringing new faculty on board over time. Relationships with colleagues in other disciplines develop as well through coparticipation in projects, teaching classes in other departments, and writing and presenting papers at conferences outside their own disciplines or departments.

Social bonding is a powerful, though underappreciated, investment in the quality of interdisciplinary work. The social lubrication of informal gatherings provides opportunities not only to get to know colleagues and others better but also to engage in mutual learning and collaboration. Jeffrey Wadsworth (*Facilitating Interdisciplinary Research,* 2004), a director at the Oakridge National Lab, called IDR "a body-contact sport": people need to run into each other to make it happen. Pierre Wiltzius, director of the Beckman Institute for Advanced Science and Technology at the University of Illinois at Urbana–Champaign, said the last thing he would shut down in the building is the cafeteria, a common space where people meet. In industry, where ID teams are more customary, arranging meeting rooms next to a cafeteria speeds up conversation and planning. "There is something about breaking bread together," Uma Chowdhry of DuPont commented, "that causes creative juices to flow" (*Facilitating Interdisciplinary Research,* 2004, p. 94). Even simple gestures such as serving cookies and coffee or tea and wine and cheese parties add to the social quality of events, whether formal programs or informal get-togethers.

Mentoring cuts across all phases of the career life cycle, though it is vital for junior faculty, graduate students, and postdoctoral fellows. In an overview of interdisciplinarity from the perspective of doctoral students and early-career academics, Graybill and Shandas (forthcoming) identify transitional stages and overarching concerns in research, pedagogy, institutional structure, and evaluation. The initiation phase raises questions about how to situate ID scholarship and define one's personal identity when moving between departments and programs. The familiarization stage entails navigating dual loyalties to disciplinary and interdisciplinary communities and projects, while balancing rigor and depth and strategizing for publication and job searches. Once in new positions, early-career academics encounter new challenges and potential benefits, requiring translation and deeper ties with new colleagues. They must also straddle the line between risk and "protected enthusiasm" while moving into the tenure and promotion process. Heralded as "agents of change" in a "new academy," this pivotal group of faculty must negotiate a career path for themselves in the context of their departments and institutions. This task requires strategies for individual success, even in the midst of collaborative work, and decisions about how to concentrate energy while identifying routes for survival through both internal and external career pathways.

The task of finding mentors can be eased if a central interdisciplinary office maintains an updated personnel bank. One of the most vital skills of an ID mentor is the ability to translate across more than one area, whether it involves two disciplines or a discipline and an interdisciplinary field. Being well versed in multiple areas means being aware of methodological and knowledge differences that aid in gaining new skills while sharing multiple perspectives on research problems and process. Whenever possible, the Ohio University guidelines urge, structured interaction with and support from at least one senior faculty member with interdisciplinary experience is needed (www.cas.ohiou.edu/facultystaff/guidelines/InterdisciplinaryFacAppt.pdf). The individual might be a member of the search committee or an assigned faculty mentor. Work with multiple mentors should be backed up by annual reviews that do not allow the experience to fall through the cracks.

The lower rate of productivity that often occurs in interdisciplinary work is of particular concern to junior faculty. A mentor can help by keeping a close eye on a candidate's grant seeking, collaborative roles, and publications—both solo-authored pieces and contributions to collaborative work. Carp (2008) underscores the importance of not being dependent on "the kindness of strangers." Even with a memorandum of understanding in place that clearly defines expectations, a mentor is crucial. Postdocs and junior faculty can also be supported by bringing visiting interdisciplinary scholars to campus, educating others in the process on the field in which a scholar works and providing mentoring. The *Guidance* document includes senior faculty in the career model. Institutions often take pride in their older ID "stars," and senior scholars are appropriate for leadership roles, but they too may require training and support. Even with the job security of tenure, senior faculty and their midcareer counterparts face many of the same challenges as junior scholars. The NAS report (*Facilitating Interdisciplinary Research*, 2004) concurs, admonishing that institutional reforms must benefit both junior and senior faculty in all areas, including the reward structure, evaluation, time, integration, and collaboration. Faculty at all stages of the career life cycle should also talk to program managers at funding agencies about their research interests and seek advice on successful strategies. They can ask colleagues for copies of successful interdisciplinary proposals as well. Here too, however, a central office would be well positioned to keep track of pertinent documents and personnel.

A closing example brings many of the elements of this chapter together. In describing two initiatives at St. Lawrence University, Cornwell and Stoddard (2001) illustrated the potential that professional development has to change both faculty culture and institutional policies. The First-Year Program (FYP), started in 1987, was a year-long living-learning program in which students took a multidisciplinary course taught by faculty from three disciplines. The Cultural Encounters faculty seminar, started in 1992, sought to create a new paradigm for the study of cultural interactions on a global scale across time. In the FYP, team teaching and collaborative learning pedagogy became powerful forms of faculty development. The process of constructing a syllabus together amounted to a kind of interdisciplinary miniseminar, as faculty confronted different questions, methods, and possibilities for texts. Further growth occurred as a teaching team translated ideas and texts into projects for students. Cultural Encounters relied on group reading, discussion, and field study in Kenya. Faculty moved beyond combining existing disciplines to creating new cross-disciplinary and transnational approaches that fostered new professional identities. The teaching and research interests of at least nine faculty trained in Eurocentric fields became more self-reflective and global. Among those in area studies, an increasingly cross-disciplinary theoretical development also became evident. A new European studies program based on multiculturalism was created, and European study-abroad programs began to take a more multicultural approach.

The process was not without strains and resistance. In the FYP, faculty moved away from the common core course, allowing each college to have a topic of interest to a particular team and a niche identity for students. Coherence across sections is now ensured by design guidelines, a commonality agreement for syllabi, and required communication skills and residential components. Greater intentionality about interdisciplinary teaching was also fostered through in-service workshops and seminars. Even with greater normalization, Cornwell and Stoddard described the faculty culture at St. Lawrence as "radically different" (p. 177) than it was prior to the two initiatives. At least one-third of the faculty experienced "transformative developments in pedagogy and/or epistemologies" (p. 163). A substantial percentage of faculty also came to share the view that questioning one's own knowledge and assumptions is important. The new commitments, though, were enacted in faculty seminars and interdisciplinary program boards, not departments. Junior faculty especially became caught between two institutional cultures when their participation in FYP and other interdisciplinary efforts was discounted. Other ranks were affected as well. One speaker in a faculty meeting likened the department to home and those invested in ID work as "prodigal sons and daughters" (p. 174). Control over hiring and tenure and promotion remains within departments, but language about ID programs was added to all job advertisements, and every search committee added a member from outside the department of hire. Some departments even tied positions to participation in FYP. ID programs were also able to write their own reviews of candidates for mid–probationary review. In the end, Cornwell and Stoddard concluded, procedural changes must be implemented if the balance of power between interdisciplinary programs and traditional departments is to take root.

Conclusion: Countering Myths and Situating Practices

A conclusion is not an end. It is a point in time. This book began with the claim that interdisciplinarity is everywhere today. Proclamations of growth and heightened importance are supported by evidence. Being the mantra *du jour,* however, is not the same as overcoming institutional barriers, doing interdisciplinary work well, being rewarded for it, and sustaining programs over time.

Responding to Myths About Interdisciplinarity

The National Academy of Sciences and other groups have admonished institutions to take a comprehensive approach to interdisciplinarity in order to create more favorable campus cultures. The book responded to that call by providing a conceptual framework and portfolio of strategies aimed at strengthening arguments and informing decision making. However, a number of myths in the form of misconceptions persist. Being able to respond to them is a crucial final strategy for creating interdisciplinary campus cultures.

Myth 1: Interdisciplinarity Is New

Interdisciplinarity is widely touted as a new priority, but exaggerated claims of the "new" disguise the longer history of developments mapped in Chapter One. Limiting developments to the singularity of the moment also renders them more vulnerable to dismissal as a fad. The willingness to engage in interdisciplinary activities is related in no small part to how familiar they seem, whether in the distant or the recent past. Hence, arguments for change should be grounded in relevant histories within the varied landscape of interdisciplinary theory and practice. In humanities, for example, older methods of interart comparison and borrowing continue. Yet expansive and innovative understandings of culture, history, and language fostered new methods and concepts that challenged traditional canons and procedures. In social sciences, problem solving, methodological borrowing, and synthetic frameworks remain powerful warrants. Yet new interactions with humanities and sciences have extended the variety of approaches. In the sciences, the historical precedent of problem focus remains prominent, but new technologies and configurations of collaborative work are changing the way research is performed and priorities for education are determined.

Several questions follow for thinking about interdisciplinary interests locally:

• What are the pertinent national histories and communities of practice for local interests?
• What forms have they taken on campus?
• What threads of continuity and shifts over time do they represent?
• How adequately are they represented in official maps of campus?

MYTH 2: GENUINE INTERDISCIPLINARITY IS . . .

Klein and Newell (1997), as noted in Chapter Three, contended that interdisciplinarity will not be a matter of agreement on campuses—conceptually, practically, or politically. Multiple forms and definitions not only coexist but have differing status in the political economy of a campus. "Much like larger societies," Cornwell and Stoddard (2001) observed, "campus communities have dominant cultures, stratification, alternative, resistant, and emerging cultures" (p. 160). The current heightened priority of instrumental forms of collaboration should not overwhelm the importance of the amorphous dynamic of change that occurs in the daily course of knowledge production or the role of critique in epistemic change. Likewise, the value of more limited forms of bridge building, such as borrowing methods and fostering multi-disciplinary breadth in the curriculum, should not be dismissed.

Here, too, questions follow for thinking about interdisciplinarity locally:

- What are the overt and sanctioned forms and practices in the surface structure of the campus?
- What are the concealed realities and less visible activities in its shadow structure?
- How looped in, to recall the words of the Interdisciplinary Programs Team at the University of Massachusetts–Lowell, are all interdisciplinary activities to the local infrastructure?
- What role do diffused interests and distributed interdisciplinary intelligence play in the operational realities of the campus?

MYTH 3: INTERDISCIPLINARY WORK IS SUPERFICIAL

The charge of superficiality stems from a number of sources. In education, the Leonardesque ambition of knowing everything has been criticized since the rise of interdisciplinary general education in the early twentieth century. In both education and research, the balance of depth and breadth is a major fault line, along with disputes over the status of particular approaches. The counterpart dismissal for myth 2—"It's not *real* interdisciplinarity"—is the lament, "It's not *really* psychology, or biology, or ..." The trail of failed programs and projects only adds to skepticism and resistance, though too many fall short of their interdisciplinary goals because the accumulated body of wisdom and practice represented in this book is underused.

Related questions follow:

- Are interdisciplinary-specific guidelines and criteria used in planning, implementing, and evaluating local programs and projects?
- Are models of particular practices consulted and adapted as needed?

- Do interdisciplinary-specific criteria and guidelines inform the evaluation of individual and collaborative work?
- Do institutional policies reflect appropriate definitions, or do criteria defer to campus-wide standard procedures?

MYTH 4: INTERDISCIPLINARITY THREATENS THE DISCIPLINES

The argument that interdisciplinarity will threaten and even undermine the disciplines perpetuates the presumption that they are not only the "natural" order of things but they do not change. Disciplines are historically constructed, they have differing degrees of openness to interdisciplinarity, and in the latter decades of the twentieth century they exhibited a broad trend toward greater porosity of boundaries. The relationship of disciplinarity and interdisciplinarity is also constructed differently. For some, they are contradictory; for others, they are complementary; and for still others, including me, the relationship has a productive tension. These differences underscore the importance of a reflexive view of disciplines, accounting for historical change and their shifting relationship to interdisciplinarity in both research and education. As this book was going to press, the American Colleges and Universities journal, *Liberal Education,* published the latest in a long line of reports tracking tradition and change in the major, including interdisciplinary developments ("Liberal Education and the Disciplines," 2009).

Further questions follow:

- Are new interdisciplinary developments in research incorporated into the curriculum?
- Are recommendations in reports from professional organizations in both disciplines and interdisciplinary fields discussed locally and considered for implementation?
- Do departments read state-of-the-discipline and accreditation reports from their national professional organizations and consider their recommendations?
- Do departments and interdisciplinary programs clarify their relationships and work in common?

MYTH 5: INTERDISCIPLINARITY IS IMPOSSIBLE TO DO

The argument that interdisciplinarity is impossible to do is both theoretical and practical in nature. To recall the discussion of institutionalization in Chapter Four, Stanley Fish's (1989) declaration of impossibility held that any strategy aiming to transgress boundaries negates itself by adopting normalizing practices. In responding to Fish, Alan Liu (2008) accepted the epistemological critique of its ideological and imperialistic operations. Yet he underscored the need for a pragmatics of interdisciplinarity capable of reconfiguring existing closures in order to respond to current urgencies. The literature highlighted in the Resources section at the end of this book provides a valuable source of pragmatics for developing new designs. Yet creating a campus culture that is conducive to interdisciplinary research and education requires more than adopting prior models and strategies. It is a form of boundary work that requires the actions presented throughout this book: weighing local variables of organizational change, identifying points of convergence, leveraging existing resources, building capacity and critical mass, platforming and scaffolding the architecture for a networked campus, benchmarking and adapting best practices, creating a resource bank, and deep structuring of a robust portfolio of strategies aimed at programmatic strength and sustainability across upper, middle, and lower levels.

A final set of questions follows:

- Are pronouncements and decisions about interdisciplinarity impressionistic or based on careful listening to the system at all levels?
- Are actions grounded in the literature, best practices, and principles for interdisciplinary design, implementation, administration, and evaluation?
- Are strategies combined, orchestrating transformative and incremental steps, as well as targeted initiatives and general loosening of barriers?
- Do actions and policies lower the accumulation of disadvantage or perpetuate it, while espousing a vague institutional commitment to interdisciplinarity?

(RE)SITUATING INTERDISCIPLINARITY

The modern system of disciplinarity is little more than a century old. It is a product of the professionalization and institution-alization of a new system of knowledge production in the late nineteenth and early twentieth centuries. Interdisciplinarity is nearing its own century mark. The first era was characterized by developments in social science-, agriculture-, and defense-related research, as well as general education and the field of American studies. At midcentury, it became more prominent in the wake of government-funded programs for problem-focused research, followed by groundbreaking educational experiments. The first widely recognized typology appeared in 1972, and the literature expanded exponentially after that. Scholarly and programmatic work would continue to test what the underlying concept meant while enlarging it in new contexts. As we near the century mark, three recent voices situate interdisciplinarity today.

One voice calls for a universal radical transformation. In an op-ed piece in the *New York Times,* Mark Taylor (2009) dubbed graduate education in the United States "the Detroit of higher learning." He faulted graduate education for mass-producing a product for which there is no market and developing skills for which there is diminishing demand, both at a rapidly increasing cost. In order to thrive, Taylor proposed, American higher edu-cation must go the way of Wall Street and Detroit. He outlined six steps: restructure the curriculum, abolish permanent depart-ments, increase collaboration among institutions, transform the traditional dissertation, expand the range of employment options for students, and impose mandatory retirement while also abol-ishing tenure in favor of multiyear contracts. Taylor's vision of a new academy is replete with cross-disciplinary teaching and scholarship, restructured fields and methods, problem-focused and topic-based programs, and partnerships among institutions. None of his suggestions is new, and variations of them appeared in previous chapters. In the midst of the current financial cri-sis, though, their cumulative force challenges the simplistic logic of downsizing by cutting dealer franchises—in this case, lop-ping off interdisciplinary programs to save departments without putting into practice the widespread rhetoric of collaborating and partnering in a web or network model.

In crafting a networked campus, it will also be important to heed a second voice. In a special issue of the *History of Intellectual Culture*, "Reconsidering Interdisciplinary Theory and Practice," Jill Vickers (2003) argued that the complex challenges of navigating interdisciplinarity in the twenty-first century require ending the search for universal and timeless characteristics. Rather than focusing on a generic whole, she contends, we can better understand interdisciplinarity by studying how it is manifested in the contexts in which particular projects emerge and evolve. In treating interdisciplinarity as an integral part of the knowledge production system, shaped and reshaped by processes of frag- mentation, synthesis, and recombination of knowledge, Vickers also underscores the plurality of generational and environmen- tal changes mapped in Chapter One. Acknowledging plurality, though, does not sidestep the need for guidelines in determining what constitutes reliable knowledge. This need, she admonishes, is all the more important today because new information tech- nologies make it more possible to do interdisciplinary work by navigating across domains of knowledge and collaborating across physical locales. Increased technological capacity, though, does not necessarily result in quality, a recurring theme of this book.

A third voice addresses two other recurring themes: institu- tionalization and self-definition. In a genealogy of science and technology studies (STS) in the *Oxford Handbook of Interdisci- plinarity* (forthcoming), Sheila Jasanoff frames the challenge of interdisciplinarity as an ongoing interplay of barriers and opportu- nities. STS emerged as a recognized field in the 1970s. Nearly fifty years later, it remains weakly institutionalized in the upper tiers of the academy, stalled by familiar institutional hurdles and the field's own contradictory self-understandings. Despite respected intellectual accomplishments, STS still faces the challenge of pop- ulating the spaces between disciplines with well-trained scholars, new offerings in the curriculum, and long-term research pro- grams. Doing so will require greater intellectual coherence, higher academic standing, and institutional stability. STS scholars must also overcome their reluctance to create potentially exclusionary boundaries and criteria of membership. The challenge of inter-disciplinarity, Jasanoff concludes, is one of strategic positioning. All interdisciplinary fields, by extension, need to establish relations to their objects of study, define relations to other disciplines, assert their own boundaries and mission, and question the self-understanding of disciplines as coherent and unified entities.

The models, best practices, guidelines, and strategies presented throughout this book offer powerful pragmatics for inter-disciplinary fields, programs, and projects. Echoing Jasanoff's admonition for fields, they all demand organization for their survival and continuity, to demarcate them from neighboring territories, and to set up internal markers by which to measure essential attributes such as originality, quality, progress, and contributions to knowledge. They all need to be able to define what makes them part of a common enterprise, make the case for what they have to offer, and situate it within the larger academic agenda. There are no magic bullets for doing so, nor is success in one moment a permanent guarantee. One overriding lesson is clear, though. In order to flourish, interdisciplinarity requires spaces where goals can be developed and sustained, not limited to weak models, reduced to service functions, or consolidated into mergers that are only economic conveniences. Partnerships have greater appeal in the current financial squeeze. They can enhance the space for intellectual synergy and organizational collaboration, while offering cost savings. However, simply moving people around and reconfiguring relations does not mean inter-disciplinarity will be the result. The defining elements of strong models are required. Moreover, Cindi Katz warned, although IDS programs have "settled in," they "continue to exist within an environment where unrelenting disciplinary claims to knowledge hold sway" (2001, pp. 521–522). Based on their analysis of institutional case studies in Chapter Four, Augsburg, Henry, Newell, and Szostak (2009) offer a conclusion that applies to all initiatives, fields, programs, and projects: "eternal vigilance is the price of interdisciplinarity" (p. 246).

RESOURCES

Facilitating Interdisciplinary Research (2004) sends a resounding message that applies to interdisciplinary research as well as education. The report exhorts individuals to indicate not only what they require; they also have a responsibility to explain and demonstrate the benefits of what they do. This section adds a final admonition: use the abundant resources that are available. It identifies materials and strategies for libraries, central oversight bodies, programs, and individuals to use in building a resource bank. It is not an exhaustive bibliography; rather, it is a representative selection of key works and strategies. Given the scope and plurality of activities covered in this book, the resources are dispersed across print publications, Web-based forums, and the gray literature of conference papers, reports, documents, and course materials. In some areas, attempts to codify literatures have been made, most notably in interdisciplinary studies, research management, and transdisciplinary team science. Particular fields, such as cognitive science and women's studies, also have defining literatures. Even with identifiable literatures, though, resources are underused. The result is a tremendous loss of knowledge and wisdom of practice.

Five sections follow: overviews and bibliographies; domains of practice; interdisciplinary studies; integration, collaboration, and evaluation and assessment; and Web-based searching and networking. The emphasis is on the past decade, though scrutiny of bibliographies will lead to earlier key publications in particular areas, and networking with organizations and Web-based searching will ensure continued updating.

OVERVIEWS AND BIBLIOGRAPHIES

Chapter One mapped major developments associated with inter-disciplinarity within science and technology, social sciences, and humanities. A number of major resources provide authoritative overviews, bibliographies, and literature reviews.

RECENT OVERVIEWS

Frodeman, R., Klein, J. T., and Mitcham, C. (eds.). *Oxford Handbook of Interdisciplinarity*. New York: Oxford University Press, forthcoming. An international collection of essays by invited experts covering common themes, issues, and knowledge production and practice in a wide range of disciplines and fields across sciences and technology, social sciences, humanities, and the professions; includes chapters on cognitive science, media and communication, environment, health science and health care, library and information science, politics-government-policy, and systems analysis and complexity.

Hadorn, G. H., and others (eds.). *Handbook of Transdisciplinary Research*. New York: Springer, 2008. An anthology on problem-driven trans-disciplinary research relating to issues such as global and local environment, migration, new technologies, health, and sociocultural change. Includes projects covering problem identification and structuring, problem analysis, and cross-cutting topics of participation, values, management, education, and integration.

Atkinson, J., and Crowe, M. (eds.). *Interdisciplinary Research: Diverse Approaches in Science, Technology, Health and Society*. Hoboken, N.J.: Wiley, 2006. A collection covering historical and theoretical contexts of interdisciplinary research with topics across the quantitative-qualitative spectrum, including complexity, sustainability, statistics, information systems, auditory-visual perception, modern history, media and cultural studies, and health science.

"Rethinking Interdisciplinarity." 2003–2004. www.interdisciplines.org/interdisciplinarity. An international virtual conference covering topics such as definition, transdisciplinarity, assessment, difficulties of doing interdisciplinary research, the evolution of knowledge domains, innovation, science and society, neuroscience, and information science.

EARLIER OVERVIEWS

Lattuca, L. *Creating Interdisciplinarity: Interdisciplinary Research and Teaching Among College and University Faculty.* Nashville, Tenn.: Vanderbilt University Press, 2001. An in-depth examination of the nature, practice, and contexts of interdisciplinary inquiry based on literature review and interviews with faculty from humanities, social sciences, and sciences.

Klein, J. T., and others (eds.). *Transdisciplinarity: Joint Problem Solving Among Science, Technology, and Society.* Basel: Birkhäuser Verlag, 2001. A collection on research and problem solving involving cooperation of academics and stakeholders, with definitions, materials from a benchmark international conference, and essays on research management, knowledge integration, mutual learning, teamwork and partnership, institutional structure, evaluation, and guidelines for practice.

Cunningham, R. (ed.). *Interdisciplinarity and the Organization of Knowledge in Europe.* Luxembourg: Office for Official Publications of the European Communities, 1999. A compilation from a major conference covering the nature of interdisciplinarity, historical perspectives, the organization of research, teaching, and public policies.

Newell, W. H. (ed.). *Interdisciplinarity: Essays from the Literature.* New York: College Board, 1998. An anthology of reprinted essays on the nature of interdisciplinary studies, philosophical analyses, administration, programs, disciplinary contexts, and research and education in social sciences, humanities, natural science, and interdisciplinary fields. Includes a guide to syllabus preparation and a closing synthesis of core questions about interdisciplinary studies and integration.

Salter, L., and Hearn, A. (eds.). *Outside the Lines: Issues in Interdisciplinary Research.* Montreal and Kingston: McGill-Queens Press, 1996. A collection of research stories covering issues and problems in interdisciplinary studies, definitions of disciplinarity and interdisciplinarity, myths, postmodern critiques, grant allocations, emerging disciplines, and the fields of women's, Canadian, and environmental studies.

Klein, J. T. *Crossing Boundaries: Knowledge, Disciplinarities, and Interdisciplinarities.* Charlottesville: University of Virginia Press, 1996. A conceptual framework for studying interdisciplinary practices, with case studies of six fields (urban, environmental, border, area, women's, and cultural studies) and interdisciplinary research in literary studies, and in science and technology, accompanied by a thirty-page bibliography updating sources since the 1990 book in the following entry.

Klein, J. T. *Interdisciplinarity: History, Theory, and Practice.* Detroit, Mich.: Wayne State University Press, 1990. A broad-based study of the history and definition of interdisciplinarity, its relationship to disciplines, and practices in problem-focused research, health care, and higher education. Accompanied by a ninety-four-page bibliography identifying literature up to the late 1980s.

ADDITIONAL BIBLIOGRAPHIES AND LITERATURE REVIEW

Holley, K. A. *Understanding Interdisciplinary Challenges and Opportunities in Higher Education.* ASHE Higher Education Report, Vol. 35, No. 2. San Francisco: Jossey Bass, 2009. An overview of literature on definitions of interdisciplinarity, the role of disciplines, learning and cognition, research practice, faculty and institutional structure, and best practices in education; with key characteristics of curriculum, teaching and learning, internal and external support, and strategies for change including tenure and promotion criteria, organizational structures, collaborative leadership, and professional development.

Chettiparamb, A. *Interdisciplinarity: A Literature Review.* Southampton, U.K.: University of Southampton, 2007. www.heacademy.ac.uk/ourwork/networks/itlg. A sixty-three-page literature review that covers the nature of disciplinarity and interdisciplinarity, realms of practice, teaching, and higher education policy context in the United Kingdom.

Klein, J. T. "Resources for Interdisciplinary Studies." *Change,* Apr. 2006, 52–56, 58. An updated "Resource Review" column identifying core print literature and defining a basic collection of materials, deepening the search for more specialized resources, and highlighting new print and Web-based material.

In addition, bibliographies are posted on the Internet by groups on individual campuses. Two examples follow:

"Literature and Resources for Interdisciplinary and Integrative Learning." Carleton Interdisciplinary Science and Math Initiative of Carleton College. http://serc.carleton.edu/cismi/literature/index .html. A collection of references focused on science and math fields, covering research on expert thinking and practice, assessment, teaching, integrative learning, and national reports and books.

"Bibliography on Interdisciplinarity." Network for Interdisciplinary Initiatives. University of Washington, 2003. www.grad.washington .edu/ acad/ interdisc_network/ ID_Docs/ NII_documents.htm. A broad-based selection of references compiled in conjunction with a campus-wide initiative.

Domains of Practice

Frodeman, Klein, and Mitcham (forthcoming), listed in the "Recent Overviews" section, provides the most recent overview of a wide range of areas, though several other works are entry points into the content areas covered in Chapter One.

Science and Technology

Facilitating Interdisciplinary Research. Committee on Facilitating Interdisciplinary Research. Washington, D.C.: National Academies Press, 2004. A report based on a major national task force surveying the drivers of interdisciplinarity today, institutional policies and strategies, evaluation, and the role of funding organizations, journals, and professional societies.

BIO 2010: Transforming Undergraduate Education for Future Research Biologists. Committee on Undergraduate Biology Education to Prepare Research Scientists for the 21st Century. Washington, D.C.: National Academies Press, 2003. A blueprint for integrating contemporary research and mathematics and physical sciences into biology education, with institutional case studies and recommendations for teaching, curriculum building, materials, administrative and financial barriers, independent research, and project-based laboratories.

Weingart, P., and Stehr, N. (eds.). *Practicing Interdisciplinarity.* Toronto: University of Toronto Press, 2001. An anthology of essays covering the topics of interdisciplinary discourse, the changing topography of science, the role of funding bodies, and international contexts of research practice, with a bibliography leading to earlier resources.

Pellmar, T., and Eisenberg, L. (eds.). *Bridging Disciplines in the Brain, Behavioral, and Clinical Sciences.* Washington, D.C.: National

Academies Press, 2000. A report on brain, behavioral, social, and clinical sciences with analysis of the potential, a review of current educational and training programs, and recommendations for public and private agencies and universities spanning funding, partnerships, organizational structure, credit and evaluation, career development, and translational research.

Kessel, Rosenfield, and Anderson (2003), listed in the "Social Sciences" section.

SOCIAL SCIENCES

Calhoun, C., and Rhoten, D. "Theoretical Knowledge, Methodological Tools, and Practical Applications: Three Agendas for Interdisciplinarity in the Social Sciences." In R. Frodeman, J. T. Klein, and C. Mitcham (eds.), *The Oxford Handbook of Interdisciplinarity*. New York: Oxford University Press, forthcoming. A historical overview of different manifestations typed as cross-fertilization, team collaboration, field creation, and problem orientation, with emphasis on research agendas, field initiatives, and mission-oriented agendas. Also considers conditions of success or failure and the current state and future prospects.

Klein, J. T. "Interdisciplinary Approach." In S. Turner and W. Outhwaite (eds.), *Handbook of Social Science Methodology*. Thousand Oaks, Calif.: Sage, 2007. An overview of the plurality and historical patterns of activity in social sciences, core terminology and differing practices, and key methodological issues, with a section on earlier works.

Smelser, N. J. "Interdisciplinarity in Theory and Practice." In C. Camic and H. Joas (eds.), *The Dialogical Turn: New Roles for Sociology in the Postdisciplinary Age*. Lanham, Md.: Rowman & Littlefield, 2004. An analysis of disciplines in behavioral and social sciences, the institutional and intellectual embodiments of interdisciplinarity, and the intellectual architecture of the *International Encyclopedia of the Social and Behavioral Sciences*.

Kessel, F., Rosenfield, P. L., and Anderson, N. B. (eds.). *Expanding the Boundaries of Health and Social Science: Case Studies in Interdisciplinary Innovation*. New York: Oxford University Press, 2003. An anthology covering conditions and strategies that promote interdisciplinary and transdisciplinary research on health at the nexus of behavioral, social, and biological sciences, with domain introductions and examples in cardiovascular health and disease, affective and cognitive neuroscience, positive health, longevity, and HIV/AIDS management.

Humanities

Klein, J. T. *Humanities, Culture, and Interdisciplinarity: The Changing American Academy.* Albany, N.Y.: SUNY Press, 2005. Study of the historical and contemporary relationship of humanities, culture, and interdisciplinarity, with case studies on the disciplines of literary studies, art history, and music, as well as the fields of American studies, African American studies, and women's studies.

Miller, R. "Varieties of Interdisciplinary Approaches in the Social Sciences." *Issues in Integrative Studies*, 1982, *1*, 1–37. A seven-category typology.

Bal, M. *Travelling Concepts in Humanities.* Toronto: University of Toronto Press, 2002. Analyzes how concepts such as meaning, metaphor, narrative, myth, and image form the backbone of interdisciplinary cultural analysis in humanities, with particular interest for art history, visual and cultural studies, literary studies, biblical studies, and feminist theory.

Moran, J. *Interdisciplinarity.* London: Routledge, 2002. An investigation of the way that disciplines divide and shape knowledge, how those divisions are transformed and transcended, and how new forms of knowledge are created, with emphasis on literary and cultural studies, theory, textuality and history, and new connections between literary studies and sciences.

Interdisciplinary Studies

The place to start for resources on interdisciplinary education is the website of the Association for Integrative Studies (AIS), www.units.muohio.edu/aisorg/. It has materials that may be downloaded, including sample syllabi, a directory of doctoral programs, guidelines for accreditation in interdisciplinary general education, interdisciplinary writing assessment profiles, a list of core publications with tables of contents, and the AIS teleconference described in this section. Older issues of the journal *Issues in Integrative Studies* and newer issues of the newsletter are also available online.

Annotated Guide to Literatures

Fiscella, J., and Kimmel, S. *Interdisciplinary Education: A Guide to Resources.* New York: College Board, 1999. The most comprehensive annotated bibliography covering K–12 and college, with more than eleven hundred entries primarily from 1990 to 1997, guided by essays on the nature of the literature and database searching and grouped into categories of educational foundations; curriculum; faculty, teacher, and team development; pedagogy and student support; and administration of interdisciplinary studies programming.

DEFINING OVERVIEWS

Chandramohan, B., and Fallows, S. (eds.). *Interdisciplinary Learning and Teaching in Higher Education: Theory and Practice*. London: Routledge, 2009. An exploration of topics in interdisciplinary learning, including quality assurance, resources, staff development, course design, assessment, student satisfaction, research support, and e-learning and distance learning. Examples in work-based learning, mass communications, computing, engineering, business, social sciences, tourism, science, and health science.

Thew, N. *The Impact of the Internal Economy of Higher Education Institutions on Interdisciplinary Teaching and Learning*. Southampton, U.K.: University of Southampton, 2007. www.heacademy.ac.uk/ourwork/networks/itlg. A thirty-three-page overview of issues in interdisciplinary programs with emphasis on the United Kingdom, covering the topics of vision and values, structures, people, processes, finances and facilities, and the student experience.

"Interdisciplinary Studies Today." Association for Integrative Studies, 2005. Teleconference and webcast. An expert panel presentation on the definition of interdisciplinary studies, outcomes, courses, programs, pedagogy, standards, and resources. www.units.muohio .edu/aisorg/Resiyrces/teleconference/.

Klein, J. T. *Mapping Interdisciplinary Studies*. Washington, D.C.: Association of American Colleges and Universities, 1999. A discussion piece for campuses embarking on change, with a survey of current trends in the disciplines, interdisciplinary fields, and general education and strategies for integrating interdisciplinary curricula, faculty development, planning processes and pedagogies, assessment, institutional change, and support activities.

Klein, J. T., and Newell, W. H. "Advancing Interdisciplinary Studies." In J. Gaff and J. Ratcliff (eds.), *Handbook of the Undergraduate Curriculum: A Comprehensive Guide to Purposes, Structures, Practices, and Change*. San Francisco: Jossey-Bass, 1997. Survey of basic definitions, origins and motivations, new developments, forms and structures, institutional change, teaching and learning, and assessment and evaluation of interdisciplinary work.

Descriptions of Educational Practice

Haynes, C. (ed.). *Innovations in Interdisciplinary Teaching*. Westport, Conn.: Oryx Press/Greenwood Press, 2002. An anthology covering curriculum design, team teaching, advising, and assessment, with additional essays on the intersections of interdisciplinary studies with writing-intensive and computer-assisted instruction, collaborative learning and learning communities, multicultural pedagogies, women's studies, inquiry- and performance-based teaching and learning, study abroad, adult education, advising, and assessment.

Klein, J. T. (ed.). *Interdisciplinary Education in K–12 and College: A Foundation for K–16 Dialogue*. New York: College Board, 2002. The first collection of essays by experts across K–16 with reports on current integrated and interdisciplinary curricula, course design, team teaching, use of technology, and administration and assessment of interdisciplinary studies programs.

Holmes, D. E., and Osterweis, M. *Catalysts in Interdisciplinary Education: Innovation by Academic Health Centers*. Washington, D.C.: Association of Academic Health Centers, 1999. A compilation of case studies of interdisciplinary health professions education at seven members of the Association of Academic Health Centers, with a focus on strategies of institutionalization aimed at creating a culture change.

Klein, J. T., and Doty, W. G. (eds.). *Interdisciplinary Studies Today*. New Directions for Teaching and Learning, no. 58. San Francisco: Jossey-Bass, 1994. Chapters by invited experts on finding resources, developing courses, administering programs, assessing learning, and networking with organizations.

Directories of Course and Program Models

Edwards, A. F. Jr. *Interdisciplinary Undergraduate Programs: A Directory*. (2nd ed.) Acton, Mass.: Copley, 1996. The most recent compilation of programs in the United States from a cross-section of institutions with examples in interdisciplinary fields, cluster colleges, and general education.

Davis, J. R. *Interdisciplinary Courses and Team Teaching: New Arrangements for Learning*. Westport, Conn.: Greenwood Press, 1995. The first comprehensive presentation of guidelines and lessons for design and implementation of team-taught courses, with close analysis of five courses from the University of Denver and one hundred models spanning general education, professional and technical programs, integrative studies programs, capstone and integrative courses, and the fields of women's and gender, multicultural and ethnic, and international studies.

Directory of IDS Doctoral Programs. Association for Integrative Studies. www.units.muohio.edu/aisorg/. A listing with website links for programs within colleges of arts and/or sciences in the United States, spanning natural sciences, natural and social sciences, social sciences, and humanities. For further resources, visit "Re-envisioning the Ph.D." University of Washington and Pew Charitable Trust, www.grad.washington.edu/envision/phd/index .html.

PROGRAM AND COURSE MODELS

Linkon, S. "Understanding Interdisciplinarity: A Course Portfolio." 2004. www.educ.msu.edu/cst/events/2004/linkon.html. An assignment model based on research into how students and faculty view interdisciplinarity and modes of facilitating integrative learning, with an incremental three-assignment sequence incorporating recursive learning to build deeper understanding of content and methods in interdisciplinary analysis.

Carmichael, T. S. *Integrated Studies: Reinventing Undergraduate Education.* Stillwater, Okla.: New Forums Press, 2004. A detailed account of the University of North Dakota's integrated general education program with details on curriculum development, pedagogy, assignments, classroom activities, faculty development strategies, and assessment that will be helpful to programs nationwide.

Smith, B. L., and McCann, J. (eds.). *Reinventing Ourselves: Interdisciplinary Education, Collaborative Learning, and Experimentation in Higher Education.* San Francisco: Anker/Jossey-Bass, 2001. A postconference collection of essays describing experiences and lessons from a cross-section of institutions, including stand-alone institutions and alternative programs in traditional institutions, as well as community colleges.

Vess, D. "Interdisciplinary Learning, Teaching, and Research." 2000–2001. www.faculty.de.gcsu.edu/~dvess/ids/courseportfolios/ front.htm. A website presenting results of a Carnegie Scholar's research project on the nature of interdisciplinary learning, outcomes, and pedagogy, with detailed presentation and analysis of two course portfolios at Georgia College and State University (*Fine and Applied Arts in Civilization* and *Global Issues in Society*).

Seabury, M. B. (ed.).*Interdisciplinary General Education: Questioning Outside the Lines.* New York: College Board, 1999. An anthology based on the University of Hartford's All-University Curriculum, with essays by faculty and staff describing course development and pedagogy, team teaching, and the dynamics of asking questions, crossing boundaries, framing issues, dealing with problems, and creating a supportive campus culture, accompanied by sample syllabi.

Hursh, B., Haas, P., and Moore, M. "An Interdisciplinary Model to Implement General Education." *Journal of Higher Education,* 1983, 5, 42–59. An older but useful model of student research on interdisciplinary problems defining the role of salient concepts that have different meaning across disciplines but provide a connecting link.

"Peer Reviewed Syllabi." In the Resources section of the AIS website. Date ongoing. www.units.muohio.edu/aisorg/. A peer-reviewed compilation of sample syllabi and other course materials.

Textbooks for Students

Repko, A. F. *Interdisciplinary Research: Process and Theory.* Thousand Oaks, Calif.: Sage, 2008. A textbook for student research covering the nature and theories of interdisciplinary studies with detailed guidelines for the research process of drawing on disciplines and integrating insights, accompanied by an appendix on resources and a glossary of key terms.

Augsburg, T. *Becoming Interdisciplinary: An Introduction to Interdisciplinary Studies.* (2nd ed.). Dubuque, Iowa: Kendall/Hunt, 2006. The first undergraduate introductory text covering the nature of interdisciplinary studies and disciplines, the writing of intellectual autobiographies, experiential learning activities, and research and problem solving, with supplementary readings and discussion of the history of programs, the process of integration, and portfolios.

Integration, Collaboration, and Evaluation and Assessment

Three cross-cutting topics loom large in discussions of interdisciplinarity: integration, collaboration, and evaluation and assessment. A number of key works provide starting points.

INTEGRATION

The topic of the 2009 conference of td-net, the Network for Transdisciplinary Research, is "Integration in Inter- and Transdisciplinary Research." Outcomes will be noted on the td-net website: www.transdisciplinarity.ch/e/.

Pohl, C., van Kerkhoff, L., and Hadorn, G. H. "Integration." In G. H. Hadorn and others (eds.), *Handbook of Transdisciplinary Research*. New York: Springer, 2008. An overview of concepts and methods of integration, covering historical perspectives, conceptual and practical challenges, a matrix for three types of collaboration, institutional challenges, and a proposed standard framework based on six core questions.

Newell, W. "Professionalizing Interdisciplinarity: A Literature Review and Research Agenda." In W. H. Newell (ed.), *Interdisciplinarity: Essays from the Literature*. New York: College Board, 1998. A synthesis of insights on the nature of interdisciplinary studies based on essays in the anthology, with sections on the nature, prerequisites, and process of integration.

Sill, D. J. "Integrative Thinking, Synthesis, and Creativity in Interdisciplinary Studies." *Journal of General Education*, 1996, *45*(2), 129–151. A model for synthesis and integrative thought, drawing on existing models for creativity and considering the implications for interdisciplinary studies with attention to the roles of bisociative thought, creative tension, complexity, interactive process, ripeness, and preinventive structures, including subconscious ideas, images, and concepts as well as an active imagination.

For descriptions of the integrative process in IDS by solo interdisciplinarians:

Repko, A. F. *Interdisciplinary Research: Process and Theory*. Thousand Oaks, Calif.: Sage, 2008. Described in the "Textbooks for Students" section.

Newell, W. H. "Decision Making in Interdisciplinary Studies." In G. Morçöl (ed.), *Handbook of Decision Making*. New York: Marcel Dekker, 2007. An ideal model of decision making by individuals in interdisciplinary studies informed by complexity theory, with a two-step process that entails drawing on disciplinary perspectives and integrating insights into a more comprehensive understanding.

Palmer, C. L., and Neumann, L. J. "The Information Work of Interdisciplinary Humanities Scholars: Exploration and Translation."

Library Quarterly, 2002, 72, 85–117. A study of interdisciplinary work patterns based on interviews, bibliometric analysis, and actor-network theory, with attention to strategies of finding and using resources, exploration and translation in boundary crossing and creativity, and the role of anchoring information and reconsideration, reformulation, and restatement.

See also Boix Mansilla (forthcoming), described in the "Evaluation and Assessment" section.

COLLABORATION

"The Science of Team Science: Assessing the Value of Transdisciplinary Research." *American Journal of Preventive Medicine*, 2008, 35(2S), S77–S249. A special issue devoted to the theory and practice of inter- and transdisciplinary research, covering definitions, social and cognitive dynamics of collaboration, assessment and evaluation, leadership, training, and case studies in health sciences.

Derry, S. J., Schunn, C. D., and Gernsbacher, M. A. (eds.). *Interdisciplinary Collaboration: An Emerging Cognitive Science.* Mahwah, N.J.: Erlbaum, 2005. A collection of postconference essays on the nature of interdisciplinary collaboration and problems and processes of inquiry, representing all seven disciplines of the Cognitive Science Society. Contains case studies of collaboration in situ and a closing section on the exemplar of cognitive science.

Amey, M. J., and Brown, D. F. *Breaking Out of the Box: Interdisciplinary Collaboration and Faculty Work.* Greenwich, Conn.: Information Age Publishing, 2004. A three-stage model of collaboration and discussion of the four dimensions of disciplinary orientation, knowledge engagement, work orientation, and leadership orientation; based on literature review, experience in postsecondary education, and an in-depth study of a research team contracted to an inner-city community council.

Multidisciplinary Learning Team Teaching Initiative. University of Michigan. www.provost.umich.edu/programs/MLTT/. A website aimed at supporting undergraduate team-teaching efforts and cross-unit degree programs at the University of Michigan, with background information for faculty, a report of the preliminary task force report, application forms, descriptions of funded program, links to funding and evaluation information, and information on funding.

See Davis (1995) in the "Directories of Course and Program Models" section.

EVALUATION AND ASSESSMENT

Huutoniemi, K. "Research Evaluation." In R. Frodeman, J. T. Klein, and C. Mitcham (eds.), *Oxford Handbook of Interdisciplinarity*. New York: Oxford University Press, forthcoming. A review of the emergent literature, incorporating insights from conceptual and pragmatic discussions, empirical studies on evaluation, and initiatives and experiences of organizations and actors. Attention is given to four overlapping questions about evaluation, merits and criteria, quality judgments, and the general problematic of research evaluation.

Boix Mansilla, V. "Learning to Synthesize: An Epistemological Foundation for Interdisciplinary Learning." In R. Frodeman, J. T. Klein, and C. Mitcham (eds.), *Oxford Handbook of Interdisciplinarity*. New York: Oxford University Press, forthcoming. A pragmatic constructionist framework for interdisciplinary learning and its assessment, focused on cognitive and epistemological dynamics with literature review and illustrations of a fourfold model of establishing interdisciplinary purpose, weighing disciplinary insights, leveraging integrations, and taking a critical stance.

Klein, J. T. "Evaluation of Interdisciplinary and Transdisciplinary Research: A Literature Review." *American Journal of Preventive Medicine*, 2008, *35*(2S), S116–S123. A review of the emergent literature, with seven generic principles highlighting variability of goals, variability of criteria and indicators, integration, interaction of social and cognitive factors in collaboration, management-leadership-coaching, iteration, and effectiveness and impact.

Research Evaluation, 2006, *15*(1), 1–80. Special issue on assessment of interdisciplinary research. An international collection with accounts of empirical studies of interdisciplinary research assessment, an expert workshop, and discussions of the challenges of interdisciplinary evaluation, standards of quality, peer review processes, and a procedure for evaluating interdisciplinary research networks, with an afterword identifying the literature.

Klein, J. T. "Assessing Interdisciplinary Learning K–16." In J. T. Klein (ed.), *Interdisciplinary Education in K–12 and College: A Foundation for K–16 Dialogue*. New York: College Board, 2002. A synthesis of findings on interdisciplinary learning assessment in primary, secondary, and postsecondary education, with definitions of desired outcomes, criteria of evaluating integrative learning, tools and models, and direct and indirect indicators, including both conventional measures and authentic student performances. Includes the logic of interdisciplinary assessment articulated in Field, M., and Stowe, D.

"Transforming Interdisciplinary Teaching and Learning Through Assessment." In C. Haynes (ed.), *Innovations in Interdisciplinary Teaching*. Westport, Conn.: Greenwood Press, 2002.

"Defining Women's Studies Scholarship." In R. M. Diamond and B. A. Adam (eds.), *The Disciplines Speak II: More Statements on Rewarding the Scholarly, Professional, and Creative Work of Faculty*. Washington, D.C.: American Association for Higher Education, 2000. An overview of assessing women's studies covering institutional contexts, national initiatives, guidelines for evaluating scholarship, and key scholarly publications, with examples of the scholarship of discovery, integration, application, and teaching.

See also other studies of assessment in interdisciplinary research and interdisciplinary studies on the Harvard Interdisciplinary Studies Project website at Project Zero: www.pz.harvard.edu/interdisciplinary.

Web-Based Searching and Networking

Web-based searching and organizational networking are vital to long-term resource banking, fostering access to up-to-date materials and collegial connections. The following essay provides an introductory framework for a multitiered approach:

Klein, J. T., and Newell, W. H. "Strategies for Using Interdisciplinary Resources." *Issues in Integrative Studies*, 2002, *20*, 139–160. A presentation of six strategies for finding resources for interdisciplinary studies: the primary literature, professional organizations and related publications, specialized literatures, disciplinary and interdisciplinary networking, electronic databases, and professional development forums.

For many professionals, electronic database searching and the Internet are first and even last resorts. Joan Fiscella (principal bibliographer and associate professor at the University of Illinois at Chicago, University Library) notes the pervasive turn to Google and Google-like searching strategies, and also starting with Wikipedia to get an overview of key terms and directions for a more critical search (personal communication, September 28, 2008). Using the search words "interdisciplinary" and "[name of field or subject area]" in Google, Google Scholar, and Wikipedia will turn up references for specific fields and domains. Two publications, though, offer detailed advice on customizing interdisciplinary search strategies and situate interdisciplinarity within the larger field of information research:

Kimmel, S. "Interdisciplinary Information Searching: Moving Beyond Discipline-Based Resources." In J. Fiscella and S. Kimmel (eds.), *Interdisciplinary Education: A Guide to Resources.* New York: College Board, 1999. An overview of strategies conducive to researching interdisciplinary topics, with a section on research sources and tools, including tips for formulating database searches and a section on trends in services and tools describing new technologies, alert services, virtual libraries, and working with library classification schemes.

Palmer, C. "Information Research on Interdisciplinarity." In R. Frodeman, J. T. Klein, and C. Mitcham (eds.), *Oxford Handbook of Interdisciplinarity.* New York: Oxford University Press, forthcoming. An authoritative account of challenges and strategies from the perspective of library and information science, including the topics of early work in the area, information scatter and literature-based discovery, bibliometric studies of patterns and flows of information within and among disciplines, information behavior research, and new directions, including implications of digital information systems, resources, and tools.

Faculty, administrators, and curriculum development groups should also be aware of the Educational Resources Information Center (ERIC), the most abundant source of published and "gray" literature, including government reports, project and program descriptions, and curriculum guides. Sponsored by the U.S. Department of Education, ERIC provides a centralized website for searching a bibliographical database of more than 1.3 million citations dating back to 1966. In 2004, ERIC began providing users free online access to full texts of approximately 107,000 ERIC documents published in 2003 or earlier. Recent updates extend further forward in years.

In addition, special journal issues on interdisciplinary topics are excellent forums for keeping up with new developments, including changes in disciplinary practices. Through the years, special issues have appeared in areas as diverse as performance studies, art history, the library, creativity, Canadian studies, and German studies. The supplement on the Science of Team Science in the *American Journal of Preventive Medicine* is a good example (listed in the "Integration and Collaboration" section). The issue appears in electronic databases in the form of entries for individual authors and for the entire number. A host of other special issues have also appeared in subject areas as wide ranging as art history, theater, Canadian studies, library and information science, and creativity. Fiscella and Kimmel's *Interdisciplinary Education: A Guide to Resources* (1999; listed in the "Annotated Guide to Literatures" section) leads to special issues on interdisciplinary studies, as well as particular subject areas. A search with the keywords "interdisciplinary" and the name of a particular subject field or topic that turns up multiple references from the same volume is a likely indication of a special section or entire issue.

For a discussion of how to link with interdisciplinary associations, see Bingham, N. E. "Organizational Networking: Taking the Next Step." In J. T. Klein and W. G. Doty (eds.), *Interdisciplinary Studies Today*. San Francisco: Jossey-Bass, 1994. Since Bingham wrote, electronic forums have become prominent sites for exploring and staying updated on shared interests. Social connections open up many possibilities for interdisciplinarity, including social bookmarking using sites such as Del.icio.us and notification systems such as Flicker. Fiscella cites the Compendium of Free, Public Biomedical Text Mining Tools Available on the Web as an example of a community of practice that mines electronically accessible tools (http://arrow smith.psych.uic.edu/arrowsmith_uic/tools.html). Browsing down the page will lead to Knowledge Environments such as the one dedicated to Alzheimer's disease research. Within communities of practice, researchers can post and call for examples, offer ideas, and link to related sites. OCLC WorldCat has a program enabling the electronic version of adding a sticky note to books of interest. The most broad-based service for locating organizations is the Scholarly Societies Project of the University of Waterloo Library in Canada. Its searchable database has links to roughly four thousand scholarly societies, websites, and essays on scholarly societies and communication (www.scholarly-societies.org/).

In addition, several groups are noteworthy:

td-net. Transdisciplinarity-Net. www.transdisciplinarity.ch/. A multilin-
gual information system devoted to transdisciplinarity in three

areas: integrative systematization of specialized knowledge, collaborations between academic research and the private sector for product development, and efforts to achieve democratic solutions to problems of society. The website has an introduction to transdisciplinarity, a forum for discussion and networking, a bibliography, and references for major projects.

The Interdisciplinary Teaching and Learning Group. www.heacademy.ac .uk/ourwork/networks/itlg. Established in 2005 to study the ways in which institutions encourage or discourage cross-disciplinary collaboration in teaching and the student experience. Key publications by Angelique Chettiparambil and Neill Thew appear above.

Association for Integrative Studies. www.units.muohio.edu/aisorg/. The first stop for resources for interdisciplinary studies and reviews of new works in both interdisciplinary studies and research. The next two listings also have strong interests in IDS.

Association of American Colleges and Universities. www.aacu.org/. Another site with a strong interest in interdisciplinary studies, it includes related topics and issues in many annual meetings and Institute on General Education. In addition, the organization's Civic Engagement project and the Diversity Web compendium of practices and resources and initiatives on Integrative Learning cosponsored by the Carnegie Foundation for the Advancement of Teaching incorporate interdisciplinary perspectives.

Association of Graduate Liberal Studies Programs. www.aglsp.org/. A professional home for master's degree programs enrolling primarily adult learners. Its valuable curriculum guides are also adaptable for upper-level undergraduate contexts. They cover popular culture, multicultural education, science, and reflections on the "good society." A separate volume presented syllabi from an AGLSP Faculty Development Institute.

H-NET. www.h-net.org/. A self-described international interdisciplinary organization that provides teachers and scholars forums for the exchange of ideas and resources in the arts, humanities, and social sciences. Over a hundred free edited listservs and websites coordinate communication in a wide variety of disciplinary and interdisciplinary fields, as well as subject and topic areas. It is also a good pathway to organizations and networks. The link to H-AMSTDY, for example, leads to the H-NET American Studies listserv, which features news and discussions of the field and its intersections with women's studies, ethnic studies, cultural studies, media studies, and related developments in English, history, and other departments.

Professional organizations with specialized interdisciplinary interests are always excellent places to start and return to periodically for updates:

American Studies Association. www.theasa.net. Provides print and Web-based resources, including *The Guide to American Studies Resources* and the *ASA Guide for Reviewing American Studies Programs.* The link to the American Studies Crossroads Project (www.georgetown.edu/crossroads/asainfo.html) leads to further pedagogical, scholarly, and institutional information as well as workbooks, videotapes, disks, and other materials.

National Women's Studies Association. www.nwsa.org/. Devoted to feminist teaching, research, scholarship, and community activism, its website keeps members posted on annual conferences, centers, caucuses, interest groups, and task forces. In addition to its news magazine and journal, the association has issued guides to practice and reports emanating from national task forces.

A multitude of other sites also lead to subject areas with interdisciplinary interests. Knowing the key organizations and people working in an area is the best means of finding authoritative sources. The National Institutes of Health, for example, has a gateway site to the growing field of translational research: http://nihroadmap.nih.gov/clinicalresearch/overview-translational.asp.

Beyond such national and international groups, individual campuses have websites with materials that are useful to a wider audience. To cite one example, the *CFIS Quarterly* at the University of British Columbia is an online publication of the College of Interdisciplinary Studies. The college supports collaborative ID research and learning in sustainability, social policy, and human health. The *Quarterly* covers related research, teaching, and events, including a series of meetings on the topic of "Imagining Interdisciplinarity." www.cfisquarterly.ubc.ca/ and www.cfis.ubc.ca/.

Other and newer social networking sites also offer researchers and educators opportunities for collaboration. The *Chronicle of Higher Education* includes stories on interdisciplinary fields and groups on a near-regular basis. http://chronicle.com/. Fiscella highlights two sites in particular (personal communication, July 7, 2009):

Common Ground. www.commongroundpublishing.com/. Committed to building new kinds of knowledge communities by encouraging interdisciplinary thinking, global conversations, and cross-institutional collaboration. Provides a shared space where participants can meet in annual conferences and social networking software that enables members of a community to stay connected virtually during the year between conferences through academic publishing processes (peer review journal publishing and books), and informal conversations (blogs and monthly e-mail newsletter).

2collab. www.2collab.com/. This online collaboration tool is a service from Elsevier designed for researchers in science, technical, and medical communities. Using the 2collab platform, groups can share within existing networks or build new ones, either privately or in public. Individuals and groups can also store and manage scholarly bookmarks in one accessible place.

GLOSSARY FOR A CORE VOCABULARY

Interdisciplinary research (IDR) and *interdisciplinary studies (IDS)* integrate content, data, methods, tools, concepts, and theories from two or more disciplines or bodies of specialized knowledge in order to advance fundamental understanding, answer complex questions, and solve problems that are too broad or complex for a single approach.

Endogenous interdisciplinarity (ID) is based on the production of new knowledge. *Exogenous ID* originates in real problems of the community and the demand that universities perform their pragmatic social mission.

Instrumental, strategic, pragmatic, and *opportunistic ID* prioritize economic, technological, and scientific problem solving, aligning interdisciplinarity with research management, national needs, and innovation in the marketplace. *Critical* and *reflexive ID* interrogate the existing structure of knowledge and education, with the aim of transforming them while raising epistemological and political questions of value and purpose silent in opportunistic forms.

Methodological ID typically aims to improve the quality of results, as in borrowing a method or a concept in order to test a hypothesis, answer a research question, or help develop a theory. *Theoretical ID* is an epistemological form that typically builds a comprehensive conceptual framework or synthesis or fosters systematic integration of propositions, models, or analogies across disciplines.

Multidisciplinary approaches juxtapose disciplinary perspectives, adding breadth and available knowledge, information, and methods. They speak as separate voices in encyclopedic alignment. The status quo is not interrogated, and disciplinary elements retain their original identity.

Narrow ID occurs between disciplines with compatible methods, paradigms, and epistemologies, such as history and literature.

Broad or wide ID occurs between disciplines with little or no compatibility, such as sciences and humanities. They have different paradigms or methods, and more disciplines and social sectors may be involved.

Transdisciplinary approaches are comprehensive frameworks that transcend the narrow scope of disciplinary worldviews through an overarching synthesis, such as general systems, feminist theory, and sustainability. The term also connotes a new structure of unity informed by the worldview of complexity in science and a new mode of knowledge production that draws on expertise from a wider range of organizations and collaborations with stakeholders in society.

Conceptual Framework of the Book

Interdisciplinarity is a pluralistic idea. It is embodied in a heterogeneity of modes and forms of work that have fostered a distributed interdisciplinary intelligence and relational pluralism in the academy. Individual activities have discrete locations, but they also diffuse and intersect with other movements, adding to the greater hybridity of knowledge today, more frequent boundary crossing, and a growing multidisciplinary thrust of faculty work. Hybrid communities of practice range from trading zones where like-minded researchers and educators interact, to matrix structures of centers and programs, to emerging fields and, with sufficient critical mass, new paradigmatic fields. Hybrid discourses range in kind from interim pidgin forms of communication to creoles that comprise a subculture or native language of a new domain. Local context results in added variability, manifested in differing degrees of in/visibility in the balance of overt and concealed interdisciplinarities across the surface and shadow structures of institutions. Creating a campus culture that is conducive to interdisciplinary research and education is a form of boundary work that requires identifying points of convergence, leveraging existing resources, building capacity and critical mass, platforming and scaffolding the architecture for a networked campus, benchmarking and adapting best practices, creating a resource bank, and institutional deep structuring of a robust portfolio of strategies aimed at programmatic strength and sustainability.

References

Addelson, K. P., and Potter, E. "Making Knowledge." In J. E. Hartman and E. Messer-Davidow (eds.), *(En)Gendering Knowledge: Feminists in Academe.* Knoxville: University of Tennessee Press, 1991.

Alkalimat, A. "Toward a Paradigm of Unity in Black Studies." In N. Norment Jr. (ed.), *The African American Studies Reader.* Durham, N.C.: Carolina Academic Press, 2001.

Archibald, D. C. "Timing Is (Almost) Everything: A Campus-Wide Movement on Hold." In T. Augsburg and S. Henry (eds.), *The Politics of Interdisciplinary Studies: Essays on Transformations in American Undergraduate Programs.* Jefferson, N.C.: McFarland, 2009.

Association of American Colleges and Universities. *College Learning for the New Global Century.* Washington, D.C.: Association of American Colleges and Universities, 2007.

Association of American Colleges and Universities and Hart Research Associates. *Learning and Assessment: Trends in Undergraduate Education.* Washington, D.C.: Association of American Colleges and Universities and Hart Research Associates, 2009.

Association of American Geographers. "Toward a Reconsideration of Faculty Roles and Rewards in Geography." In R. M. Diamond and B. E. Adams (eds.), *The Disciplines Speak: Rewarding the Scholarly, Professional, and Creative Work of Faculty,* Washington, D.C.: American Association for Higher Education, 1995.

Augsburg, T., and Henry, S. (eds.). *The Politics of Interdisciplinary Studies: Essays on Transformations in American Undergraduate Programs.* Jefferson, N.C.: McFarland, 2009a.

Augsburg, T., and Henry, S. "Preface." In T. Augsburg and S. Henry (eds.), *The Politics of Interdisciplinary Studies: Essays on Transformations in American Undergraduate Programs.* Jefferson, N.C.: McFarland, 2009b.

Augsburg, T., and Henry, S. "Introduction." In T. Augsburg and S. Henry (eds.), *The Politics of Interdisciplinary Studies: Essays on Transformations in American Undergraduate Programs.* Jefferson, N.C.: McFarland, 2009c.

Augsburg, T., Henry, S., Newell, W. H., and Szostak, R. "Issues, Challenges, and Prospects: Beyond the Politics of Interdisciplinarity." In T. Augsburg and S. Henry (eds.), *The Politics of Interdisciplinary Studies: Essays on Transformations in American Undergraduate Programs.* Jefferson, N.C.: McFarland, 2009.

Bailis, S. "The Social Sciences in American Studies: An Integrative Conception." *American Quarterly,* 1974, *26*(3), 202–224.

Bal, M. *Travelling Concepts in Humanities.* Toronto: University of Toronto Press, 2002.

Becher, T. "The Counter-Culture of Specialization." *European Journal of Education,* 1990, *25*(2), 333–346.

Bechtel, W. "The Nature of Scientific Integration." In W. Bechtel (ed.), *Integrating Scientific Disciplines.* Dordrecht: Martinus Nijhoof, 1986.

Bender, T., and Schorske, C. E. "Introduction." In T. Bender and C. E. Schorske (eds.), *American Academic Culture in Transformation: Fifty Years, Four Disciplines.* Princeton, N.J.: Princeton University Press, 1997.

BIO 2010: Transforming Undergraduate Education for Future Research Biologists. Committee on Undergraduate Biology Education to Prepare Research Scientists for the 21st Century. Washington, D.C.: National Academies Press, 2003.

Boisot, M. "Disciplines and Interdisciplinarity." *Interdisciplinarity: Problems of Teaching and Research in Universities.* Washington, D.C.: Organization for Economic Cooperation and Development, 1972.

Boix-Mansilla, V. "Assessing Expert Interdisciplinary Work at the Frontier: An Empirical Exploration." *Research Evaluation,* 2006, *15*(1), 17–29.

Boix-Mansilla, V., Feller, I., and Gardner, H. "Quality Assessment in Interdisciplinary Research and Education." *Research Evaluation,* 2006, *15*(1), 69–74.

Boxer, M. J. "For and About Women: The Theory and Practice of Women's Studies in the United States." *Signs,* 1982, (3), 661–695.

Boyer, E. *Scholarship Reconsidered: Priorities of the Professoriate.* Princeton, N.J.: Princeton University Press, 1990.

Brew, A., "Disciplinary and Interdisciplinary Affiliations of Experienced Researchers." *Higher Education,* 2008, *56*(4), 423–438.

Brint, S. G., Turk-Bicakci, L., Proctor, K., and Murphy, S. P. *The College Catalog Study Database.* Riverside: University of California, Riverside, 2008. www.higher-ed2000.ucr.edu/.

Brint, S. G., Turk-Bicakci, L., Proctor, K., and Murphy, S. P. "Expanding the Social Frame of Knowledge: Interdisciplinary, Degree-Granting

Fields in American Colleges and Universities, 1975–2000." *Review of Higher Education,* 2009, *32*(2), 155–183.

Brown, J. S., and Duguid, P. "Universities in the Digital Age." *Change,* 1996, *24*(4), 11–19.

Burkhardt, P. "Administering Interdisciplinary and Innovative Programs: Lessons from the Rise and Fall of Arizona International College." *Issues in Integrative Studies,* 2006, *24,* 159–176; and unpublished additional comments on "Interdisciplinary Studies at Arizona International College, University of Arizona."

Bystrom, V. "Teaching on the Edge: Interdisciplinary Teaching in Learning Communities." In C. Haynes (ed.), *Innovations in Interdisciplinary Teaching.* Westport, Conn.: American Council on Education/Oryx Press, 2002.

Caldwell, L. K. "Environmental Studies: Discipline or Metadiscipline?" *Environmental Professional,* 1983, *5,* 247–259.

Calhoun, C. "Sociology, Other Disciplines, and the Project of a General Understanding of Social Life." In T. C. Halliday and M. Janowitz (eds.), *Sociology and Its Publics: The Forms and Fates of Disciplinary Organizations.* Chicago: University of Chicago Press, 1992.

Calhoun, C., and Rhoten, D. "Theoretical Knowledge, Methodological Tools, and Practical Applications: Three Agendas for Interdisciplinarity in the Social Sciences." In R. Frodeman, J. T. Klein, and C. Mitcham (eds.), *Oxford Handbook of Interdisciplinarity.* New York: Oxford University Press, forthcoming.

Camic, C., and Joas, H. "The Dialogical Turn." In C. Camic and H. Joas (eds.), *The Dialogical Turn: New Roles for Sociology in the Postdisciplinary Age.* Lanham, Md.: Rowman and Littlefield, 2004.

Capaldi, E. "Intellectual Transformation and Budgetary Savings Through Academic Reoganization." *Change,* 2009. www.change mag.org/July-August%202009/full-intellectual-budgetary.html

Carp, R. "Relying on the Kindness of Strangers: CEDD's Report on Hiring, Tenure, Promotion in IDS." *Association for Integrative Studies Newsletter,* 2008, *30*(2), 1–6.

Carp, R. M., and Wentworth, J. "Phoenix: From Ashes to Reincarnation at Appalachian State University." In T. Augsburg and S. Henry (eds.), *The Politics of Interdisciplinary Studies: Essays on Transformations in American Undergraduate Programs.* Jefferson, N.C.: McFarland, 2009.

Caruso, D., and Rhoten, D. "Lead, Follow, Get Out of the Way: Sidestepping the Barriers to Effective Practice of Interdisciplinarity and

Transdisciplinarity. A New Mechanism for Knowledge Production and Re-Integration in the Age of Information." 2001. www.hybridvigor.net/interdis/pubs/hv_pub_interdis-2001.04.30. pdf.

Casey, B. A. "The Administration and Governance of Interdisciplinary Programs." In J. T. Klein and W. Doty (eds.), *Interdisciplinary Studies Today*. San Francisco: Jossey-Bass, 1994.

Casey, B. A. "Developing and Administering Interdisciplinary Programs." In J. T. Klein (ed.), *Interdisciplinary Education in K–12 and College: A Foundation for K–16 Dialogue*. New York: College Board, 2002.

Casey, B. A. "The Administration of Interdisciplinary Programs." In R. Frodeman, J. T. Klein, and C. Mitcham (eds.), *Oxford Handbook of Interdisciplinarity*. New York: Oxford University Press, forthcoming.

Civian, J. T., and others. "Implementing Change." In J. G. Gaff and J. L. Ratcliff (eds.), *Handbook of the Undergraduate Curriculum: A Comprehensive Guide to Purposes, Structures, Practices, and Change*. San Francisco: Jossey-Bass, 1997.

Clark, B. R. *Places of Inquiry: Research and Advanced Education in Modern Universities*. Berkeley: University of California Press, 1995.

Clark, L., Lacey, P., and Bingham, N. "Alternative Conceptions, Experiences, and Outcomes of Interdisciplinary Programs at Earlham." In *Papers: Evergreen Conference on Interdisciplinary Education*. Tacoma, Wash.: Evergreen State College, 1997.

Clayton, K. "The University of East Anglia." In L. Levin and I. Lind (eds.), *Inter-Disciplinarity Revisited: Re-Assessing the Concept in Light of Institutional Experience*. Stockholm: OECD/CERI, Swedish National Board of Universities and Colleges, Linköping University, 1985.

Consortium on Fostering Interdisciplinary Inquiry. Minneapolis: University of Minnesota. http://academic.umn.edu/provost/interdisc/inquiry.

Cornwell, G. H., and Stoddard, E. W. "Toward an Interdisciplinary Epistemology: Faculty Culture and Institutional Change." In B. L. Smith and J. McCann (eds.), *Reinventing Ourselves: Interdisciplinary Education, Collaborative Learning, and Experimentation in Higher Education*. San Francisco: Anker/Jossey-Bass, 2001.

Coyner, S. "Women's Studies." *NWSA Journal* [National Women's Studies Association], 1991, *3*, 349–354.

Davis, J. W. "From Cutting Edge to Cutting Board: The Inter-Arts Center at San Francisco State University." In T. Augsburg and S. Henry (eds.), *The Politics of Interdisciplinary Studies: Essays on Transformations in American Undergraduate Programs*. Jefferson, N.C.: McFarland, 2009.

Dogan, M., and Pahre, R. *Creative Marginality: Innovation at the Intersections of Social Sciences.* Boulder, Colo.: Westview Press, 1990.

Downes, M. "The Humanities Program at the University of North Carolina at Asheville." In M. Nelson (ed.), *Alive at the Core: Exemplary Approaches to General Education in the Humanities.* San Francisco: Jossey-Bass, 2000.

Dubrow, G. "Facilitating Intellectual Mobility over the Course of Faculty Careers." Interdisciplinary Initiatives Working Group, Network of Interdisciplinary Initiatives. Seattle: University of Washington, 2005.

Dubrow, G. "'Institutionalizing' Interdisciplinary Research." *Inside Higher Education,* July 25, 2007. www.insidehighered.com/layout/set/print/news/2007/07/25/interdis. Citation by Elizabeth Redden.

Dubrow, G., and Harris, J. "Seeding, Supporting, and Sustaining Interdisciplinary Initiatives at the University of Washington: Findings, Recommendations and Strategies." 2006. www.grad.washington.edu/acad/interdisc_network/ID_Docs/NII_documents.htm.

Edwards, A. F. Jr. *Interdisciplinary Undergraduate Programs: A Directory.* (2nd ed.). Acton, Mass.: Copley, 1996.

Elam, D. "Ms. en Abyme: Deconstruction and Feminism." *Social Epistemology,* 1990, *4*(3), 293–308.

Elam, D. "Taking Account of Women's Studies." In R. Wiegman (ed.), *Women's Studies on Its Own: A Next Wave Reader in Institutional Change.* Durham, N.C.: Duke University Press, 2002.

Elam, H., and Ross, C. "The Area One Program at Stanford University." In M. Nelson (ed.), *Alive at the Core: Exemplary Approaches to General Education in the Humanities.* San Francisco: Jossey-Bass, 2000.

The Engineer of 2020: Visions of Engineering in the New Century. Washington, D.C.: National Academies Press, 2004.

Evenbeck, S., Jackson, B., and McGrew, J. "Faculty Development in Learning Communities: The Role of Reflection and Reframing." In J. Levine (ed.), *Learning Communities: New Structures, New Partnerships for Learning.* Columbia, S.C.: National Resource Center for the First-Year Experience, 1999.

Facilitating Interdisciplinary Research. Committee on Facilitating Interdisciplinary Research. Washington, D.C.: National Academies Press, 2004.

Feller, I. "New Organizations, Old Cultures: Strategies and Implementation of Interdisciplinary Programs." *Research Evaluation,* 2002, *11*(2), 109–110.

Feller, I. "Multiple Actors, Multiple Settings, Multiple Criteria: Issues in Assessing Interdisciplinary Research." *Research Evaluation*, 2006, *15*(1), 5–15.

"Final Report of the Transition Team on Interdisciplinarity." University of Massachusetts–Lowell, June 1, 2007.

Firpo, A. "Tools for Effective Leadership in the 21st Century." In D. E. Holmes and M. Osterweis (eds.), *Catalysts in Interdisciplinary Education: Innovation by Academic Health Centers*. Washington, D.C.: Association of Academic Health Centers, 1999.

Fish, S. "Being Interdisciplinary Is So Very Hard to Do." *Profession*, 1989, *89*, 15–22.

Fisher, D. *Fundamental Development of the Social Sciences: Rockefeller Philanthropy and the United States Social Science Research Council*. Ann Arbor: University of Michigan Press, 1993.

Frank, R. "'Interdisciplinary': The First Half-Century." In E. G. Stanley and T. F. Hoad (eds.), *WORDS: For Robert Burchfield's Sixty-Fifth Birthday*. Cambridge: D. S. Brewer, 1988.

Furtado, A., and others. "'To Educate the People': The Rise and Fall of the Department of Interdisciplinary Studies at Wayne State University." In T. Augsburg and S. Henry (eds.), *Disciplining Interdisciplinary Studies? The Politics of Interdisciplinary Transformation in Undergraduate American Higher Education*. Jefferson, N.C.: McFarland, 2009.

Gabelnick, F. "Achieving Interdisciplinary Innovation: Leading and Learning in Community." In C. Haynes (ed.), *Innovations in Interdisciplinary Teaching*. Westport, Conn.: American Council on Education/Oryx Press, 2002.

Gaff, J. *New Life for the College Curriculum*. San Francisco: Jossey-Bass, 1991.

Gaff, J. "Tensions Between Tradition and Innovation." In J. G. Gaff and J. L. Ratcliff (eds.), *Handbook of the Undergraduate Curriculum: A Comprehensive Guide to Purposes, Structures, Practices, and Change*. San Francisco: Jossey-Bass, 1997.

Gaff, J. G. *General Education: The Changing Agenda*. Washington, D.C.: Association of American Colleges and Universities, 1999.

Gaff, J. G., and Ratcliff, J. L. "Preface." In J. G. Gaff and J. L. Ratcliff (eds.), *Handbook of the Undergraduate Curriculum: A Comprehensive Guide to Purposes, Structures, Practices, and Change*. San Francisco: Jossey-Bass, 1997b.

Galison, P. "Computer Simulations and the Trading Zone." In P. Galison and D. J. Stump (eds.), *The Disunity of Science: Boundaries, Contexts, and Power*. Palo Alto: Stanford University Press, 1996.

Gardner, H. *Changing Minds: The Art and Science of Changing Our Own and Other People's Minds.* Boston: Harvard Business School Press, 2004.

Geertz, C. "Blurred Genres: The Refiguration of Social Thought." *American Scholar,* 1980, *4*(2), 165–179.

Goldsmith, H. "Interdisciplinarity, Teacher Preparation, and Liberal Studies at San Francisco State University." In T. Augsburg and S. Henry (eds.), *The Politics of Interdisciplinary Studies: Essays on Transformations in American Undergraduate Programs.* Jefferson, N.C.: McFarland, 2009.

Grant, G., and Riesman, D. *Perpetual Dream: Reform and Experiment in the American College.* Chicago: University of Chicago Press, 1979.

Graybill, J. K., and Shandas, V. "Doctoral Student and Early Career Academic Perspectives on Interdisciplinarity." In R. Frodeman, J. T. Klein, and C. Mitcham (eds.), *Oxford Handbook of Interdisciplinarity.* New York: Oxford University Press, forthcoming.

Grayson, C. J. "Benchmarking in Higher Education." In J. W. Meyerson (ed.), *New Thinking on Higher Education: Creating a Context for Change.* San Francisco: Anker/Jossey-Bass, 1998.

Gunn, G. "Interdisciplinary Studies." In J. Gibaldi (ed.), *Introduction to Scholarship in Modern Languages and Literatures.* (2nd ed.). New York: Modern Language Association, 1992.

Habib, H. B. *Towards a Paradigmatic Approach to Interdisciplinarity in the Behavioral and Medical Sciences.* Karlstad, Sweden: Center for Research in the Humanities, University of Karlstad, 1990.

Harris, E. "The Arts." In J. G. Gaff and J. L. Ratcliff (eds.), *Handbook of the Undergraduate Curriculum: A Comprehensive Guide to Purposes, Structures, Practices, and Change.* San Francisco: Jossey-Bass, 1997.

Heckhausen, H. "Discipline and Interdisciplinarity." *Interdisciplinarity: Problems of Teaching and Research in Universities.* Washington, D.C.: Organization for Economic Cooperation and Development, 1972.

Heilbron, J. "A Regime of Disciplines: Toward a Historical Sociology of Disciplinary Knowledge." In C. Camic and H. Joas (eds.), *The Dialogical Turn: New Roles for Sociology in the Postdisciplinary Age.* Lanham, Md.: Rowman and Littlefield, 2004.

Hendershott, A. B., and Wright, S. P. "The Social Sciences." In J. G. Gaff and J. L. Ratcliff (eds.), *Handbook of the Undergraduate Curriculum: A Comprehensive Guide to Purposes, Structures, Practices, and Change.* San Francisco: Jossey-Bass, 1997.

Hendra, R. F. "The Devolution of the Individualized Degree at the University Without Walls/University of Massachusetts–Amherst: A Case History." In T. Augsburg and S. Henry (eds.), *The Politics of*

Interdisciplinary Studies: Essays on Transformations in American Undergraduate Programs. Jefferson, N.C.: McFarland, 2009.

Henry, S. "Disciplinary Hegemony Meets Interdisciplinary Ascendancy: Can Interdisciplinary/Integrative Studies Survive, and If So, How?" *Issues in Integrative Studies,* 2005, *12,* 1–37.

Holley, K. A. *Understanding Interdisciplinary Challenges and Opportunities in Higher Education.* ASHE Higher Education Report, Vol. 35, No. 2. San Francisco: Jossey Bass, 2009.

Hollinger, D. A. "The Disciplines and the Identity Debates, 1970–1995." In T. Bender and C. E. Schorske (eds.), *American Academic Culture in Transformation: Fifty Years, Four Disciplines.* Princeton, N.J.: Princeton University Press, 1997.

Huy, Q., and Mintzberg, H. "The Rhythm of Change." *MIT Sloan Management Review,* 2003, *44*(4), 79–84.

Hyman, S. Invited address at workshop on "Quality Assessment in Interdisciplinary Research and Education." Washington, D.C.: American Association for the Advancement of Science, February 8, 2006.

Interdisciplinarity. London: Nuffield Foundation, 1975.

Interdisciplinarity: Problems of Teaching and Research in Universities. Washington, D.C.: Organization for Economic Cooperation and Development, 1972.

Interdisciplinary Research: Promoting Collaboration Between the Life Sciences and Medicine and the Physical Sciences and Engineering. Washington, D.C.: National Academies Press, 1990.

Jasanoff, S. "A Field of Its Own: The Emergence of Science and Technology Studies." In R. Frodeman, J. T. Klein, and C. Mitcham (eds.), *Oxford Handbook of Interdisciplinarity.* New York: Oxford University Press, forthcoming.

Kann, M. "The Political Culture of Interdisciplinary Explanation." *Humanities in Society,* 1979, *2*(3), 185–300.

Katz, C. "Disciplining Interdisciplinarity." *Feminist Studies,* 2001, *27*(2), 519–525.

Katz, S. "Beyond the Disciplines." Address to the meeting on "The Role of the New American College in the Past, Present, and Future of American Higher Education." Saint Mary's College of California, Moraga, Calif., June 17, 1996.

King, C. J. Written Comments for workshop on "Quality Assessment in Interdisciplinary Research and Education." Washington, D.C.: American Association for the Advancement of Science, February 8, 2006.

Klein, J. T. *Crossing Boundaries: Knowledge, Disciplinarities, and Interdisciplinarities.* Charlottesville: University of Virginia Press, 1996.

Klein, J. T. *Humanities, Culture, and Interdisciplinarity: The Changing American Academy.* Albany, N.Y.: SUNY Press, 2005.

Klein, J. T. "Interdisciplinary Approach." In S. Turner and W. Outhwaite (eds.), *Handbook of Social Science Methodology.* Thousand Oaks, Calif.: Sage, 2007.

Klein, J. T. "Evaluation of Interdisciplinary and Transdisciplinary Research: A Literature Review." *American Journal of Preventive Medicine,* 2008a, *35*(2S), S116–S123.

Klein, J. T. "Integration in der inter- und transdisziplinären Forschung." In M. Bergmann and E. Schramm (eds.), *Transdisziplinäre Forschung: Integrative Forschungsprozesse verstehen und bewerten.* Frankfurt: Campus Verlag, 2008b.

Klein, J. T., and Newell, W. H. "Advancing Interdisciplinary Studies." In J. G. Gaff and J. L. Ratcliff (eds.), *Handbook of the Undergraduate Curriculum: A Comprehensive Guide to Purposes, Structures, Practices, and Change.* San Francisco: Jossey-Bass, 1997.

Klein, J. T., and others (eds.). *Transdisciplinarity: Joint Problem Solving Among Science, Technology, and Society.* Basel: Birkhäuser Verlag, 2001.

Kleinberg, E. "Interdisciplinary Studies at a Crossroads." *Liberal Education,* 2008, *94*(1), 6–11.

Landau, M., Proshansky, H., and Ittelson. W. "The Interdisciplinary Approach and the Concept of Behavioral Sciences." In N. F. Washburne (ed.), *Decisions: Values and Groups, II.* New York: Pergamon, 1962.

Lange, P. Comments at workshop on "Quality Assessment in Interdisciplinary Research and Education." Washington, D.C.: American Association for the Advancement of Science, February 8, 2006.

Lattuca, L. *Creating Interdisciplinarity: Interdisciplinary Research and Teaching Among College and University Faculty.* Nashville, Tenn.: Vanderbilt University Press, 2001.

Laufgraben, J. L. "Faculty Development: Growing, Reflecting, Learning, and Changing." In J. O'Connor and others (eds.), *Learning Communities in Research Universities.* Olympia, Wash.: Evergreen State College, 2003.

Lemert, C. C. "Depth as a Metaphor for the Major: A Postmodernist Challenge." Paper presented at the Association of American Colleges meeting, San Francisco, January 11, 1990.

Leshner, A. I. "Science at the Leading Edge." *Science,* February 6, 2004, p. 1729.

"Liberal Education and the Disciplines." *Liberal Education,* 2009, *95*(2), Special issue.

Lindquist, J. "Strategies for Change." In J. G. Gaff and J. L. Ratcliff (eds.), *Handbook of the Undergraduate Curriculum: A Comprehensive Guide to Purposes, Structures, Practices, and Change.* San Francisco: Jossey-Bass, 1997.

Liu, A. *Local Transcendence: Essays on Postmodern Historicism and the Database.* Chicago: University of Chicago Press, 2008.

MacNeal, A. P., and Weaver, F. S. "Interdisciplinary Education at Hampshire College: Bringing People Together Around Ideas." In B. L. Smith and J. McCann (eds.), *Reinventing Ourselves: Interdisciplinary Education, Collaborative Learning, and Experimentation in Higher Education.* San Francisco: Anker/Jossey-Bass, 2001.

Mahan, J. L. "Toward Transdisciplinary Inquiry in the Humane Sciences." Unpublished doctoral dissertation, United States International University, 1970.

McKeon, R. "The Uses of Rhetoric in a Technological Age: Architectonic Productive Arts." In L. F. Bitzer and E. Black (eds.), *The Prospect of Rhetoric: Report of the National Development Project.* Upper Saddle River, N.J.: Prentice Hall, 1979.

Messer-Davidow, E. *Disciplining Feminism: From Social Activism to Academic Discourse.* Durham, N.C.: Duke University Press, 2002.

Messer-Davidow, E., Shumway, D., and Sylvan, D. "Preface." In E. Messer-Davidow, D. Shumway, and D. Sylvan (eds.), *Knowledges: Historical and Cultural Studies in Disciplinarity.* Charlottesville: University of Virginia Press, 1993.

Miller, J. H. "The Role of Theory in the Development of Literary Studies in the United States." In D. Easton and C. S. Schelling (eds.), *Divided Knowledge: Across Disciplines, Across Cultures.* Thousand Oaks, Calif.: Sage, 1991.

Miller, R. "Varieties of Interdisciplinary Approaches in the Social Sciences." *Issues in Integrative Studies,* 1982, *1*, 1–37.

Miller, R. "Interdisciplinary Studies at San Francisco State University: A Personal Perspective." In T. Augsburg and S. Henry (eds.), *The Politics of Interdisciplinary Studies: Essays on Transformations in American Undergraduate Programs.* Jefferson, N.C.: McFarland, 2009.

Minnich, E. *Liberal Learning and the Arts of Connection for the New Academy.* Washington, D.C.: Association of American Colleges and Universities, 1995.

Mitchell, W.J.T. "Interdisciplinarity and Visual Culture." *Art Bulletin,* 1995, *77*(4), 540–544.

Muir, J. K. "Turning Points: The Story of New Century College at George Mason University." In T. Augsburg and S. Henry (eds.),

The Politics of Interdisciplinary Studies: Essays on Transformations in American Undergraduate Programs. Jefferson, N.C.: McFarland, 2009.

Musil, C. M. (ed.). *Students at the Center: Feminist Assessment.* Washington, D.C.: Association of American Colleges and Universities and National Women's Studies Association, 1992.

National Women's Studies Association. "Defining Women's Studies Scholarship." In R. M. Diamond and B. E. Adam (eds.), *The Disciplines Speak II: More Statements on Rewarding the Scholarly, Professional, and Creative Work of Faculty.* Washington, D.C.: American Association for Higher Education, 2000.

Newell, W. H. "Miami University's School of Interdisciplinary Studies." In T. Augsburg and S. Henry (eds.), *The Politics of Interdisciplinary Studies: Essays on Transformations in American Undergraduate Programs.* Jefferson, N.C.: McFarland, 2009.

Newell, W. H., and others. "Apollo Meets Dionysius: Interdisciplinarity in Long-Standing Interdisciplinary Programs." *Issues in Integrative Studies,* 2003, *21,* 9–42.

Nowotny, H., Scott, P., and Gibbons, M. *Re-Thinking Science. Knowledge and the Public in an Age of Uncertainty.* Cambridge: Polity Press, 2001.

O'Connor, J. "Learning Communities in Research Universities." In J. O'Connor and others (eds.), *Learning Communities in Research Universities.* Olympia, Wash.: Evergreen State College, 2003.

Ostriker, J. P., Holland, P. W., Kuh, C., and Voytuk, J. A. (eds.). *A Guide to the Methodology of the National Research Council Assessment of Doctorate Programs.* Washington, D.C: National Academies Press, 2009.

Ostriker, J. P., and Kuh, C. V. (eds). *Assessing Research-Doctorate Programs: A Methodology Study.* Washington, D.C.: National Academies Press, 2003.

Palmer, C. "Information Research on Interdisciplinarity." In R. Frodeman, J. T. Klein, and C. Mitcham (eds.), *Oxford Handbook of Interdisciplinarity.* New York: Oxford University Press, forthcoming.

Palmer, C. L., and Neumann. L. J. "The Information Work of Interdisciplinary Humanities Scholars: Exploration and Translation." *Library Quarterly,* 2002, *72,* 85–117.

Panel on Modernizing the Infrastructure of the National Science Foundation's Federal Funds for R&D Survey. *Data on Federal Research and Development Investments: A Pathway to Modernization.* Washington, D.C.: National Academies Press, forthcoming.

Pellmar, R., and Eisenberg, L. (eds.). *Bridging Disciplines in the Brain, Behavioral, and Clinical Sciences.* Washington, D.C.: National Academies Press, 2000.

Pfirman, S., and Martin, P. "Facilitating Interdisciplinary Scholars." In R. Frodeman, J. T. Klein, and C. Mitcham (eds.), *Oxford Handbook of Interdisciplinarity*. New York: Oxford University Press, forthcoming.

Pfirman, S., and others. *Interdisciplinary Hiring, Tenure and Promotion: Guidance for Individuals and Institutions*. Council of Environmental Deans and Directors, 2007. www.ncseonline.org/CEDD/cms.cfm?id=2042.

Plumwood, V. *Feminism and the Mastery of Nature*. London: Routledge, 1993.

Powers, E. "Alice's Adventures in Tenureland." *Inside Higher Ed*, January 28, 2008. www.insidehighered.com/news/2008/01/28/aacu.

Readings, B. *The University in Ruins*. Cambridge, Mass.: Harvard University Press, 1997.

Reardon, M., and Ramaley, J. "Building Academic Community While Containing Costs." In J. G. Gaff and J. L. Ratcliff (eds.), *Handbook of the Undergraduate Curriculum: A Comprehensive Guide to Purposes, Structures, Practices, and Change*. San Francisco: Jossey-Bass, 1997.

Repko, A. F. *Interdisciplinary Research: Process and Theory*. Thousand Oaks, Calif.: Sage, 2008.

Repko, A. "Transforming an Experimental Innovation into a Sustainable Mainstream Academic Program: The New Interdisciplinary Studies Program at the University of Texas at Arlington." In T. Augsburg and S. Henry (eds.), *The Politics of Interdisciplinary Studies: Essays on Transformations in American Undergraduate Programs*. Jefferson, N.C.: McFarland, 2009.

Report of the Commission on Interdisciplinary Studies. Detroit: Wayne State University, June 30, 1993. www.research.wayne.edu/idre/report_ids.htm.

"Rethinking Interdisciplinarity." Virtual seminar sponsored by Centre National de la Recherche Scientifique, Paris, France. 2003–2004. www.interdisciplines.org/interdisciplinarity.

Rhoten, D. "Interdisciplinary Research: Trend or Transition." *Items and Issues*, 2004, *5*(1–2), 6–11.

Rhoten, D., Boix-Mansilla, V., Chun, M., and Klein, J. T. "Interdisciplinary Education at Liberal Arts Institutions." Brooklyn, N.Y.: Social Science Research Council, 2006. www.teaglefoundation.org/learning/pdf/2006_ssrc_whitepaper.pdf.

Rhoten, D., and Pfirman, S. "Women in Interdisciplinary Science: Exploring Preferences and Consequences." *Research Policy*, 2007, *36*, 56–75.

Rich, D., and Warren, R. "The Intellectual Future of Urban Affairs: Theoretical, Normative, and Organizational Options." *Social Science Research*, 1980, *17*(2), 53–66.

Rodgers, S., Booth, M., and Eveline, J. "The Politics of Disciplinary Advantage." *History of Intellectual Culture*, 2003, *3*(1). www.ucalgary .ca/hic/.

Rosenfield, P. "The Potential of Transdisciplinary Research for Sustaining and Extending Linkages Between the Health and Social Sciences." *Social Science and Medicine*, 1992, *35*(11), 1343–1357.

Roy, R. "Interdisciplinarity in America 1949–1999: Experiences of a Proactive Champion of the Cause." In R. Roy (ed.), *The Interdisciplinary Imperative: Interactive Research and Education, Still an Elusive Goal in Academia.* Lincoln, Neb.: Writer's Club Press, 2000.

Sá, C. "Interdisciplinary Strategies at Research-Intensive Universities." Unpublished doctoral dissertation, Pennsylvania State University, 2005.

Salter, L., and Hearn, A. (eds.). *Outside the Lines: Issues in Interdisciplinary Research.* Montreal and Kingston: McGill-Queen's University Press, 1996.

Sarkela, S. "Alternative Ways of Organizing: The Importance of Organizational Culture." In B. L. Smith and J. McCann (eds.), *Reinventing Ourselves: Interdisciplinary Education, Collaborative Learning, and Experimentation in Higher Education.* San Francisco: Anker/Jossey-Bass, 2001.

Schneider, C. G., and Shoenberg, R. *Contemporary Understandings of Liberal Education.* Washington, D.C.: Association of American Colleges and Universities, 1998. No. 1 in the Academy in Transition series.

Schorske, C. E. "The New Rigorism in the Human Sciences, 1940–1960." In T. Bender and C. E. Schorske (eds.), *American Academic Culture in Transformation: Fifty Years, Four Disciplines.* Princeton, N.J.: Princeton University Press, 1997.

"The Science of Team Science: Assessing the Value of Transdisciplinary Research." *American Journal of Preventive Medicine*, 2008, *35*(2S), S77–S249.

Scientific Interfaces and Technological Applications. Panel on Scientific Interfaces and Technological Applications. Washington, D.C.: National Academies Press, 1986.

Seabury, M. B. "Introduction." In M. B. Seabury (ed.), *Interdisciplinary General Education: Questioning Outside the Lines.* New York: College Board, 1999.

Smelser, N. J. "Interdisciplinarity in Theory and Practice." In C. Camic and H. Joas (eds.), *The Dialogical Turn: New Roles for Sociology in the Postdisciplinary Age.* Lanham, Md.: Rowman and Littlefield, 2004.

Spear, K. "Liberal Education by Proclamation or Design?" In K. Spear and others (eds.), *Learning Communities in Liberal Arts Colleges.*

Olympia, Wash.: Evergreen State College, Washington Center for Improving the Quality of Undergraduate Education, in cooperation with the American Association for Higher Education, 2003.

Star, S., and Griesemer, J. "Institutional Ecology, 'Translations,' and Boundary Objects: Amateurs and Professionals in Berkeley's Museum of Vertebrate Biology." *Social Studies of Science,* 1989, *19*(3), 387–420.

Stocking, G. W. Jr. "Delimiting Anthropology: Historical Reflections on the Boundaries of a Boundless Discipline." *Social Research,* 1995, *62*(4), 933–966.

Stoddard, E. R. (ed.). "Legitimacy and Survival of a Professional Organization: The Association of Borderlands Scholars." *Journal of Borderlands Studies,* Spring 1992.

Stokols, D., and others. "Evaluating Transdisciplinary Science." *Nicotine and Tobacco Research,* 2003, *5*(Suppl.), S21–S39.

Szostak, R. "The Office of Interdisciplinary Studies in the Faculty of Arts at the University of Alberta." In T. Augsburg and S. Henry (eds.), *The Politics of Interdisciplinary Studies: Essays on Transformations in American Undergraduate Programs.* Jefferson, N.C.: McFarland, 2009.

Taylor, M. C. "End the University As We Know It." *New York Times,* April 26, 2009, p. A23. www.nytimes.com/2009/04/27/opinion/27taylor.html?pagewanted=1&_r=3.

Teddlie, C., and Tashakkori, A. "Major Issues and Controversies in the Use of Mixed Methods in the Social and Behavioral Sciences." In A. Tashakkori and C. Teddlie (eds.), *Handbook of Mixed Methods in Social Behavioral Research.* Thousand Oaks, Calif.: Sage, 2003.

Tierney, W. G. *Building the Responsive Campus.* Thousand Oaks, Calif.: Sage, 1999.

Toombs, W., and Tierney, W. *Meeting the Mandate: Reviewing the College and Department Curriculum.* ASHE-ERIC Higher Education Report No. 6. Washington, D.C.: School of Educational and Human Development. George Washington University, 1991.

Trow, M. "Interdisciplinary Studies as a Counterculture: Problems of Birth, Growth, and Survival." *Issues in Integrative Studies,* 1984/5, *4,* 1–15.

Trowler, P. R. "Introduction: Higher Education Policy, Institutional Change." In P. R. Trowler (ed.), *Higher Education Policy and Institutional Change: Intentions and Outcomes in Turbulent Environments.* Buckingham, UK: Society for Research into Higher Education/Open University Press, 2002.

Trowler, P. R., and Knight, P. T. "Exploring the Implementation Gap: Theory and Practices in Change Interventions." In P. R. Trowler (ed.), *Higher Education Policy and Institutional Change: Intentions and Outcomes in Turbulent Environments.* Buckingham, U.K.: Society for Research into Higher Education/Open University Press, 2002.

The University and the Community: The Problems of Changing Relationships. Paris: Organization for Economic Cooperation and Development, 1982.

Unsworth, J. "University 2.0." In R. N. Katz (ed.), *The Tower and the Cloud: Higher Education in the Age of Cloud Computing.* Washington, D.C.: EDUCAUSE, 2008.

Vickers, J. "'[U]framed in Open, Unmapped Fields': Teaching and the Practice of Interdisciplinarity." *Arachne: An Interdisciplinary Journal of the Humanities,* 1997, *4*(2), 11–42.

Vickers, J. "Diversity, Globalization, and 'Growing Up Digital': Navigating Interdisciplinarity in the Twenty-First Century." *History of Intellectual Culture,* 2003, *3*(1). www.ucalgary.ca/hic/.

Wagner, C. S., Roessner, J. D., and Bobb, K. "Evaluating the Output of Interdisciplinary Scientific Research: A Review of the Literature." Prepared for SBE/SRS National Science Foundation by SRI International Science and Technology Policy Program, May 2009.

Wakefield, P. "Interdisciplinarity with Emory University's Critical Academic Community." In T. Augsburg and S. Henry (eds.), *The Politics of Interdisciplinary Studies: Essays on Transformations in American Undergraduate Programs.* Jefferson, N.C.: McFarland, 2009.

Warhol, R. R. "Nice Work If You Can Get It—and If You Can't? Building Women's Studies Without Tenure Lines." In R. Wiegman (ed.), *Women's Studies on Its Own: A Next Wave Reader in Institutional Change.* Durham, N.C.: Duke University Press, 2002.

Wátzlawick, P., Weakland, J. H., and Fisch, R. *Change: Principles of Problem Formation and Problem Resolution.* New York: Norton, 1974.

Weingart, P. "Interdisciplinarity: The Paradoxical Discourse." In P. Weingart and N. Stehr (eds.), *Practicing Interdisciplinarity.* Toronto: University of Toronto Press, 2000.

Wentworth, J., and Carp, E. M. "Phoenix: From Ashes to Reincarnation at Appalachian State University." In T. Augsburg and S. Henry (eds.), *The Politics of Interdisciplinary Studies: Essays on Transformations in American Undergraduate Programs.* Jefferson, N.C.: McFarland, 2009.

White, L. M. "The Humanities." In J. G. Gaff and J. L. Ratcliff (eds.), *Handbook of the Undergraduate Curriculum: A Comprehensive Guide to Purposes, Structures, Practices, and Change.* San Francisco: Jossey-Bass, 1997.

Winter, M. "Specialization, Territoriality, and Jurisdiction in Librarianship." *Library Trends,* 1996, *45*(2), 343–363.

Wubbels, G. G., and Girgus, J. S. "The Natural Sciences and Mathematics." J. G. Gaff and J. L. Ratcliff (eds.), *Handbook of the Undergraduate Curriculum: A Comprehensive Guide to Purposes, Structures, Practices, and Change.* San Francisco: Jossey-Bass, 1997.

Yates, S. J. *Doing Social Science Research.* Thousand Oaks, Calif.: Sage, 2004.

INDEX

Note to index: An *e* following a page number denotes an exhibit on that page; an *f* following a page number denotes a figure on that page; a *t* following a page number denotes a table on that page.

CPSIA information can be obtained
at www.ICGtesting.com
Printed in the USA
LVOW10*0004050318

568655LV00006B/43/P